Geography of Hearts

A Honeymoon Bicycle Crossing of America

By Jim Crawford

Geography of Hearts

A Honeymoon Bicycle Crossing of America

ISBN 13: 978-1-955338-17-2

Cover design by Cathy Crawford

Printed in the United States of America

pp

POCAHONTAS PRESS

DUBLIN, VA

POCAHONTASPRESS.COM

*This book is dedicated to the many folks who
blessed us in our crossings.*

Contents

Prelude

Saturday, September 14, 1996

Noon in Nashville, Illinois, 26 miles down the road. We've been riding straight south on Rt. 127 with a crosswind. As we've ridden along, I've been thinking about traveling.

Cathy and I are travelers that choose to travel on bicycles, not bicyclists per se. I think bicyclists tend to focus on the mode of travel more than the why of travel. To me, this mode of travel is more on a human scale. It is faster than walking, and I can carry more gear to make the experience more varied and comfortable.

The why of our travel is curiosity, to experience new places, new people. It is not based on the physical, in fact physical holds only a minor part in this play. This travel is the geography of hearts, the vital center and source of our beings, emotions, and sensibilities.

Prologue

"Does this look familiar? Anywhere along here?"

"What does it say in the journal?"

"...Oh wait, look over there."

Cathy was scrutinizing the landscape out of the passenger window, straining to match her memories with our current surroundings. I concentrated on keeping the car on the road. It was a scenario that played out over and over for the next 4,000-plus miles.

In June of 1996, Cathy and I got married. I was 45, and she was 36. For our honeymoon, we embarked on a bicycle journey, camping as we rode across the country from Seattle, WA to our home in Roanoke, VA. Twenty-six years later, we were back. This time, our camping gear was not packed in panniers but crammed into our 2014 Prius which we called Evee. This time, we carried iPhones and were guided by Google Maps, Yelp, and Booking.com. And this time, we were accompanied by our 12-year-old Airedoodle, Jetta.

We had planned this retrace trip for a year earlier, as a 25th anniversary milestone. However, we were forced to delay. For me, 2021, the year of my 70th birthday, was marked by serious heart problems. My pacemaker had been implanted the year before. Then, the week of our 25 th anniversary, I had open heart surgery, receiving a new aortic valve and three bypassed coronary arteries. Thus, I was made fit and ready for adventure.

I contemplated the future and regarded the past. It amazed me how 26 years had flown by. But how much had changed, really? How much had stayed the same?

"Never go back," my grandmother tearfully told me a long time ago. Her comment was upon visiting the home where she had grown up, a place she had known intimately. Our going back, our retrace, would be to places we had glimpsed for mere moments, rarely more than a few hours, but places that touched our hearts. I wondered if we would feel the same way.

What follows is my daily journal from our bicycle crossing, interspersed with moments from our 2022 Retrace trip. I have changed some names to protect the privacy of the people we met along the way. My journal begins when our flight lands in Seattle, WA on June 18, 1996 and ends with our arrival back home in Roanoke, VA, 3 1/2 months and 4,276 miles later. Our two trips reflect the unique social, technological, and cultural milieux through which we progressed, not to mention the difference between viewing the country by bicycle versus car.

Journey: Beginning

The Pacific Northwest

Tuesday, June 18, 1996

Three days after our wedding, the happiest day of my life, we are sitting in a Denny's in Seattle, three hours after landing. Our boxed bikes and gear made it in good shape, and we took our time assembling them at the airport. It felt great to be starting our adventure home. We have been anticipating this cross-country trip for months. It is sunny and cool, 58 degrees, the air nice and dry. We're heading up to my friend Debbie's in North Seattle.

Wednesday, June 19, 1996

It's great seeing Debbie again and meeting her partner Angi.

Yesterday, the ride up here was fun, especially after getting into the city. We rode up along the bay by Pike's Market and the Port Docks with container ships being loaded and unloaded, and rode five or six miles on a bike trail along the bay. I had two flats, prompting a cry for Kevlar tires and new tubes. We finally arrived here at 7:00. Debbie fixed us spaghetti and salad, and we ate on her patio.

Today we had a busy shopping day, buying many needed items: For me—two new touring tires (32mm Conti Top Touring), three tubes, two pairs of socks, biking vest, two shirts (all on sale), water bottle and cage, a beautiful front handlebar bag, instructions for my bike computer (free), Seattle bike map (free), rain hat, Swiss army knife; for Cathy—a nice rear rack trunk, bike shirt (moose print, matching mine), socks, silk long-john shirt, fleecy purple sweatshirt, shades for her prescription glasses, and

Gramicci pants. Five hundred dollars total! Wow!

We rode our bikes 18 miles around the city on errands to Greg's Bicycle Shop and REI. We visited the outstanding Center for Wooden Boats, checking out the variety of small wooden boats, where their designs originated, and what the boats were used for, all this on Washington Lake in the city. Seattle is incredibly bike friendly. At one point we were in a line of eight bikers in the bike lane during rush hour. There were more bikes than cars at the light!

Tonight, we took Debbie and Angi out for Mexican on the bay at sunset. We are only partially adjusted to this time zone.

I'm thinking this trip is like molecular physics compared to the experience of jetting out over the same territory that we will bicycle. The bike trip back will be slow and deliberate, all senses receiving information, scenery constantly changing, many elements impacting us beyond our control (climate and geography being the two biggies).

Retrace 2022

August 2-19, 2022
Roanoke, VA to Seattle, WA

For our 2-month long retrace trip, we packed Evee's interior space to accommodate a large, soft foam bed for Jetta. She is the sweetest and most companionable travel-loving dog either of us has ever known. Her bed fit just behind the driver's seat so that she could scootch up between Cathy and me. With a big grin, she watched America unfold in front of us, occasionally delivering wet kisses in our ears.

We mounted a Thule cargo box on new roof racks. On a removable platform on the rear hitch, we loaded a large cargo box, nicknamed Burt Backrack (Yes, we tend to name our prized possessions). Every square inch of these boxes, as well as the car's interior, was packed with gear. We were going for comfort, including a large 6-person tent, a double cot, a luxurious ExPed Megamat Duo mattress with nice sheets and pillows, three chairs, a table, a two-burner Coleman stove, a cooler, fairy lights and candles, a tablecloth, a full kitchen, lots of food, many changes of clothing and shoes, and a set of folding steps to help Jetta into the car. Of course, we also found just enough room for my guitar. With all this weight and added wind drag, we drove just under 9,000 miles on this retrace trip and averaged 45 mpg. Go Evee!

Of course, this was all luxurious compared to our bike trip. Then we had carried backpack size equipment in our panniers (front and rear) and in my single-track trailer BOB (Beast of Burden). At that time, our 3-man tent and Therm-a-Rest sleep system carried us through. We balanced comfort with weight, indulging in a few nonessentials like books, musical instruments, and nice cook pots.

For our retrace trip, Cathy had planned a full and fun trip from Roanoke to get to our original starting point in Seattle. I won't go into detail, but our route included a stay in New Jersey with Cathy's college-mate, Eileen (also our maid of honor at our wedding). In upstate New York, our old friends Scott and Beth had organized a reunion with pals from my college years for a great few days of music and comradery. Outside of Minneapolis, our niece Susan and her husband Ross took us for a leisurely kayak float on the St. Croix River.

Cathy has a desire to visit as many National Parks as possible, so she routed us by Indiana Dunes in Illinois, Theodore Roosevelt in North Dakota, and Mt. Rainier in Washington.

Near Mt. Rainier, while hiking the trail to Sheep Lake, a jet flew overhead. I looked up at the Seattle-bound plane, and having an epiphany, said to Cathy, "That was us twenty-six years ago, landing in Seattle."

In Seattle, we splurged on a room in a boutique hotel that was walking distance to Pike's Market, Seattle Center, and The Center for Wooden Boats. Our nephew Brian and his sweetheart Kim were travelling from Denver, and we met them for dinner near Pike's Market.

Much of our two-day experience in the city centered on locating places for Jetta to relieve herself and eateries where she was welcome, both in short supply. We were surprised and saddened by the large homeless population camping on the downtown sidewalks, mostly heavy-lidded young adults showing obvious signs of addiction and heavy drug use.

Thursday, June 20, 1996

We're on our way to the Edmond's Ferry and the Olympic Peninsula. Mount Rainier is bright and looming behind us to the south.

We took the Edmund's Ferry, crossing the Puget Sound to the Olympic Peninsula, then had a fine bike ride 38 miles northward to Port Townsend. We got to Port Townsend around 6:30, tired and hungry, and set up camp in the overflow area at Fort Worden. We had a great meal at Blackberries Restaurant, as we talked and nourished ourselves. There's a Blues festival this weekend and lots of folks were jamming, including a great Cajun band. Folks were still dancing when we trundled off to our tent and sleep.

Friday, June 21, 1996, Summer Solstice

We're in Port Townsend's Uptown Coho Cafe having breakfast. It feels good to be in this maritime climate. Outside it is overcast, grey and cool, while inside John Hyatt is urging us to, "Have a little faith in me," on the sound system. We got great news from our waitress about my old friend Daryl, who lives here (we will try to find him while we are in town); he and his mate, Hilda, have a new baby!

It was wild last night seeing all the festival folks walking around with guitars and other instruments. It made me ache for a guitar to play, though last night I was too tired. We slept ten and a half hours, like angels. During the night Cathy woke me, and we lay with our heads out the tent door, looking up at a starry, starry night sky. What a world.

We rode to Daryl and Hilda's house mid-morning and met three-month-old Dawn. Then Daryl took us to Dock A to board the sloop *Eliza Nelson*, which he had built. As we sailed, we talked about their plans to move to Orcas Island and set up a charter business while Hilda sets up a sail loft.

There are many people here that are putting a dream together around wooden sailing craft. The pace is slow, tidal, and friendly. The boats in dry dock look to the bay, awkward and braced on the "Hard", hopeful and dreaming of the buoyant, chaotic sweep of the water's surface, beautifully mated to the fluid tension.

Cathy is in Thriftway buying spaghetti for dinner and maybe a bottle of wine. We just got in from a great sail with Daryl, twenty knots and flying. Good time all around. The *Eliza Nelson* is heavy, 22,000 pounds, but lies over easy. Daryl still has lots of work to make her a comfortable cruiser. She has already sailed to Alaska, which is where Dawn was conceived.

I like Daryl. He is a kind and aware guy. He maintains his identity with his hippie past, and doesn't sacrifice his value system, which seems to be, "Do more with less; be fair and hard-working at what you love; savor friendships; live life large."

Saturday, June 22, 1996

We got up this morning around 7:00 and ate a camp breakfast. After packing up, we rode over to Daryl's for a short visit before we started heading east. Hilda showed up on her bike as we were leaving—more pictures and best wishes. From an internet cafe in Port Townsend, I e-mailed a friend in Roanoke. The fee for this service—three dollars!

We left Port Townsend on the 11:45 a.m. Keystone Ferry,

crossing the corner of the Strait of Juan de Fuca to Whidbey Island. Port Townsend is the westward most point of our bike trek, and today we start riding into the rising sun along Route 20 through the beautiful and mountainous North Cascades.

We ate lunch at Rhododendron Park along Padilla Bay, in a quiet, dark-green fir forest. We were hungry and consumed two bagel sandwiches, one with peanut butter, the other with cheese, followed by figs, nuts, raisins, granola bars, a half-apple each, and lots of water and Gatorade mix.

A little while back, Cathy's glasses lens popped out as she was riding along. As she was stopping, she had trouble unclicking her left foot, and she fell over sideways onto the edge of the road, *Laugh-In* style. From my biking position behind, I saw this and felt helpless. It scared me. She wasn't hurt. Since it is chilly, she was padded by several layers of clothes. She explained she got disoriented with one eye seeing through her prescription lens and the other eye without!

<<<<< >>>>>

Retrace 2022

On this retrace trip, we rode the Edmund's ferry, but didn't go straight to Port Townsend. We took a four-day side trip to Olympic National Park, meeting up with Brian and Kim again. Although we had a glorious time there, I will not elaborate since this was not part of our bike trip.

After this diversion, we returned to retracing our original route at Port Townsend, staying at Fort Worden State Park. Walking around the campground, we expected to clearly discern where we had pitched our tent 26 years ago. We were surprised how unfamiliar it all seemed. Later we learned that this would be the case in many places.

We enjoyed walking around town and through the neighborhoods. Daryl and Hilda had moved away from Port Townsend, but there were still other active backyard boatbuilding setups.

Twenty-six years brings enormous technological advances. Gone are the internet cafes, once so amazing. Now, nearly everyone, even children, carry a pocket-sized computer with a host of tools including phone, email, maps, books, and games. Communication is now instantaneous, and we have access to libraries of information at the touch of the screen.

Sunday, June 23, 1996

We made it to Deception Pass State Park around 5:00
yesterday and set up in the cyclist camping area. Then we rode
out to a restaurant and had salmon sandwiches and a beer. We
are cheap drunks now! After dinner we took turns showering and
massaged each other before drifting off to deep sleep.

At 6:00 this morning we were awakened by rain drops on
the tent. We scrambled out and brought in the towels and Cathy's
handlebar bag, then drifted back to sleep to the sound of light
rain. We slept on and off until 9:30 when the rain stopped.

We've eaten breakfast—yogurt, bananas, Pop-Tarts,
granola, and water. Now to pack up and roll on.

We just crossed Deception Pass. Cathy is perfecting her
unorthodox dismount. The "Just go ahead and do it, it's not as
bad as you think it will be" dismount is indeed exciting as she fell
once again. This time she failed to lean the bike over to the right
when she un-clicked her foot from the pedal. She went right over,
much more relaxed than the first time.

We still are in the land of espresso. Seattle is the cultural
hearth of gourmet coffee. Even this far from Seattle, there is
very little distance decay of the phenomena. Many restaurants
advertise espresso on plastic banners hanging by the side of the
road so passers-by, who must be caffeine junkies, can see them in
time to whip in for another cup. Drive-through espresso shacks
are plentiful.

We rode along Padilla Bay, which was home to the
Swinomish and Samish Indians before the white man came. The
coastal Indians of the Pacific Northwest had some metal knives
and tools when first observed by explorers. The metal came from
shipwrecked Chinese junks, carried to these shores by the Japan

Current. It is not known when the first metal was introduced in this gift-of-the-sea manner or how the gift was interpreted, but they knew a good tool material when they saw it.

This is fertile land. We rode past apple and blueberry orchards and fields of soybeans and spinach. People are friendly and blame the lack of accurate weather forecasting on a bad satellite and don't seem to worry. It showered briefly, the dark clouds rolling in from the Pacific, heading eastward. As they bumped into the Cascade Mountains, thunder could be heard, and a more serious rain event was in the making. Into this area is where we are going, across mountain passes named Rainy Pass and the like.

I've been thinking of many things as I am settling into the physical routine. As I think about biking less, my mind is left to see and contemplate. Tomorrow we really start heading east. I like the Pacific Northwest. I like the enclaves of independent folks, "slightly indigent," as Daryl said. There is a slower pace. Maybe it is the weather, the rhythm of tides and storms, or long days—sixteen or so hours of daylight now—and very short days in winter. Maybe island consciousness has impacted most people out here on the coast who have waited for a ferry or been stranded when one breaks down. Patience is a virtue.

Sixteen miles down the road, at Bay View State Park, we decided to stop for the day, dry out our tent, and rest some. This is a nice, quiet park—five dollars for us cyclists and twenty-five cent showers. Cathy tried to call home, but the pay phone was broken, and there are no pay phones anywhere within a three-mile radius.

Right now, a great blue heron wings overhead, ravens shriek and cavort, and songbirds lighten the evening air. I think back to the two Bald Eagles perched on the bare limbed apex of a fir tree overlooking Padilla Bay, their source of food and hope.

We heard that their massive nest harbored chicks. The male was drying his wings after the shower, looking like the eagle on a quarter, and he seemed oblivious to the roar of a nearby tractor in the field and to us stopped by the side of the road below, gawking. And yet we are interwoven, man, eagle, and this ecosystem of the bay which is now protected as a nature reserve from developers wishing to "condo-ize" the estuary. This is our work, this balance, this harmony.

Retrace 2022

August 24-25, 2022
Deception Pass to Bay View, WA

We have good memories of the salmon sandwiches we ate at Deception Pass, but on this retrace, we never found that restaurant. We did however spend a few hours at Deception Pass State Park, hiking around rocky Rosario Head. This was a treat, since on our bike trip we hadn't explored this territory on the bay before hitting the road. The area was so immense we couldn't take the time then.

We laughed to realize that 26 years ago, we were not familiar with the now ubiquitous coffee drive-throughs.

At Bay View State Park, we set up camp and took a short walk to get our bearings and to reconcile our memories with what we now saw. Again, very vague. Much to our relief, we could see Padilla Bay had not been developed. Padilla Bay National Estuarine Research Reserve is located near the State Park and has trails and an interpretive center.

When we came back to our camp, another tent was set up in the site beside us. We met Jill, age 65, and her mom Ann, 92. Accompanying them was their French Bulldog, Murphy.

We appreciated their calm campsite activities. Ann enjoyed sitting in a comfortable chair by their fire, talking with Jill who was preparing food and keeping their camp neat. Ann often would "make suggestions", and Jill would agree, though I could tell she had accrued a lifetime of Ann's suggestions. Jill let the long pattern of Mother-Daughter guidance pass. I saw Jill smile, more inside than out, thankful that her mom was alive and well. Such understanding in this sweet theatre of life spoke to me to consider my own friendships with understanding.

Murphy strolled purposefully past our site, ignoring Jetta's obligatory comments. They easily worked it out. This is one of Jetta's personality strengths.

The next morning, Jill and Ann were preparing to leave. Cathy and I offered to take down their large tent and pack it into their car. They accepted and thanked us sincerely. They left us with an abundance of firewood, enough for several nights.

That night, Cathy and I had some wine and sat by the fire and talked of our trip and many other things in our lives. Such is the offering of sitting by an evening fire in a campsite.

The North Cascades

We left Bay View State Park by 8:45, an early start for us. We are now 60 miles further east. We set up camp at Rockport State Park—$5, a beautiful spot in the mountains. We are within view of snow-covered peaks, and tomorrow we will start the climb to Rainy Pass.

The ride today was spectacular as we left the marine coastal biome and rode along the Skagit River into a lush rainforest climate. It rained several times on us, a slow steady rain that fit the environs. Then the day burst forth with sunshine. We saw cedar waxwings playing in a slough. White, blue, and purple foxgloves were taking advantage of clear cuts to reign over the stumps that were hunched into the green decomposing cycle. As we entered the Cascades, I felt small and at the mercy of the surrounding topography.

This section of the Cascades Highway generated a series of long steep climbs and swift descents. There was heavy overgrowth. The encroaching vegetation required cutting back trees on much of this section of the Highway.

After a full day of ups and downs, we found this small park and campground, Rockport State Park, and we set up our tent. Since we'd heard from a biker that there was a restaurant and laundry only a mile from the park, we decided to ride out to get something to eat. Instead, the ride was six miles downhill, and to top it off, the restaurant was closed! We were weak with hunger and realized we'd have to pedal back up the mountain to our campsite. We were just setting forth when a pickup truck stopped. The driver offered to take us to get a burger and give us (and our bikes) a ride in his truck back up to our tent. His name was Jerry, and his offer was a blessing.

Jerry works in Seattle, a two-and-a-half-hour commute which he used to do daily; now he stays the workweek in an apartment in the city. He and his wife, Willow, own a 40-acre farm with chickens and a menagerie of farm animals, including a donkey they had just gotten. When I asked Jerry why he got a donkey, he said, "There is no reason to get a donkey, except for the hell of it."

This is a lush area in these upper reaches of the Skagit River Valley. The highway we are on, the Cascade Mountains Scenic Highway, is closed in the winter just east of here which gives this valley an isolated feel. There are many alternative-living folks in this area, "So it's hard to say how many live here," Jerry says to my inquiry. Jerry didn't want us to tell people about this place.

When we got back to the campground, Jerry walked back with us to setup. We talked more with this man whose curiosity with life made him glow. He offered to leave some eggs out for us by the road so we could eat them in the morning. Saying that we were blessed is a huge understatement.

We met our first fellow cross-country cyclist today, a Canadian named Bert, who is riding to Maine. We also heard about a couple on a tandem bike who are a few days ahead of us. They are going to Pennsylvania.

Retrace 2022

A few years ago, I Googled Jerry and learned that he had passed away of heart failure in Seattle in 2017, at the age of 74. I tried, unsuccessfully, to contact his wife, Willow, who still owned their 40-acre farm in the Skagit Valley. On our retrace, although we did not know its exact address, we meandered through this valley of small farms and imagined life there. While in the area, we stopped briefly at Rasar State Park, letting Jetta wade in the milky blue river.

We picnicked in Rockport State Park. In 2007, it had been closed to camping due to the age of the trees. Danger from deadfall was too high. At one downed tree, I counted 476 rings. How many of those were added between the last time we visited and when it fell? Rockport is still open for day use, and we hiked through the ancient trees dripping with moss and lichens. In the defunct campground, the tables were covered in green life as well.

Around this point along our retrace route, I grew aware of a type of detachment in our current mode of travel. As we drove our car through this beautiful terrain, along bays and bluffs, past people, birds, flowers, and the beauty of all nature under the sky, it became abundantly clear to me that walking, hiking, and bicycling are much better modes of travel, hands down. When hiking or riding a bicycle, our minds and bodies become part of the land, its hills and valleys, creeks, and meadows. We feel our bodies work as we climb a long mountain ascent. Deer pause to watch, birds skip along in front, playing. This rhythm of breathing and pedaling establishes a synergy within the terrain. The smell and feel of the forest and the fields of grasses and flowers speak to the mystery of life itself.

Of course, detachment occurs, but other lessons from our retrace mode of travel were enlightening. We began to understand this travel puzzle was an opportunity for us to honor this time, this place, our love of each other, our dog, and life itself. This mindfulness nurtured our hope and faith in the beauty of the Here and Now. We have so much to be thankful for. We released ourselves into this journey. How fortunate we were to be able to experience America together again.

Tuesday, June 25, 1996

We started our ride at 9:45 on this pretty day. We met a vendor at a scenic overlook who was selling jewelry from his old van. His name was Art. He was in his late fifties yet looked older with his leathered skin and graying beard. His son lives nearby and drives a logging truck. I bought a cut-bronze caravel sailing ship cut from an English half-penny from this character. I sensed a talisman for our journey. I stowed it in my handlebar bag which had a clear plastic window showing our current bike map. As I biked along, it was fun to look at the talisman sailing across the map of this beautiful country.

Art is on his way to Montana and then down to Arizona this winter to a winter-long flea market where he will camp out in his van, hang out and do jewelry. Art showed me scars from when he hit an armadillo on his motorcycle and went down. I photographed him with his wares standing beside his rig.

Our ride up to Colonial Creek Campground was fine, four miles of steep grade, but it wasn't bad. We went through a tunnel on the grade that was especially dark and spooky. Then I realized I had my sunglasses on!

We stopped at the North Cascades Visitor Center and enjoyed the exhibits. We bought a book about the geology here. The large-scale display maps were fun too. Cathy ran her finger along the course of Route 20 on the huge North Cascades National Park relief map, feeling the grade.

I copied this from a display:

Rocks of the North Cascades

> Gneiss Skagit -- complex metamorphic
> Granodiorite
> Granite -- rarely found
> Greenschist -- ocean floor volcanic rocks forced
> under the continent

Yellow Aster Complex -- oldest, 100s of millions of years
Schist -- metamorphism of shale, sandstone, limestone
Talc -- magnesium rich

Cascade terrains collided with the North American continent 90 million years ago, thrusting up and then leveling to a plain. During the past 40 million years, heavier oceanic rocks were thrust beneath the edge of this region, pushing up the Cascades, causing volcanic activity.

Reading this geologic information really added to my understanding and excitement of this beautiful ancient terrain.

We made it to the campground by 6 p.m. and set up by 7. Our tent is pitched next to Colonial Creek, and the sound of water crashing over the boulders is a constant, pleasant backdrop to our activities.

It started raining as we were cooking macaroni and cheese, but we were under some tall fir trees, and the water wasn't making it down to us. After dinner, we went to bed. Soon drops began hitting our tent and continued for hours after it stopped raining.

We have been talking about this trip, how most of the time in life we have a destination and then go back. We are realizing and coming to peace with the understanding of not going back but continuing onward each day. I think it causes us to be more observant, go slower, and savor the moment.

Wednesday, June 26, 1996

We were up at 7 a.m. Now, we are packing. The sun is out, and mist is rising. The tent is upside down in the sun, drying. We ate breakfast in the tent, and we're almost packed by 9. In the bathroom, I spoke to a father and son from Philly. They are in a rented car touring around the country. Like us, they have the glow of travelers.

It's 9:51 p.m. We're at Lone Pine Campground, four miles east of Washington Pass (elevation, 5,457 ft.). We got here around 6:15, set up, and cooked spaghetti with a garlic clove, onion, and tomato sauce.

Today we climbed a mile in elevation on the bikes, riding 39.6 miles, averaging 7.5 mph, and actual riding time was 5:14. Quite a day. We both feel pretty good.

This terrain is stupendous. Everywhere there are tremendous vistas, and the sound of cold clear cascading water is a constant backdrop for the beautiful flowers blooming along the wayside. We took a short hike up Happy Creek, seeing deer and much beauty. It is early spring here. There is snow at this elevation, about 4,000 feet.

Retrace 2022

August 26-28, 2022
North Cascades, WA

I wore the half-penny talisman on a cord around my neck on this retrace trip. In the car, we zoomed along the North Cascades Highway, past pull-offs, not recognizing where we had met Art.

To slow down our retrace journey through the North Cascades, we stayed for three nights at Colonial Creek, giving us more time to explore this special place. Our campsite was situated on a boulder strewn dry streambed. We followed a trail up the creek to the spectacular view from Thunder Knob. Years ago on our bikes, we kept our momentum, moving steadily through this area, focused on the road ahead. This time we got to appreciate the brilliant aqua of Diablo Lake. Nearby, we took a short uncrowded hike to Rainy Lake, enjoying the mirrored reflections of the surrounding Cascades.

The part of the North Cascades beyond Colonial Creek did not exactly match to my journal. For example, we did not find Lone Pine campground which I had recorded, but we did find one named Lone Fir at the location I had described. We accepted that we may not recognize the landscape. The pictures in our minds from so long ago, often as not, did not match the scenery we experienced now. We resolved to concentrate on having fun exploring new scenes. We also began appreciating that our car allowed us to explore further from our defined route than our bicycles had permitted.

The West

Thursday, June 27, 1996

It drizzled during the night and was quite cool. The sound of cascading water was constant through the night. We got up, ate some granola bars, nuts, and water, and took a 2-mile hike through the woods. Water flows everywhere. Decaying detritus and damp green moss carpet the forest floor. The moist air smells rich and dank with pine overtones. We paused over each creek crossing, astonished and in awe of the flood of clear water crashing over rounded boulders of gneiss and granite. Some sections of the rapids were a curling white froth, licking back on its mother wave—a reflection of bottom geography of strong boulders being diminished over time, to what, I cannot fathom. Looking through the clear icy blue water at the rocks, I was reminded of our kitchen window with its old glass, rippling and bubbling the world beyond.

After our walk, we packed up and snacked again, then rode off, bundled up for what we perceived to be a brisk downhill of 15 or so miles. Shortly into the descent, we rode into a warmer, dryer climatic region. Our clothes came off to shorts and t-shirts. Sagebrush and golden-brown grasses flanked the mountainsides. Elder replaced fir as the dominant tree shape, and silence greeted us. No longer were we riding by sonorous creeks. Here were dry streambeds and smoother flowing green rivers. We have moved into the West. We have seen the last climatic ecosystem of the Pacific Maritime. This is a Continental region—chaparral, open sky, ranches, horses, the culture facing the big sky West. We ride beside the sage banks of the bold Methow River, a thirty-year-old holding down his first job with health benefits, not the rambunctious cavorting of the Cascade rebellious youth.

We descended 25 miles into Winthrop, an unabashed tourist trap that by all outward appearances seems to be successful. The shtick is the Western motif, complete with wild west facades and toilets that flush with the tug of a rope. This is RV land, and our bikes look alien chained to the wood rail fence on Main Street. We ate a curry chicken special with salad and water, ordered a mocha and a malt, and watched from the deck above, as kids played in the maze that a clever speculator built in two days last winter out of 4"x4" posts and canvas partitions.

We rode out of town on Highway 20, stopping at an IGA where we stocked up on three days' worth of food ($45). We're happy riders leaving this town.

We made it to the Methow River Campground two miles west of Twisp around 5 p.m. There was a touring bicycle and tent that I recognized as Bert's, the Canadian from several days back. We set up nearby and eagerly took showers; it had been two days since a hot shower. Bert came over, and we talked. He offered to take us out to dinner for our honeymoon.

Though we had bought baked beans and Ball Park Beef Franks, we consented to his kind offer, put the franks in a plastic bag in the cold river, and rode two miles into Twisp to the Roadkill Cafe. Bert is an interesting guy. He has cycled around the US several times, but he looks out of shape. He hardly made it over the last pass and is avoiding Loup Loup Pass and Sherman Pass by some roundabout, but seemingly leveler, routes. He is a CA (like a CPA in the States) from Vancouver BC, and he developed a software package that helps quarterly tax filers. He talked about French (Francophile) secession from Anglophile Canada, and how there was too much immigration which is breaking up the culture of Canada.

Dinner was delicious. Afterwards, we hopped on our bikes for the pleasant ride back to our tent. Our campsite is 30 feet from the Methow River which is proud in her banks, the sound of the water monotone and soothing. Cathy and I are incredibly comfortable in our little ecosystem on the road. She is my harmony to our heart song.

Friday, June 28, 1996

We're up early, 7 a.m. The sun on the tent warmed us enough to get Cathy stirring. We're packed and having breakfast by the swift-flowing Methow. The Methow doesn't freeze during the winter because its frigid flow from the mountains is mixed with warm waters coming from ground fissures under the riverbed. Thus, the river provides a wintering place for waterfowl and land creatures as well.

Yesterday, in Winthrop, I bought a *USA Today*. All in all, a disquieting experience—the car bomb blast in Saudi Arabia, US politics, the VMI case to remain all male (VMI lost), and all this US-centric, anal, analyzing, society pains. There is nothing of the beauty of the purple orchids we found, nor the humorous bellowing and blustering of the bull across the ever-flowing river, nor the chirps of the flycatchers flitting amongst the branches of the alders along the river, nor the call of the meadowlark in the distance. What self-contemptuous, ego-slavered drivel fills the paper. Money and power blind the spirit of all but the most aware. No more papers! I like being disconnected from the political madness. It fits the speed at which we travel across the earth. The land is our teacher; it sets the pace and direction.

Around 10:30 a.m., Twisp. We've stopped in the Cinnamon Twisp Bakery for some goodies and a cup of coffee. I talked to the young woman working there about Twisp. She described lots of snow and many miles of cross-country skiing (she is a cross-country racer). There's no theater in the Methow Valley, including Winthrop, which explains the videos being rented in every gas

28

station and grocery store.

9 p.m., Margie's RV Campground in Riverside. We rode a total of 49.7 miles today. Loup Loup Pass was a stout climb. We met Neville and Abby at the top. They are on a tandem Cannondale and biking to Boston. They are from England but have been in New Zealand and Australia for three years, working. They are both doctors.

The countryside continues to be a dry landscape. Green areas are achieved by irrigation or direct contact with the river. We are camped in the RV park alongside the Okanogan River. We set up camp, showered and had beans and weenies, our whole pack of Ball Park Franks.

We stopped in Okanogan at a bike shop, and I got some Triflow lubricant for chains and other moving parts. The guy adjusted Cathy's brakes and shaved some off the lower part of the pad.

Dinner was great. We had some wine, sat in our Therm-A-Rest chairs, and watched the flycatchers and western orioles zip around; the sun was golden on the ridge to the east. Many times today I rode up beside Cathy and watched her ride against the backdrop of this stark eastern Washington terrain. It is such a joy to know we are here in this place and in this time.

We have developed a pattern of riding. As we ride, I follow behind Cathy, four or five feet, towing our BOB trailer which flies a homemade bright yellow triangular pennant atop a five-foot-long fiberglass rod. We want to make sure cars approaching from behind will see us. It works. Most cars give us a wide berth. (BOB—Beast of Burden—is our detachable single-wheeled trailer attached to my bike's rear hub.)

Ultimately, our pace is determined by the terrain we traverse. We aren't in a hurry, but as we get in better shape, we will naturally be able to keep a faster, steadier pace.

Saturday, June 29, 1996, Our Two-Week Anniversary!

8:30 a.m. We loaded and rolled down to Molly's Cafe for coffee and homemade cinnamon rolls. At one time Riverside was the head of steamboat navigation on the Okanogan River. In 1904, one and a half million pounds of produce crossed the docks. Pictures on the walls of Molly's show the city in its heyday, the steamboat days, before the railroad made Riverside inconsequential.

Today the town is small and slow. Many of the buildings pictured in the old photographs are now only a memory. Molly's Cafe is the unofficial meeting place for the town. The place is packed, meaning about 20 people in the 25-foot by 30-foot room. Molly rides herd over all that transpires in the cafe. She waits the tables and collects the money. She has an incredibly loud voice; we could hear her from outside announcing someone's order of eggs over easy. There are no secrets in Molly's; everyone knows what everyone else is eating or saying to Molly. She repeats our questions like a public announcement system, yelling out, then laughing a grating laugh. Molly is a card. Riverside appreciates Molly and endures her. As I was paying her at the cash register, I made the mistake of quietly asking her what the population of Riverside was. "Hey Bill," she shouts out over the room to a man at a far table, "What's the population of Riverside?" Everyone looked up at the obvious visitor, drawing his or her own conclusions as to why I wanted to know in the first place. "Right now, about 202," Bill says. "202!" Molly repeats, shouting. We retreated to our bikes, frazzled by Molly's high blood pressure sideshow. If only her cinnamon rolls and coffee had been good, but the tasteless rolls lacked salt in the dough, and the coffee seemed to have the salt in it.

Today we are looking at 17 miles of flat and a 25-mile climb of 3000 feet over Wauconda Pass. At breakfast, Cathy leaned over the table and offered, "I'm kind of scared about today."

6:45 p.m. I am sitting in the grocery store parking lot in Republic. Cathy's inside buying wine and pancake mix with maple syrup. We're going on about nine miles to Curlew Lake State Park and resting tomorrow. We've ridden 58 miles today, thus far. As we made the long climb to Wauconda Pass (elev. 4310'), the dry landscape gave way to more pines and grasses. It was much greener. This side of the pass is greener also, even at lower elevations; we've dropped back down 2500 feet. This was one heck of a day of riding, long climbs; it was warm but refreshing. We stopped often to eat snacks to keep our energy up. We both are working hard; this is the most riding Cathy has ever done.

8:45 p.m., at the Curlew Lake showers waiting for Cathy. Nice place. The ride today was great. When we came into Wauconda (pop. 25) before the last steep push of four miles to the pass, we stopped at the Wauconda Cafe and Store, a neat old place with great food, and ordered Dan's Special—one cup of chicken and dumplings soup, nice salad, and homemade bread for $2.67! I also got a jumbo chocolate shake with real ice cream. We needed that food.

Sunday, June 30, 1996, Blue Moon

Curlew Lake State Park. On this day of rest, we made coffee and great pancakes with maple syrup and butter.

We met a couple from north of Seattle, Russ and Alice. Russ has done some riding and is very friendly. He took some photographs of us with his camera on a tripod and wide-angle lens. He's an interesting person and so is Alice.

Russ is into heirloom plants, especially apples. He talked of how in the 1700-1800s there were over 300 genetic strains of apples, but they are being lost. The same is true of wheat varieties. In the past, there were hundreds of varieties of wheat. Now there are eight varieties of wheat grown in the US. Talking with him increased my desire to learn more natural history, naturalist information. Russ told us about Ponderosa Pine and Jeffery Pine, two interesting pines of this area. He pointed out that the bark of the Jeffrey Pine smelled like cream soda. Scratch and sniff.

Cathy and I talked of taking a geology course at our local community college to give a base to understanding geologic patterns. I'd like to take a general biology course to help my learning of plant life. There's so much to learn and do.

After lunch now. I'm writing letters, visiting with Russ, and relaxing. I cleaned and oiled both bike chains and lubed all other moving parts. Both bikes are doing perfect jobs hauling us and our gear around. Fine machines.

Cathy's mapped out a course to make it to Sandpoint, Idaho by the 3rd of July, and we'll weather over the 4th there. We should be in Glacier a week from tomorrow and we plan to stay there 3 or 4 days.

Retrace 2022

Winthrop is still a thriving tourist attraction with lots of up-scale Western clothing stores and cafes with cowboy hat wearing waitresses. We ordered lunch at Rocking Horse Bakery and sat on the wood-planked sidewalk out front to eat with Jetta at our feet. It felt like Dollywood's little Western brother, and it mostly matched our memories of it.

In Twisp, I asked around for information on the Roadkill Restaurant. No one in town that day remembered it. I asked in an art gallery, the food co-op, and Cinnamon Twisp Bakery, where I purchased a couple delicious cookies. Twisp has become a center for arts, food, hiking, mountain biking, and wintertime activities like snowshoeing and cross-country skiing. There were several art galleries and restaurants serving fine food, microbrews, and world-class wine.

The Methow River campground is now an RV village with access for residents only. After explaining our mission to the manager, she reluctantly gave us special limited permission to drive around the loop. We were not allowed off the pavement, so we couldn't venture over to the river that had cooled our hotdogs.

Striking up conversations has been more difficult in general. Is it because we're going at a faster pace? Is it the lingering effect of Covid and social distancing? Is it because with a dog, there are many places we cannot enter?

Molly's Cafe in Riverside is now Appaloosa Restaurant with a barnwood sided façade and cowboy theme. Nothing is left of the old cafe vibe with its period photos. Molly does not live here anymore. According to Riverside's Clerk-Treasurer, Molly's Mom used to be an

RN at a hospital in Australia.

We spent a couple of nights at Curlew Lake State Park. Although we couldn't be precise on where our campsite had been on our bike trip, the park was very much as we remembered it. The campground was not crowded, being the end of the season. When we cooled off with a quick swim in the lake, we were the only ones in the beach area. At night, the lake reflected a beautiful crescent moon. We enjoyed our neighbor, a fellow from Spokane who was spending the final week before school started, camping and fishing with his grandson. They laughed when they saw us bathing Jetta on the expansive green lawn of our campsite. We took time to go into Republic to do our laundry.

Monday, July 1, 1996

Up around 7 a.m. We made coffee and a big batch of pancakes. Last night we called home and found out that our friends, Cathryn and David are going to fly out on the 4th of August to meet us in Great Falls, Montana for a 5-day canoe trip on the Missouri River. Great! We will contact them soon. Today we will cross Sherman Pass.

7 p.m., Kettle Falls State Park. We made it over Sherman Pass in the Kettle Range in pretty good shape, a 17-mile climb of 3000 feet. I had a bad flat in my rear tire and changed to a new tube about three miles from the summit.

We met Neal, Randy, Sharon, and Beth. We were having lunch on the ascent, when Neal and his son Randy came riding up the grade and stopped to talk. Sharon and Beth were driving support and soon joined us. It was good to see other bikers. They are carrying less and keep a faster pace than Cathy and me. Neal teaches 5th grade in Framingham, Massachusetts.

The downhill was fun, about 24 miles down to the Columbia River. We are camped on the banks of the Columbia about 100 miles upstream from the Grand Coulee Dam. We're camped in Ponderosa Pine barrens, a nice spot, not too buggy with plenty of shade amongst the trees.

We just got back from a stroll along the Columbia, throwing rocks in and watching the ripples harmonize. The ride today was fun. We saw Bert again as we left the campsite this morning. He was going a round-about route up into Canada to avoid Sherman Pass.

There were several information kiosks along our route describing the White Mountain Fire of 1988, in which twenty thousand acres of the Colville National Forest burned. We rode through a section of this burned-out forest with green undergrowth rising between the blackened trunks. After 8 years, the seedling trees were only about 16 inches tall or less.

We stopped at the Camp Growden CCC site farther along the forested roadside. There were very informative displays and information kiosks about the history of the CCC. According to the kiosks, Franklin Roosevelt started the Civilian Conservation Corps in 1932 to create jobs and to improve America's infrastructure. In nine years, 300,000 young men passed through its ranks. Most men received $1.00 a day plus food and lodging for their labors. They were required to send most of this back to their respective families; there weren't many opportunities for them to spend it in the CCC anyway. In the Pacific Northwest, the CCC built 677 lookout structures, 85,000 miles of road, 42,000 miles of hiking trails, planted millions of trees, improved wildlife habitat, fought fires, and constructed many recreational facilities still used today. In 1942, under the shadow of war and an improved economy, Congress diverted money from the CCC to the war effort, and the CCC became a footnote in history.

Further down the road, nearer the Columbia River, we stopped at a logging re-enactment site. We hiked a trail viewing ruins and exhibits showing how, in the 1920s, loggers used railroads and flumes to get logs down to the Columbia and onward to the sawmill. Human ingenuity is impressive, be it exhibited by logger barons seeking huge profits or a social experiment called the Civilian Conservation Corps.

We're having some Fig Newtons before heading to bed as dusk dims, and the few mosquitoes come out. I can hear the train leaving the Boise Cascade Wood Products Plant, which we passed a few miles upriver. It was the destination of the 20 or so logging trucks that passed us, pulling tandem trailers loaded with barked-up pine trees—always a precarious situation.

Tuesday, July 2, 1996

Up early, 6:30. Cathy is still snoozing. The temperature is 62 degrees. I can hear the bustle of enterprise; the mill is humming as a train approaches in the distance. The Columbia is glassy calm, due to the Grand Coulee Dam.

The dam (24 million tons of steel and concrete) is a mile long and twice as high as Niagara Falls. It backs up the Columbia River forming Roosevelt Lake which stretches 137 miles northward to the Canadian border and continues for miles into Canada, offering them recreational use of US facilities. The Coulee Dam National Recreational Area is surrounded, for a good part, by the Colville and Spokane Indian Reservations. Historically, Kettle Falls, where we are, was a major gathering place for Native Americans as they harvested salmon.

A few days back, I read about the young man, Bill Miner, who at 16 robbed his first stagecoach netting $25,000. He graduated to trains. Considered a "gentleman robber", ole Bill Miner left a legacy that any child playing cowboys and Indians still honors to this day; he is credited with first using the phrase, "Hands Up!" Unfortunately, he couldn't stop his thieving ways and spent many years in San Quentin, dying there an old man.

Cathy and I are perfecting our campground entrance. We ride in, survey sites, choose one near water and facilities, dismount (normally, I hope). Off comes BOB, then panniers. Out of BOB comes our ground cloth, tent, poles, and fly. Within minutes the tent is up, sleeping bag strewn across the top to air. Trips to get water are made. Within another 15 minutes, the kitchen is functioning, stove hissing, and water heating for spaghetti, Ramen noodles, macaroni and cheese, or hot drinks. Out come maps, books, etc., and we get the Therm-A-Rest chairs together, then showers—either the hot 25-cent variety, or sponge and water bottle kind at the site, in cold water. We can have this done and be eating within an hour of riding into the campground; this depends on our hunger quotient, of course.

"I'm up," I hear faintly from the tent. Time to pack, eat some granola bars and stop for coffee later.

It's 8:45 a.m. We're rolling out. So long, Columbia.

We're having breakfast in Kettle Falls. We've come 512 miles since Seattle. We saw a plastic relief map of Washington State this morning at the Park Ranger's office revealing a very mountainous terrain ahead of us.

9:51 p.m., Panhandle National Forest Service Campground. We arrived here an hour ago under threatening skies. Mosquitoes buzz everywhere. We set up and paid the two hosts with the miniature schnauzer who walked down to collect the fee. They were covered with bug spray; we weren't. In the cloud of mosquitoes and darkening skies, we took cold and hasty water bag showers, standing on the wooden table, our state of undress hidden by the brush growing along the Pend Oreille River.

I feel great now, the last mosquito is smashed against the tent wall, blood smeared across the nylon.

What a day! In Colville we bought Coleman fuel and a water bottle, then we had a great cup of coffee and conversation at Steve's Talk and Coffee. We talked about Colville (pop. 7,000). The town is run by the old power people, mainly in logging and wood products, but this is a declining enterprise now. There is no one to step up with a vision for the town. Business the old way is not the answer.

From Colville to the top of the mountain was 20 miles of hard climbing, more than we thought. Plus, it was hot and sunny, around 92 degrees. We got up to this funky tavern called Cree-ations, nestled beside the otherwise solitary two-lane highway amongst the pine forests. We were surprised to meet Bert there. He was having a beer and complaining bitterly about the climb and heading for the nearest motel, which was still 25 miles away. We had a couple Cokes and two tacos that were excellent. We left there feeling good with cold spring water in our bottles. Eight miles or so later we finally dropped down into the Pend Oreille River Valley.

We rode up to Ione, a small logging town 19 miles from the Canadian border. This is not the heyday for this town, but the surrounding countryside was beautiful. We ate at the Waterfront Inn on the Pend Oreille River by which the town rests. The food was good, despite the hot muggy temperatures out on the deck. Inside it was even hotter, a stale, musty heat, so we sat out on the deck along with two other small groups at tables. This was the only place to eat dinner in Ione.

At the table next to us, talking loudly enough for us to clearly overhear, were three men and one woman. One man appeared to be Asian, the rest white Americans. They were working on a deal. The Asian man, Chinese it turned out, represented a Chinese company that wanted to buy a shutdown sawmill in Ione and rebuild it in China. I wondered how many conversations were taking place in America like this one, a harbinger of economic trends to come. It was sadly humorous though. The Chinese man had the savvy; he spoke seven languages, including English, very well. The Americans (who had already bungled a deal in Russia) knew enough about China to fill a post card. But they were loud, Anglo-centric, and the fools.

There's some learning that's going to come down on that deal, I thought. The woman, in an Oregon Ducks sweatshirt, and one of the men were from Salem, Oregon. The other American— taut leathery brown skin, blue jeans, plaid shirt (not tucked in) and New Balance tennis shoes—smoked Kools and did most of the talking. Their main emphasis was that they wanted their salaries deposited in an "offshore" bank of their choosing with "offshore" money by the 25th of each month. If not, they were leaving.

Later it came out that the Americans thought they would still own the buildings, but the Chinese man said, "No, not at first." This caused some commotion amongst the Americans, and they agreed to check on it. Their arrogance was a sad expression of a global economic powershift in the making. China's population currently is 1.2 billion. One in five humans is a Chinese citizen. Its annual population growth is 14 million, equivalent to Australia's total population. Demand for economic growth in China is unprecedented since the dawn of the Capitalist Dream.

We left there before 8 p.m. and still had 18 miles of riding to come to this campground. We rode down the east side of the river on a great road, very quiet. Only six vehicles passed us the whole hour it took us to get here. The roadside was a lush pine forest, and we saw several deer. We were told to keep an eye out for moose, but alas, we saw none.

Cathy is sleeping now. It is drizzling and a little breeze is picking up which is great to cool this tired ole boy. We gave each other full body rubs then studied our maps, looking forward to the 60-mile ride to Sandpoint, Idaho tomorrow. We looked back to the Washington map. Again, Cathy traced our route across the North Cascades and all those memories, some 583 miles, saying names as she went—Port Townsend, Bayview, Sedro Woolley, Concrete, Rockport, Diablo, Mazama, Winthrop, Twisp, Okanogan, Omak, Tonasket, Wauconda, Republic, Kettle Falls, Tiger, Ione, Lost Creek. I love that, and I can feel that finger from my heart to my throat.

Ten seconds between last lightning and the thunder. It's getting closer.

Wednesday, July 3, 1996

We got up and packed up fast to avoid the mosquitoes. We were on the road by 8 a.m. and rode 15 miles to Usk. I'm writing this in the Usk Bar and Grill. We had a huge breakfast of omelets, pancakes, and coffee. We both are a little sore and tired this morning. We're resting up here in the bar, relaxing a bit. I think Cathy got up a little too early. We've got the water bottles in here now, going to fill them and hit the road to Idaho.

We're in Newport, Idaho, it's 1:15 p.m. Cathy's eating a banana split. I had a milkshake. We both are sore-butted and low energy. We had two tough days in a row. We climbed over Sherman Pass, the highest road pass in Washington, and yesterday we had a 25-mile hot climb and about 7 hours of actual riding time, clocking 76 miles. But Washington and the Cascade Mountains are behind us now.

Thursday, July 4, 1996, Independence Day

We were about a mile out of Newport yesterday around 4:00 when we stopped to check our maps. We were riding to a State Park, 20 miles further on. The road wasn't very well marked. I spotted a Park Ranger truck stopped at an intersection and rode over to ask directions. He told us all the campsites were full down the way toward Sandpoint, and we had better go to the Priest River Campground; they had sites reserved for bikers. This was four miles away in the same direction we were heading so it was very timely advice. We later admitted, "We're blessed."

Priest River (pop 1,560) is at the confluence of the Priest and Pend Oreille Rivers. The Pend Oreille flows northward into Canada from its headwaters around Missoula, Montana. It is the

41

only local river with a French name, which refers to the name that French trappers gave to the indigenous people living in this area who adorned their ears with shell ornaments.

This place is great, with swimming and good showers. The bicycle sites are the best sites in the campground, and we are the only bikers in the area, so we have it to ourselves. I built a fire for dinner, and we ate Ramen noodles and played harmonicas together. We went for a swim, which was cold and refreshing, then we cleaned up with 25-cent showers.

Today we're at the Village Kitchen in Priest River having breakfast. We loaded up BOB with our dirty laundry and rode 2 miles into town. I had a flat along the way. The laundromat was closed for the holiday, so we'll have to wash our clothes tomorrow. Today will be a day of rest, reading, swimming, and eating. All much needed.

I called my dad and my stepmom Annah Lee at home. They sounded good. Dad is being treated for prostate cancer, and he said his doctor told him his PSA count was down. The doc wants him to have a bone marrow examination next week. It was great hearing his voice. I want so much for him to be well and feel good this summer, and we can show them slides when we return. I pray for this.

Friday, July 5, 1996

We have been riding through a very sparsely populated region of the country with little towns of less than a thousand people. The logging industry is the main source of income, but it is declining. Many restaurants display "We Support the Timber Industry" signs by their front doors. The restaurant in Usk was dark and depressing; worn red tablecloths safety-pinned together in the middle served as sun-blocking curtains. Behind the bar was a counter lined with different chance games for money. The more economically depressed, the more we see that people are given chances to play, thus the more people play. Is just having a chance, though so pitifully small, a mental placebo or pacifier, that last step before construction of the Church of Our Lady of Perpetual Sorrows that we saw beside the headquarters of the Kalispell Indian Reservation?

The Kalispell Reservation (pop. 400) has been allowed to operate gambling casinos. They have been financially successful, yet the overall impact on their chances of being satisfied is nil. The liquor bottle feeds the sorrow, a new cycle begins. Some get out, mainly kids, through the school system.

I was told by the guy at the history museum in Newport that Indian kids, given the chance, excel at computers. He said that there are no full-blooded Pend Oreille Indians left, but are mixed with the Kalispell, Colville, and Cree. He said 100 years ago, following in the tradition of the "earless" Indians of the 1700s, if an Indian got in trouble, "they would cut off his ear and send him to the Kalispell reservation, from which they couldn't return to their own."

5 p.m., Sandpoint Idaho. We had a nice 31-mile run here to Sandpoint where we bought supplies at a bike shop—two tires for Cathy, rim tape for me, two tubes, two water bottles, and pepper spray. We're having a sandwich now then we'll move on.

The bike trail on Highway 95 coming into Sandpoint was great. There were two lanes for bikes and pedestrians after the bridge over Lake Pend Oreille. A trail dropped down to water level on a paved path. We began passing folks carrying chairs, tables, floats, and rafts, along the path toward the lake. It was a motley looking crew for sure, not many acknowledgments to my greetings. When we got to town, we came upon Barnum Circus trucks all packed up and parked by the lane. We realized that they were getting in a picnic and a swim before moving on.

Retrace 2022

Driving up Sherman Pass, we were hugely impressed with our past selves. This truly was a long climb. We stopped to walk the interpretive trails of Camp Growden and the logging reenactment site. Both were overgrown and underwhelming. But still, they made good places for all three of us to stretch our legs. We noted that Steve's Talk and Coffee doesn't exist now in Colville.

As we approached Ione, we decided to look around to see if the Waterfront Inn was still functioning. We pulled into the gravel parking lot of a neglected structure that soon became more recognizable to us. The back of the old wood-sided building overlooked the Pend Oreille River like we remembered. Nestled adjacent to the old building was a newer motel, The Riverside Inn. I noticed a young woman through the open door of the laundry room, across the parking lot from us. I walked over, motioning toward the old building, to confirm that it was the same Waterfront Inn as twenty or so years ago. She smiled timidly as she verified our conclusion. I got the feeling no one had spoken to her in a while, especially about the old Inn. I told her about our own connection there.

Her name was Brittany. She was too young to have experienced those days 26 years ago. While Cathy waited with Jetta, Brittany and I walked around the other side of the Inn. The old deck was (sort of) still there, though it was on its way to rotting off.

We thanked her for talking with us. I took a couple photos of her with a coy smile. We took a last look around, then loaded back into Evee and drove 17 miles south alongside the Pend Oreille River to the Panhandle Campground pondering the changes that 26 years can *exert.*

We took time to talk briefly with the camp hosts as they were readying for Labor Day weekend. Then we drove on to the Priest River Campground where we'd stayed 26 years ago.

When Jetta jumped out of Evee at Priest River campground, she hit the ground awkwardly and came up limping painfully on her left front leg. As I've said before, we adore her, and this concerned us. We stayed close to our tent that evening, venturing only across the camp loop road to admire the sunset over the Priest River; the smoky haze turned the setting sun bright red. The next morning, she was not limping as badly, but we were glad to have several undemanding days ahead for her to heal more completely.

We took a day trip into Sandpoint to get some groceries and explore the area. We found the Serenity Lee Trail that runs along the Pend Oreille River. It was hot, and we were still concerned about Jetta's leg, but we walked a short distance down the paved greenway to try to find the bridge where we had seen the circus crew. It did not seem familiar. I think the bridge we remembered had been dismantled, but maybe not. After a slow drive through town and an unsatisfactory stop at a Sandpoint history museum, where we didn't learn anything about the old bridge, we were ready to return to our tent in Priest River.

The next day we visited the Priest River Museum, located in a two-story wood framed house offering a front porch with rocking chairs to take in the calm activity of the town. I went in and met Joy the docent of the museum. Because of the heat, Cathy stayed outside in the open car with Jetta, letting her rest and stay off her front leg. Joy doesn't get many visitors to the well-ordered museum and was happy to show me around. She was raised in Priest River. Her father and brother were in the logging business. The first floor had nicely displayed toys, dolls, clothing, and old photographs of life and livelihoods in Priest River in the early 1900s. Upstairs was a room with walls filled with displays of chain saws from the old days; one saw had an eight-foot chain and it took two people to handle that monster. Ironically, it was quiet inside the museum. I felt we were looking at Joy's own belongings from childhood. I donated a couple of dollars and thanked her for her work preserving bits and pieces of the past of Priest River.

Saturday, July 6, 1996

8:30 a.m. We just brewed a cup of dark French alpine roast coffee, not bad for bicycle touring. We're at the Sam Owen Campground on the NE corner of Lake Pend Oreille. We got in around 8:30 last night after a 20-mile ride from Sandpoint. In Sandpoint's outskirts, we stopped for film at a Kmart. I got four rolls of slide film at a good price. When I came out, Cathy was fixing a flat; her tire had blown out. Turns out the guy at the bike shop had put 110 pounds of air pressure in her tire that called for 85 pounds. Cathy went in while I finished fixing the flat. All they had were huge puncture resistant tubes, so this is what she got.

This area of Idaho, the Panhandle, is very interesting. There are warnings for moose on signs along the highway. We didn't see any moose, just one big-racked buck deer. The Pend Oreille Lake was formed by glacial action 10 to 20 thousand years ago. The glacier dammed up the present Pend Oreille River causing a huge lake, a thousand feet deep in areas. Periodically, the dam broke, sending torrents of water that scoured the eastern Washington valleys along the present river. This is a natural lake, a remnant of the ice age, and it is huge. In the old days, boatyards and builders dotted its shore; little passenger steamboats plied the waters. Larger craft moved goods and lumber, crisscrossing the waters tucked within these mountains. The coming of the railroad began the decline of the working watercraft. Today, tourists are motored around the lake, keeping to schedule.

In the campground last night, we met Larry and Nancy from Boise, 450 miles to the south. Larry looks a little like Richard Simmons. He's out jogging now. He had run to the top of Going-to-the-Sun Road in Glacier Park and told of RVs driven by old men careening off the waist high wall that edges the narrow road. We really didn't want to hear this report, given that in a week or so we will be biking over the Going-to-the-Sun Road, and we will be riding extra close to the edge of the road.

The weather this morning is sunny and warm. Yesterday was cool, perfect riding temperature. We packed up and ate breakfast at the picnic table, with deer wandering through the campsite, tame enough that we must shoo them away.

On the way out of the campground, riding in the bright morning light, our bones and muscles just beginning to accept their fate, we stopped at the historical marker pointing out the Kullyspell House site. Built by David Thompson in 1809, this was the site of the earliest fur trade outpost in the Pacific NW. Thompson was a geographer and surveyor who mapped vast fur regions for the Northwest Company of Montreal.

11:45 a.m. We're in Clark Fork at Buck's Tavern and Cafe having lunch. Clark Fork (pop. 450) is the first place with the name of the famous explorers that we have encountered on this trip. Cathy's looking over our map for a grocery stop and camping.

I heard the cook say, "Been there, done that, going to do it again tomorrow." First time I've heard that phrase, and I think it is probably a very accurate statement. The waitress seemed unable to fathom that we didn't know where to buy groceries in Clark Fork. "Well, there's only one place..."

The ride from Clark Fork was beautiful, gradually climbing into the Rockies. When we turned left off Rt. 200 onto Highway 56, we immediately saw snow on the peaks in the distance. The Montana state line marked the beginning of Mountain Time; we lost an hour. This stretch of road was remote, and the anticipation of the Rockies intensified this feeling. Still, we pedaled on, stroke by stroke, breath by breath.

Cathy was having a tough day; her back was aching. She had loaded up on groceries at Clark Fork, putting most of them on her bike. We stopped along Highway 56 at some logs by the roadside, near a dirt road turn off. It was hard to find shade near the road on this stretch of highway. The right-of-way for the road cut a wide swath through the conifer forest. These logs had an edge of cool shade for our hot tired bodies, and we lounged on the logs as if they were Lazy Boy recliners. We ate peanut butter and crackers, summer sausage, bananas, and mixed Kool Aid. Occasionally a car or logging truck would approach along this desolate stretch of asphalt.

After our snack, I convinced Cathy to let me carry the trunk of food on BOB. This worked well since the weight didn't seem to matter to my overall load and effort. We will need to pare down our load for the Going-to-the-Sun climb.

When we entered Montana, we saw the speed limit signs. During the day the limit is "Reasonable and Prudent." We groaned, envisioning cars and trucks speeding past on this two-lane road just inches from our bodies. But to our surprise, it seemed most people did drive reasonably. Maybe this was because it was Saturday and most of the vehicles that passed were nearing their second decade, and it was Saturday.

We got to Bad Medicine Campground around 5:30 and set up camp. These USFS (United States Forest Service) campgrounds don't have showers, so we hiked down to Bull Lake in our sandals and swim trunks with soap and washcloths in tow to freshen up. A couple from Spokane assured us that the water was "not bad, surprisingly so." Under the snow-capped Ibex Mountains, we crept into the lake. Wow, a toe-cramper for sure! We got in as far as we dared and dipped and splashed and lathered and dipped again and GOT OUT! I was expecting, after the warm recommendation of the Spokane folks, Cave Mountain Lake water, like back home—warm-on-the-top-foot-layer kind of lake. Of course, I hadn't factored in the Spokane Factor; they don't know warm water!

Sunday, July 7, 1996

Up at 9 a.m. It is a chilly 54 degrees. Some folks pulled in last night; their mountain bikes have some wear on them. One bike has a sticker on its fork, "Free Your Mind."

We're becoming breakfast/energy-bar test monkeys. We have as choices this morning: Carnation Breakfast Bars (Chewy Chocolate Chip, not bad, had one already); Little Debbie low fat chewy Granola Bar (Apple); Sun-Ripe Yogurty-dipped Granola Bar (Wildberry); Quaker Chewy Granola Bar (chocolate chip); Kellogg's Nutri-Grain Cereal bars with wheat, whole grain oats and fruit (peach, cherry, and raspberry). All this washed down with orange flavored Gatorade, and we are in biker heaven. Throw in a few mosquitoes and voilà, the experience is real. Oh, add some sore leg, arm and back muscles that need stretching. Bananas too.

After breakfast at Bull Lake, we left our tent and gear at the campsite and rode empty up to Ross Creek Cedar Grove. This was a pretty good climb, and we both were a little sore. The cedars were magnificent, clustered in small stands of three or four trees. Many were 500 years old, and 4 to 6 feet across. These massive trees were seedlings when Columbus came over. We walked the mile-long nature trail, enjoying the special feel of these gentle giants, touching them, and sitting amongst them, feeling the solitude of their haven.

On the way back to camp a car stopped, and the driver warned us he saw a bear cub up the road and to be careful. We, of course, wanted to see the cub and equally so, we didn't want Mom to maul us on the bikes, so we rode on with heightened awareness at every bend. We saw no bear cub but did stop several times to appreciate its environs of sprawling conifer forest, falling streams, and searing blue sky. This ride reinvigorated us. We returned and quickly packed up our gear onto the bikes, watered up our bottles, and rode onward into the new day.

We're at the intersection of Highway 56 and Rt. 2, two miles along the road at York. York is the lowest point in Montana, which doesn't bode too well for our grade from here. Cathy just called Lake McDonald in Glacier Park to see if we could reserve a site for Thursday night. They said they reserve the hiker/biker sites until 9 p.m. We're planning to stay four days before going over the top of the continental divide.

Cathy is calling home now. I look forward to hearing about the conversation. I ask questions periodically for miles, seeking clarification, nuances to all that was said. Sometimes this drives Cathy crazy.

She's done. Let the questions begin. "They say hello. They still have colds." What? That's it? Well, I'm going to have to fire her, not nearly enough information!

Today, we stopped in Libby at a medium-sized grocery store and stocked up on food, including steaks. We rode on Rt. 37 along the Kootenai River, a beautiful river that is a scenic Montana postcard. There were several drift boats, flat bottomed dory-type boats with sweeping high bows. In one, a guy was working the oars, and two guys were fly fishing, one in the bow, one in the stern. Both fishermen stood, working the water with their fly rods, drifting along with the frisky current of the mountain-born river. This is how I like to fish, standing in a boat. We rode by scenes like these several times in the long afternoon light of summer.

Osprey were fishing the river too. Once, one arced down tangent to a section of deep glassy water; its claws touched the surface, parting the water for twenty-five feet. Ospreys are beautiful hunters, the most successful of North American predatory birds. Their claws are adapted to fishing such that one of the front three claws can rotate and face the same way the rear claw faces. The two opposing pairs of claws are better for plucking a fish from the water. They also dive for fish, bringing them to the surface. Osprey can take off from the water with bigger fish because they turn the fish headfirst into the direction they want to fly. The struggling fish might aid the osprey's takeoff by helping it to get going in the water.

On the shore opposite us were heavily wooded pine and fir mountain ridges. We climbed up to the Kootenai Dam. Kootenai is the name of the Native Americans that lived in this region in the late 1700s and early 1800s. The waters of Lake Kootenai flooded an old railroad line that was used to bring mineral ore out of Canada and Montana. The dam also flooded three or four whistle-stop towns, complete with churches, schools, and homes that vanished beneath the rising waters. The lake is long and narrow, flooding the upland valley for 60 miles further into Canada. The dam was constructed in 1958. The electricity generated by the hydro-electric dam is cabled directly with Seattle, some 840 miles away (by our odometer).

We passed a biker heading west. He started in Maine ten weeks ago. His name was Carl, and he was from South Africa. We don't see many tourers and when we do, whoever sees them first says, "Bikers!", and we both prepare to stop. Talking to a fellow traveler is a tradition as old as mankind. Carl wasn't too much into that tradition; he never stopped. He slowed enough to pass the basic info back and forth. He said Logan Pass wasn't too bad, but we noticed that he wasn't carrying a tent or cooking supplies. He asked us to tell his two brothers further back that he was going on into the nearest town and to meet him at the first bar, and he was off. Well, we enjoyed the stop anyway.

11 p.m. at Lake Koocanusa Resort. It's just getting dark! We ended up going 20 miles farther than we had planned. We

were whupped when we pulled in here at 9:00. We quickly set up camp, walked down for hot showers (Ahh, heaven!), came back and cooked Spanish rice and green beans, and pan-fried 2 sirloin steaks. We ate just a step above wild dogs.

Dusk lasts a long time, and by the time dishes were done and everything ready for bed (lock bikes together, food in the tent), we still didn't have to use our headlamps at 11:00!

Monday, July 8, 1996

We were up by 8:30; it's another beautiful morning. I hustled down and put a load in the washer. Now I'm back having coffee and breakfast bars, a banana, and an apple. I'm feeling great; Cathy is too, but we're stiff. We're looking at maps and ciphering.

We met Dick from Ontario, Oregon in the campground. He and his wife have been spending summers here for 20 years and have occupied the same site for 10 years. They have a large RV camper and Dick has built a small deck off the front. Dick fishes and chops wood. He has a friend in Libby, and he takes his fish there to smoke them. He gave us two preserved whitefish about 8 inches long. He used to run a Ford tractor dealership. He sold it 20 years ago and he's "been bumming ever since."

7:12 p.m. We are at the Mariners Haven Campground near Rexford. We biked 38 miles today, averaging 10.9 MPH, and rolled the wheels for 3:28. It was a tiring ride, somewhat up then down, then up again. It was sunny and warm, in the high 80s. We have biked 841 miles from Seattle.

We saw osprey along the ride, several nests atop pine trees overlooking the lake. And, at one point, four deer—two big bucks and two smaller does—jumped up on the road from the lake side; the opposite side of the road was the vertical rock wall side of the mountain. They saw us fifty yards off and froze. At the same time, an empty logging truck rounded the curve, coming down the grade toward us. The bucks decided to go back down over the guardrail toward the lake, but one of the does was slow to move, and the driver locked the brakes on his huge machine. He missed her by a hair, literally. As he passed us, I made the "close call" signal—the motion of wiping sweat from my brow. I saw him in the cab right beside us and he was simultaneously making the same motion! That was close.

We ate one of Dick's fish for lunch on a bagel with mustard, and it was tasty. Speaking of eating, Cathy has made lemon pepper pasta with chili con carne on top, corn on the side. Plus, we're having a couple red eyes. Mmm, life is sweet.

Retrace 2022

September 3, 2022
Lake Pend Oreille, ID to Lake Koocanusa, MT

When we left Priest River, the smoky haze from forest fires was the thickest we'd experienced. We drove on to Sam Owen. We saw the marker for the Kullyspell House site on our way into the campground. At least that made us feel like we were in the right place because the camping area had changed drastically. A year earlier, over the Labor Day weekend, a storm had blown through, downing many trees. Photos of the extensive damage showed RVs, tents, and vehicles buried among the branches and trunks of uprooted trees. Remarkably, no one was hurt. The campground closed for the massive cleanup. An assessment by the forest service identified other weakened trees and those were also removed. The area had reopened but this operation had left the forest much thinner. Stumps seemed to outnumber standing trees.

We picnicked at Bad Medicine Campground on Bull Lake, then we drove over to Ross Cedar Grove Scenic Area. We hiked into the spectacular Cedar Groves on the interpretive loop trail. The paths were filled with lively families happily sharing this special place. Some of the ancient western red cedars are more than 8 feet in diameter and loom 175 feet above Ross Creek. At one spot, three Cedar trees grew so close that their roots combined. We recognized it as one where we had snapped a photo 26 years ago. I climbed into the base of these three 500-year-old trees and felt a timeless connection with these ancient beings. Later, we compared the pictures from the two eras and were amazed to see that the trees were visibly larger. Well, over a quarter century had passed, maybe we shouldn't have been surprised.

We drove down through the Lake Koocanusa Resort where we had met Dick. It is still an active summer retreat full of semi-permanent campers, fishing boats, and folks living the dream.

Mariner's Haven had been turned into a residential lake development. Although not included in my original journal, (I must not have had the opportunity to write at the time) we had camped in one of the campground's teepees, for the fun of it. Strangely, that night water began puddling around the perimeter of the teepee. We woke up to see water rising toward our sleeping bag. After realizing that it was only getting higher, we dragged our gear outside to higher ground and spent the rest of the night under the stars. The next day we learned that an irrigation dam had burst, creating a small flood—small in that we were probably the only ones affected by it. Revisiting the area, we thought we could identify where the teepee had been, but the surroundings had changed; Mariner's Haven was now a subdivision.

On this retrace, we stayed nearby at a NFS campground Rexford Bench. We were looking forward to nice facilities with showers. But when we got there, the sewer line had just broken, so there were no working facilities at all. The closest available pit toilet, in the parking lot of the swimming area, was a mile from our campsite. The next day, staff finally brought porta-potties into the campground. With the showers still closed, Cathy took an abbreviated bath in the lake with her bathing suit on. It was too cold for me.

Staying here for two nights afforded us time to hike on the bluffs above the fantastically turquoise Lake Koocanusa. Jetta's paw seemed mostly recovered and she happily jaunted along with us.

<<<<< >>>>>

Tuesday, July 9, 1996

Today is another warm sunny day. We are about seven miles down the road from Mariner's Haven in Eureka at the Sunflower Bakery and coffeehouse having the Breakfast No. 2. We met Tom and Debbie, avid rock climbers and New Yorkers. Tom guides at a climbing school near Lake George. We also met a fellow Virginian, Mike who owns a cafe in Richmond. His sister is an artist and bakes bread at a cafe near our home in Roanoke. She biked cross country years back. It's a small world.

From the little town of Fortine, we mailed a package home—one cassette tape (fully recorded), five rolls of exposed film, maps, souvenir brochures, two t-shirts (one is Cathy's great t-shirt of a woman coming out of the surf carrying a male mermaid), a pair of gloves, and two harmonicas. This lightened our load a bit in preparation for Going-to-the-Sun Road.

Wednesday, July 10, 1996

10 a.m. We're at Dog Creek Campground about three miles west of Olney, Montana. Whitefish is 21 miles east.

This morning I fixed a flat on Cathy's rear tire and put in the huge puncture resistant tube. We had breakfast at Pards meal-trailer behind the campground store and met Cindy, the owner. I taped her talking while she made a big breakfast for us. She has a great big laugh and friendly smile. I hope things go well for her. She is giving this meal-trailer a try, but it seems she is out in the middle of nowhere, with little chance of many customers. She stays in a trailer along Dog Creek.

I'm in a deli in Whitefish. Cathy is at an optometrist trying to get her glasses lens fixed because it keeps popping out. At the bike shop here, she bought a mirror and spare tube. The shop was busy and well run. The repair person was hard at it, and his workman-like pace and obvious skill were refreshing compared to some of the shops that we have seen that are just trying to sell bikes, mainly "mountain" bikes, which is the current trendy thing to have. Outside the shop we met a couple from British Columbia who are cycling the continental divide route. They both pulled BOB trailers and have used them for several years. Like me, they are very enthusiastic about them.

Whitefish is a small tourist resort town with golf courses, a Nordic center, and skiing trails. The atmosphere is casual. Several restaurants have tables outside to take in the local color. We see professional outdoor adventure groups, their vans bristling with mountain bikes and gear. Hiking shoes are in, as are shorts with tights for women.

The roads here are terrible though, many potholes and crumbled edges. The 20-mile ride from the campground to Whitefish, over a serious climb on a narrow, twisty road with the noon logging truck rush, was as perilous a stretch as we have ridden thus far. Maddening is a good description also.

With the abundance of caution required by these dangerous road conditions, we put our faith in drivers seeing BOB's yellow flag. On this road, with blind curves and no shoulder, I look ahead to Cathy, riding strong and steady, and a prayer goes out for her safety.

Cathy is back from the optometrist but no luck on her glasses; looks like a job for duct tape.

Retrace 2022

The campground store and Cindy's meal-trailer have been re-placed with a small motel, Dog Creek Lodge.

As for the package that we had mailed to our home from Fortine described in my journal, the package never made it to our home. Such a loss is hard to accept. The worst for us was losing all the photos and tape recordings from this first leg of our trip.

We drove into Whitefish on Labor Day, and lots of people were out and about. We got a salad at Thriftway and ate it in a nearby city park along the Whitefish River. Since Jetta's paw was now much better, we decided to take a hike on the popular Lion Mountain Trail. This would have been fun on a mountain bike, but it was not a particularly scenic walk. We laughed remembering a time when we thought mountain bikes were just a trend.

The Rocky Mountains

Thursday, July 11, 1996

We are staying in Glacier Campground, about 1½ miles from the town of West Glacier and the entrance to Glacier National Park. This is a nice campground, $3.50/person, including good showers. Bert from Canada left here yesterday morning; we found his receipt in the campfire ring. There were two recumbent bicyclists last night, but they left this morning. We talked with cyclists Robert and Mike who teach junior high school science and are riding for a few weeks in this area. They left this morning for Logan Pass.

I'm having trouble with BOB's tube. I called the shop back in Whitefish, and Nancy there is seeing if anybody is coming this way who could bring a tube out to me at the campground. We were just there yesterday, but I didn't have this problem until we were almost here. I need a spare BOB tube anyway; it is a 17-inch tube.

It is funny, this time space paradigm we are in. To us, the distance to Whitefish (50+ mile round trip) is a good day's ride, given that we are carrying our home with us, about 230 pounds between the two of us. But to an automobile driver, it is less than an hour away! Hills are of little consequence to a car, but terrain is a major factor to us, and this is hilly country. I am surprised each time something like this strikes me. I am in the slower paradigm; things make more sense to me at this speed. To us we are traveling too fast at times to take it all in.

We're spending this morning doing laundry, writing some postcards, and moving our tent site. There is a group of 30 kids coming to the bike area today and the campground manager is letting us move to a regular (and quieter) campsite for the same biker rate.

7 p.m. We rode down to Apgar at Lake McDonald for an outing. We got maps at the information center and sat by the lake pondering our hikes and looking up toward the towering, craggy, snow draped peaks of the Rockies. I could see Going-to-the-Sun Highway far off, angling up the side of the Garden Wall range. The angle of ascent is 6%. I started to want a nap, so we rode back to the tent. We both took naps, and then showered.

I'm rested but still groggy. Cathy is counting and registering our traveler's checks, and soon we will know how much we have spent thus far.

I called Glacier Cyclery, and they said a friend would bring the BOB tube up in the morning. I ordered two tubes and a tire, so now we have extras for all the wheels in the Crawford vehicle ensemble.

We also called Cathryn and had a good chat about our planned river trip. It looks like the whole trip will cost us $500 including two nights in a motel, food, and the river trip. What fun. She's also willing to bring things out to us, hopefully the guitar and fiddle.

The report is in: After 23½ days on the road, including our shopping spree in Seattle, we have spent $1,210. This averages to $55 per day. There are some expenses that are not normal—tires, mirror, bags, etc.—but this isn't bad. Food is our big expense. We have $2,800 left.

Friday, July 12, 1996

I was up early and walked down to the office for a cup of coffee and to see what Hurricane Bertha was doing. She's weakening and hitting the NC and SC coasts today around noon.

I was glad to hear it is weakening. I was watching the Today Show on the office TV. The radar images of the Southeastern seaboard seemed so far removed from here.

Looking at the wall of granite around me, thrusting rock into the heavens, I realized the temperature difference from here to the ridge is not 5 degrees like the Blue Ridge, but is 40 degrees. The Rockies are a huge natural barrier, a divider of weather systems, the terminus of ecosystems, and mother of a drier, harsher climate. The eastern side of the Rockies up to the 98th meridian is the warren of the Great Plains, incubator of the western myth, the insulator of a continent, a definer of cultures.

Time/Distance. These two concepts are readjusted in our minds as we cycle across America. Cycling creates a black hole, where time is sucked in and lengthened until we stop and stay put for a few days. Then all that stretched out time de-accordions into now, and memory and reflection dance. Images from Port Townsend, Bayview, Rockport, have as much immediacy as those of yesterday, two days ago, last week.

Furthermore, the impact of the internal combustion engine on space, its warping, is unfathomable. I overheard a woman yesterday, checking in to the campground. She and her husband left here in the morning in their car driving over Logan Pass to the east. Then they turned north to Calgary, then west across the Canadian Rockies, then south into Idaho down to Bonner's Ferry and then they decided to come back here, to the same campground. All this in ONE DAY! If we so determined to take this course on our bikes, we would surely take two to three weeks.

It is 52 degrees. The sun is up a little more, beaming into the forest floor through the birch, aspen, small maples, alder, larch, and pine. Cathy has just made two bowls of fruit, yogurt, and granola—perfect. Our empty containers become little refuse units for our trash. I imagined if we had to carry it with us and Cathy said, "We couldn't do it in America, too much packaging."

Wow! The proprietor of the campground just drove up in his golf cart with BOB's tubes and tire. Just 14 dollars for all that, plus campsite delivery!

We rode empty bikes to the east side of Lake McDonald and hiked up, over and down to Trout Lake. The hike was 8.4 miles round trip, up 2,100 feet, down 2,100 feet to the lake then back to the bikes. We biked 33 miles round trip. The hike was beautiful, through thick areas of beargrass in perfect bloom. Beargrass was misnamed by Lewis and Clark as bears don't like it at all. Native Americans made watertight baskets from its grassy leaves. We saw two avalanche paths from last winter.

We ate lunch out on a log jam of driftwood at the downstream side of the lake. A loon swam in the crystal blue water, another called from beyond. A mink-like animal scurried along the logs, dipping into the water, washing its front feet, and moving on. The silence and reverie lasted about 20 minutes, when another hiking group, three kids and two adult men, showed up. The logs beckoned the kids. They scampered around barefoot, threatening to dump our picnic, which was balanced on the logs interconnected like floating pick-up sticks.

We left shortly after an older man came, and having no water, he scooped a cupful of lake water and guzzled it down. Giardia is a common organism in water that is untreated. I hope his guts are OK today.

Tonight, we had the BBQ, salad, and beans all-you-can-eat deal ($5.95) for the 3rd dinner in a row at the BBQ joint in the campground. We met Phil, a Soils master's student at VPI. He had a Tech t-shirt on, and I walked up to him and said, "How 'bout them Hokies?" Later, Cathy and I went back to the restaurant to an interesting and informative wildflower talk.

Saturday, July 13, 1996

3 p.m., Avalanche Falls Campground. We got up before 7:00, had breakfast, and packed up camp. We stopped in West Glacier and bought three days' worth of food. Cathy had to pee so bad in the grocery store that it hurt me to see her dancing around in the aisles unable to think.

The short 18-mile ride up to here wasn't too bad. A biker passing from the other direction cautioned us to be careful, a cyclist had gotten hit up ahead. The road is not very wide and has no bike lane. I ride about five feet behind Cathy, both of us riding with our tires oh so close to the white line marking the edge of this narrow road, hoping cars behind us will see BOB's yellow pennant flying, and praying they aren't just sight-seeing but are being aware of the road they travel. I hope there is less traffic on Monday when we go over the pass.

I took a nap shortly after putting up the tent and eating lunch. I'm pretty beat and sore from yesterday's hike; Cathy is too. We are surprised at how out-of-shape our hiking muscles are. We are stiff little puppies today. We did take a short walk up to the Avalanche Creek Falls where it twists, tumbles and leaps through and down a narrow solid rock channel.

The bike area ($6/night) is located near the entrance across from the hosts' RV. Behind them is a constantly running generator that supplies electricity to run the hosts' RV. We'll have to put up with it. They said it didn't bother them. They just think of it like it is the sound of a waterfall. Here they are in a pristine wilderness, 9,000-foot peaks majestically tower above, and they sit in this sound-polluted zone until they don't notice anymore.

The camp hostess has articles posted by her RV about grizzly attacks, "I'll never go hiking again," one headline shouts. Another article is titled "Can't see the trees for the RVs." It's about the current superintendent of Glacier National Park and his plan to remove this campground, along with its grove of 300-year-old cedars and pave it over to form an RV park. She was very critical of it, saying he came from Mammoth Cave in Kentucky, and this is his mark he wants to make—allow the big RVs to get up into the mountains this far. Wilderness through the windshield and *Days of Our Lives* on the tube, Heaven!

Cathy has added more fluorescent paint to her bags to aid visibility, and I think I'll work on mine too. We've carried those paint tubes all this way; we're not carrying them over the pass.

Dinner is under way, spaghetti with stir-fried broccoli, mushrooms, and garlic. The roar of our cook stove adds to the clamor of the host's generator.

Retrace 2022

September 5-7, 2022
Glacier Campground, West Glacier, MT

It was gratifying to be back in Glacier Campground where we had enjoyed our time on the west side of Glacier 26 years earlier. Covid protocols meant that there was no socializing inside the campground office this time. A new concessionaire had taken over the BBQ restaurant, but it had just closed for the season, so we missed out.

Since we had Evee, we pondered driving through the Canadian Rockies and back again, like the couple I had overheard 26 years ago. But we shied away from the idea when Google maps calculated 8-plus hours of driving, not including stops. That was more than we were willing to do.

A truck with a big camper, pulled in beside our campsite. I went over to visit with Andy and Lynn. Andy has a fishing boat in Alaska and trawls for crab, halibut, and other species. I couldn't believe my ears when he said he'd also fished on Glover's Reef, five miles across the channel from Hopkins, Belize. In the early 1990s, Cathy and I stayed several times in Hopkins while I was working on my master's degree, so I knew that area well.

Although it's a vastly different experience in a car, Glacier is still truly beautiful through the windshield. The Going-to-the-Sun Road was breathtaking. Surprisingly, it seemed narrower and more treacherous driving a car than riding a bike. The views on that day were somewhat hazy. We could see a small forest fire burning on a mountainside across the valley.

On our tour that day we checked out the Visitor Center at Logan Pass, and we picnicked at Sprague Creek overlooking Lake Mc-Donald. I hung out with Jetta while Cathy hiked the short loop at Av-

alanche Falls. She snapped a few photos showing the water flow much lower than our previous visit. At Lake McDonald Lodge it was shady and cool enough to leave Jetta in the car while we went in for a quick marvel at the craftsmanship of the building and the extensive decor of mounted trophies of elk, deer, moose, pronghorns, bighorn sheep, and mountain goats.

Avalanche Campground was closed and we couldn't enter. But we were glad to see it seemed intact and still fully wooded, not an RV parking lot.

To hike at Glacier with Jetta, we had to be creative. Most of the park was not accessible to us. Generally, dogs can go only where cars can go. The paved trail we had used on our bikes between the West Glacier entrance and Apgar Village permitted dogs. The three of us strolled through woods to Lake McDonald, then along the shore.

Cathy had researched and found some hiking options outside the park where dogs are allowed. So, on our second day, we traipsed up to Staunton Lake in Flathead National Forest and Great Bear Wilderness. The steady climb brought us to a placid, idyllic lake. We passed a few other hikers, but mostly had the lake to ourselves. We lounged on the bank and ate our lunch while Jetta enjoyed wading along the shallow shore.

Sunday, July 14, 1996

It is 53 degrees in the tent this morning at 7:30, cool mountain temperatures. We mixed some Bisquick pancakes (we didn't know you needed milk and eggs) and had them with maple syrup. I'm on my second cup of coffee. It is a beautiful day again, sunny, not a cloud in the sky. We're getting ready to hike up to Avalanche Lake.

The sheer peak just to our east, Cannon Peak, is a vertical mile above us here in the campsite. In 1901, a couple climbed it on their honeymoon. They wrote their names, date, and honeymoon information on a piece of paper, put it in a medicine bottle, and left it on the peak. It was found up there a few years back, and the peak was renamed for them.

After breakfast, we hiked to Avalanche Lake, rimmed with 5,000-foot peaks. Five waterfalls cascade into the basin. The water is turquoise-clear blue. The only drawback? People. This is the most heavily used trail in the park, with an elevation gain of only 500 feet. There aren't many easily accessible hikes, thus multitudes descend in all shapes, sizes, and ages. Yet it was still pleasant, the awesome spectacle overwhelming all other thoughts, the mossy green forest bottom lying in wait under rustic rowdy pine trunks as the sharp sunlight, succumbing to forest mist and hue, filters to the ground in soft patches. In brighter areas, where an old fir, larch, or ponderosa pine has lain to the earth leaving a sun gap, ferns abound, and Devil's Club turns its large maple-shaped leaves toward the light. Queen's Cup Bead Lilies like this moist haven too.

This evening, two bike tourers arrived, Lilly and Chloe. They are from the San Francisco Bay Area. We had a good time talking with them about their trip and comparing notes. They are heading to Michigan.

Linda, a small woman on a recumbent also biked in. She had a cool rig. Her gear fit in two panniers plus a bag for her tent and sleeping bag. She is so little that she uses a child's sleeping bag. Like Chloe and Lilly, she hails from the Bay Area, so they chatted it up.

We attended the naturalist's talk tonight in the campground. It was weak, not much substance. I'm looking forward to biking over the Continental Divide on the Going-to-the-Sun Road in the morning. I've lubed my pedals, aired up both bikes, and put a new tube in BOB's tire. We are ready!

Monday, July 15, 1996

6:17 p.m., Johnson's Campground, St. Mary. We rode over Logan Pass this morning. We got up around 6:30, packed, ate, and left camp at 8:00. We rode steady; the serious grade started about five miles from camp. Several bikers were on the Going-to-the-Sun Road today, two different groups, one supported, the other not. I'd say about 35 bicyclists in all were making the crossing with us this morning. Cathy and I hung with the best of them. We were so excited at the whole scene, the incredible vistas, the road itself creeping up the side of the Garden Wall, waterfalls, rainbows, snow walls, mountain goats, a grouse hen and her chicks clucking along the precipice. We hardly felt our weight it was so exciting.

Logan Pass was beautiful, the snow fields bright in the rare air. We ate lunch sitting on a rock, in awe of where we were and how we had gotten there. We rested a bit, watching two dudes hiking up to a snow field with their skis strapped to their backs. Then we mounted our bikes for the descent down the eastern side of the Continental Divide. Dropping down, we immediately sensed it was warmer, the smaller trees and aspen groves indicating a change in biomes. The wind increased and the sun intensified on the dry land. Such a change in environments in one day by riding a bicycle is exhilarating and awe-inspiring.

We saw the Triple Divide Peak, a three-sided peak that divides the waters to the Pacific on the west, the Gulf of Mexico on the east and the Hudson Bay to the north. We took lots of photos on the way up the pass, and I made periodic tape recordings. On the way down, I was recording when I hit a pothole and the tape recorder flew up. I almost caught it, but alas, it crashed to the road. I was able to retrieve it before a car smashed it, and I think it is OK!

At a deli in St. Mary, we met and talked with Robert from Natchez, Mississippi. Robert, who is retired, rode a train up here and has been hiking and camping the back trails here and in Waterton, Canada. He said he came through Glacier on a train in the army and always wanted to come back and hike. He is only the second Black man we have seen in Montana.

We are doing laundry at the campground. I'm in a shaded grassy area with a nice breeze and a bench swing. I tried to nap in the yard, but the little bugs and flies put an end to that.

Stats for today: 36 miles; Av. 8 mph; Mx 35.9mph; Odometer 1029; Time 4:00.

Tuesday, July 16, 1996

8:26 a.m. We're at Johnson's Cafe having the breakfast special. I feel great. Cathy reports feeling good, but she's sleepy faced. Last night, Cathy was awakened by a guy from a youth group that was staying here. He was wandering around in the dark muttering to himself, unable to find his tent. After a short time, she got up and helped him locate it.

This morning, the folks in a truck camper came over to

71

talk to Cathy while I was in the restroom. They're from south Texas and are vacationing in Montana. As they left, the lady said, "As you get further south, watch out for vandalism." I took it as a slight to Mexican folk.

Wednesday, July 17, 1996

Just boiled coffee water with the jet stove—quiet returns. It is overcast this morning, the first overcast morning in several weeks. The campsite is great. Swift Current Ridge towers to the north and Boulder Ridge is hunkered to the south. The valley to the west terminates with the Grinnell Glacier still present in the bowl-shaped cirque.

Yesterday, after breakfast at Johnson's Cafe, we headed along Lower Saint Mary Lake, northward toward Babb, ten miles away. As we left the Cafe, so did six bikers, retired folk from California, who are friends and are on a two-week bike tour heading into Canada. A couple of them drive a support van and they switch off on this duty. It was fun talking with them. They rode stronger than I expected. BOB and I led for a time, but they kept my pace and eventually, I fell back to join Cathy coming along. I had been throwing the wood to it going 20+ mph, making the best of a tailwind and rolling terrain—much faster than our normal sustainable pace. But it sure got the heart pumping.

We got to Babb quickly. Babb consisted of one bar, one Sinclair gas station with its green dinosaur sign, and a tiny grocery store which was not too bad, as it turned out. We spent sixty dollars there for three days of food. We bought Canadian and Montana flags; I mounted the Montana flag on the top of BOB's standard and off we flew. The owner of the store was from Georgia and had attempted hiking the Appalachian Trail but got blood poisoning from a burst blister and ended up in a hospital for two days. He wants to try it again.

We left Babb on a secondary road toward the northwest and the Many Glacier section of the park. We rode in the teeth of the twenty-mph headwind, but the road climbed only a hundred feet in the ten miles to the park. We eased along well for the circumstances and made it to the campground in less than two hours, including stops to view the Swiftcurrent River flowing out of the valley we were entering.

Upon arrival, we reconnoitered some, set up camp, loaded the metal bear resistant food box, and went on an eight-mile hike up to Grinnell Glacier. The trail was closed by snow so we couldn't actually get to the glacier. We could see where the park rangers were dynamiting the snowbank to clear the trail.

What a beautiful place. Wildflowers are at their peak—Beargrass, Indian paintbrush, Queen's Cup Bead Lily, and Aspen trees. The views are amazing. It is almost too much, sensory overload! We hiked by three little glacial lakes aligned along the valley like turquoise jewels on Mother Earth herself. The Blackfeet name for this area translates to "Land of the Walled-in Lakes." Waterfalls misted, sprayed, and roared into the valley from both sides of the rocky ridges—prime mountain goat territory. We thought we spotted several, but they turned out to be the bleached white, twisted shapes of Alpine fir deadwood. We freshened up at one petite falls, the nooks revealing salmon-colored columbine and tiny orchids, life perfectly adapted to this biome of the high plains and mountains.

We got back and met Sam from Seattle, a sixth-grade inner-city schoolteacher. He took a train to East Glacier and is hiking around. He is eating at the restaurant here and can't believe the thoroughness of our kitchen and gear. I can't either! Cathy is amazing; she has organized an Outdoor Kitchen bag, the herbs and spices, everything we need for good food which she prepares with little hassle and such enjoyment. Uh oh, I hear the zipper fanfare of her entrance to the new day. I am so lucky. We are so lucky.

Thursday, July 18, 1996

We're eating muffins and sipping camp-brewed coffee. Cathy checked the temperature; it's 55 degrees. It is overcast, the gray mist lapping the mountain ridges. We are feeling fine after yesterday's great hike. Kio, a Japanese bicyclist who rolled in yesterday evening, is packing up his bike and heading on toward Alaska, quietly.

Yesterday morning we got up and fixed blueberry pancakes with maple syrup. We invited Sam to join us for breakfast and we had a good time eating and talking.

Afterward, the three of us hiked up to Ptarmigan Lake, about 12-miles round-trip. The lake is named for the bird which turns white in the winter. The hike was beautiful. The day was sunny and in the 70s. We are at peak wildflower season.

When we got to the lake, situated in a bowl rimmed with snow fields, a fifth of the lake was frozen. Cathy and I, still warm from the hike, decided to dive in. This was the coldest and briefest swim either of us has experienced—a real toe-cramper! Afterwards, we sat by the lake's edge trying to take in this place. We ate a packed lunch and talked, while spotting mountain goats traversing the scree in the far distance. Cathy and I hiked on up to Ptarmigan Tunnel and looked out into Canada across the stunning Rockies.

This place is so magnificent. The scale is beyond comprehension of distance or time. The folded and colorful layers of sedimentary rock exposed and soon to be scree are ribbons of time. Looking into the throat of a tiny orchid with the magnifying lens—another glimpse of time, delicate, intelligent time. Scanning a slab of stone with the lens over a colony of fungus pods, metallic black round spires holding forth bits of genetic wisdom, the depth of field so flat on the little lens such that two or three black shiny orbs come into focus at a time, their surfaces creased slightly, ready to spew forth their riches, their hopes, their life into the liquid airy sea.

There, in with the buttercups, the same juicy yellow, the glacier lilies, their petals curling back open, happy. The flowers nod in the breeze. This is their domain, these snowy glades. In early spring, while the snows still cover the frozen ground, the glacier lily concocts its juices in a warm brew, generating enough heat to melt away the covering snow, freeing its thin corkscrewing leaves into the sun's life-giving light—already the stem rising with its promising bud into the alpine sky.

Or there, with the others, small delicate plants growing in harmony with the moist rock ledge, tucked and clinging effortlessly, exerting only as needed in the rare air, using this place without resistance to unfold its pure light forms. There rises on its minute streak of stalk, the burst of the Sticky Shooting Star, the size of a small dream, its fuchsia petals streaming back, the thrusting, streaking yellow center with its stamen parting the coming space—another glimpse of time too mysterious to comprehend.

Looking up to the jagged rims of the circling ridges, patterns of an ancient glacier which three million years ago ground this cirque. The stark, naked edge between ridge and sky, solarized in time, ever-changing perspective of stars. And there along the steep sloped snowfield, up there, a mountain goat, its white coat grayed by the blinding white snow, nimbly step/slides diagonally down to the angled alpine meadow. Distance draws the figure back, away toward a black and white image, a shape, a goat form.

The clear air gives little hint of space. Indeed, things

flatten, layer, overlay till you are left with time, time to be here, on this ground, within this ancient paradigm. This rhythm, this unfathomable scale, permeates one's reason, questions reality. Is it not mid-July, surrounded by flowers of native wildness, superimposed over barren rock scree, and ridges and fields of frozen water, white marbled fields, its edges pocked with blue ice hovering over the ground inches or more like a loose-fitting cap on a lad's furtive head?

But what of this place? What of this time? And this scale? Is it not a function of focus, perspective, a crystal dream you can't forget to remember its beginning or its end? What is the meaning of this stacked, layered, lifted, crumbling time, like a catch of breath in the chest of time? Does it not say to the habitual thought, be here, be gone? Why not accept this challenge, slip back from preconceived structure and smile at the wisdom of the anther and pistil, the molting fur of the summer goat, the shriek of the raven flying backward into the raucous gusts of wind, yielding, and bearing off to the lee of a fir stand? Let our wisdom be realized as a lens, layering, lengthening our vision, bringing what is between, beyond, beside into focus. In this time, let the joy well up, bend and touch the ground, its life is but an eon to the moment of man.

Our trek yesterday also took us to Iceberg Lake. The lake, set in a three-quarter round bowl of vertical cliffs, was filled with ice. The snow and ice were covered with fallen debris; the ground was wet, an alpine bog. A buck and doe foraged along the water's edge in the brush, the buck's antlers molting and fuzzy, like a felt toy.

Today I sit writing inside the grand and historic Many Glacier Hotel. The SW wind of a massive front pounds the aged building from a running start across the lake. This is part of the picture here, a moment, one step on a sunken trace. All the hotels in Glacier were built in the early 1900s by the Great Northern Railway to draw tourists. The Swiss Chalet-style Many Glacier is the largest (240 rooms). I am very comfortable in my spot by the window.

Sam, Cathy, and I walked up to Red Rock Falls, a three-mile level hike, but mainly today we've rested. We met Debbie and Doug, who are from Indiana and rode the train in. If tomorrow's weather continues to blow like this, we will wait to leave.

It is 10:30 p.m. The wind outside the tent more resembles a squall. We are tucked in this pine and fir grove, young sturdy trees, stiff to the coursing wind, yet moaners and howlers they are. The wind swirls; we can hear it roll on down the valley of trees, the howl diminishing, then another wave. Yes, this is a fluid medium, washing out of Canada, down these icy peaks, hissing as it passes.

Wow, the last gust had to be fifty mph. These young spruce deflect most of it above this little pod that has been our sweet home for thirty-one days now. Everything except for the bikes and trailer is inside, lining each side of the bed.

These are passion days, bliss days, followed, found, and set free. Sometimes I feel so happy, I hear myself moan out loud, a deep sigh, like in Malololili, Fiji, after several coconut bowls of kava: a release. We're like cats playing with bliss in America's pantry—this secret Crown of the Continent.

This evening, we cooked a fine meal of macaroni and cheese, chili beans, and green beans. Sitting at the table, clothed for the cold, the wind still breached our bulwarks. We huddled, sitting opposite each other, talking, listening, quickly eating the warm food. We cleaned up and heated water for cider and tea. Mmm, perfect. We have lots of cooking fuel now; I had to buy a gallon in St. Mary.

Cathy bought a Montana Gazetteer at the Lodge today

and we studied and schemed about the next ten days of travel. This is great fun, the topo map telling of contours, mining sites, and desert areas. We can detect flat land approaching, the roads become straight with ninety-degree corners.

Bicycles contort space and time. Contour, headwinds, all these forces, be they geographical, cultural, ecological, or political, are like spokes in the medicine wheel which we turn with our desire and our bodies. The quest now is the harmonious linking of these forces and our willing spirits to purely travel. Each day is a craft, and the craft person first must center. We have reduced our needs to fit our bikes. Sam said our mission statement was "to be wherever you are and at some point, be in Roanoke."

Friday, July 19, 1996

In Swiftcurrent Restaurant having the breakfast special. Well, the mountain gods are continuing their valley-bowling tournament, careening their massive gusty wind balls down the valley floor until they spill out onto the plains in a fanfare of dust devils and scattering sage. To the west, the sky, for two days now, has been a dark mass of grey, shrouding the peaks beyond Red Rock Falls and cradling Iceberg Lake. Opposite this cloud dam, groups of swirling bright white cumulus clouds cloaked in a turquoise blue sky march forward from the east.

Are these clouds Pacific moisture sucked along over the Canadian tundra and Rockies by a youthful high-pressure system to our south? No matter, we won't try to ride in this. We are staying put, doing laundry, writing, reading, and tenting it. We are thankfully in no rush. We are in a beautiful place with a few new friends and time to enjoy, rest, create, and craft another day onto our lives.

Cathy is off doing the laundry or trying to. Seems others

are doing similar things. I am lying in the tent writing, the door open to a small meadow of beargrass, thistles, Indian paintbrush, and more green unknowns.

Bicycle touring is the exhilaration of destinations reached or changed by circumstances beyond our control, where the unknown progresses with us. Maps, legends of geographic possibilities, are key; they're to be read and mulled over, interpreted freshly with each day's experience. The fine lines are the paths over unknown terrain, coursing by towns and crossroads where lives, land, and tradition co-mingle to give a flavor unique to each place.

Speed is relative. Cars whiz by, soon disappearing over the horizon or around the bend. Contour dictates our pace, but steady we ride, scanning the byways, pointing out flowers, birds, waterfalls, vistas. Or we sing to each other, just a verse or chorus— neither of us adept at remembering whole songs. Melodies linger, sometimes conjured up by the rhythmic pedaling or the monotonous breathing of a long climb.

Climbs, especially if they keep a steady grade, are places to contemplate, to view the road and land, to hear. The slow pace means passing through gentle air, with little noise in our helmets or by our ears. In such quiet, the tires hum softly, the pedals and chain drive system emit a soft higher pitched tone, relaxing and pleasant, yet quiet, so that the welcome cry of an approached osprey atop its branchy, twiggy nest, its clear high whistle, lifts us up to see. Maybe the mate soars silently above, but now we know to investigate their realm, their territory.

Along Koocanusa Lake, osprey nests seemed to be every quarter mile. They often flew along with us, high up, calling, much like the bluebirds who follow us, leapfrogging ahead to a limb, turning to watch, then as we draw opposite them, off they fly, swooping ahead another 20 yards to watch us again; bluebird play.

Saturday, July 20, 1996

Weather Report (copied from the bulletin board at the ranger station):

Today: Partly sunny on East side, a few showers in mountains.

Hi: 65-70 Lo: 40s

Tonight: Mostly clear East side, showers over mountains, diminishing winds.

Tomorrow: Mostly sunny and warmer.

Hi: 70s Lo: 40s;

Extended: Dry and warmer.

We will not be leaving until tomorrow. Throughout the night, the winds howled and rolled through the valley, and it rained hard for a while. When we got up around 3:20 a.m. to go to the bathroom, stars peeked through the blackness. Really, a pretty and massive feeling.

The front passed during the night. There was a slight dusting of snow on Hinkle Peak and several others this morning. We walked up to the restaurant, got large coffees and muffins, and ate in the tent using our chairs, a very comfortable nest in here.

Sam leaves this afternoon. He is an interesting man, quiet with a slightly cynical city-type humor. His son is fifteen and weighs 215 pounds; he is a lineman on the high school football team. He makes good grades and Sam thinks a possible scholarship is in the works if he doesn't get his knee torn sideways.

Up on Ptarmigan Trail the other day, we were stopped overlooking the maze of valleys below. Sam has hearing aids in both ears. I heard a helicopter drawing closer from its high-altitude flight, probably a scenic tour from West Glacier to view the National Park. As the singular sound of the chopping blades intensified, I noticed Sam staring off to a different time. I knew then that he had been in Vietnam. I said, a little to break his reverie, "You were in Vietnam." He said, "Yeah, I was just flashing back with that helicopter." I said nothing. The flash was over. He was back and we walked on. He was dealing and healing by being here, and I knew it.

Later we talked. He had been eighteen, and "didn't know better." "If I'd been two years older, I wouldn't have gone," he said. He joined the Navy in 1967. He fell in with fellow booters and alliances were formed, friends. At the end of boot camp, each man was allowed to give a wish list of where he wanted to be stationed, three wishes. At the time the Navy couldn't send anyone to Vietnam unless they requested it. Sam filled out his card and turned it in. Vietnam wasn't on his list.

A few weeks later he found himself along with his buddies shipped out to Vietnam. They ran patrol boats up and down Vietnamese rivers, Howitzer machine guns mounted on the bows. After a couple months over there, his friends confessed over beer that they had intercepted his card and wrote VIE, the code for Vietnam, across his list. He then knew why he had been stationed there, but he was still too young to be upset. He lost 70% of his hearing in both ears with the blasts from the Howitzers. He is still dealing with that twist of fate. He didn't apply for aid on the hearing loss. "I decided to deal with it on my own," he said.

At 44, Sam returned to school, got a master's degree in education and a teaching certificate. He teaches 6th-grade social studies in the poorer schools of Seattle to mostly Black, Asian, and Latino kids. He has immersed himself into Black urban street culture. He's the "blackest white dude" the kids know. There is a friendly calm to Sam to match his loping gait.

Sunday, July 21, 1996

We were up at 7 a.m. The front has passed. Winds are calm to moderate, mostly blue sky, a great day for a bike ride.
We rode 12 miles with the wind down to Babb, bought $31 worth of groceries in Thronson's General Store, and decided to have breakfast across the road at the cafe. The six or seven cars parked outside seemed like a good sign.

The owner of the West Wind Cafe—sunglasses on, jeans and taut red t-shirt—sat opposite us at the counter and struck up conversation. I asked about Babb. He said the number of people stopping is down by half. He guessed it might be due to the Olympics, but the price of gas ($1.59/gal) was brought up. "Oil companies are ripping us off," he said, "started when Carter was in and is continuing with Clinton. I don't trust him," he offered. "Uh oh," I think.

He was as tight as his t-shirt, and he needed to get it off his chest. He launched into a now familiar harangue that includes the East runs the West; Montana is suffering; these environmentalists are putting us out of work. "Hell, most of 'em work for the government; they get their paycheck," he drones. "Hell, I used to put in logging roads, but I got out of it. They come and shut you down." Ted Turner, along with all those Californians, buying Montana land boiled up. "I might just drive south. Born and raised in Montana, but it ain't the same. And if *she* ever came in here, I wouldn't serve her. I'll never forget, with our boys over in Vietnam, what she did." (Jane Fonda, I'm guessing.)

By that time, we were just nodding at the complexity of emotions from this man. Thankfully, a friend sat down, and they started a conversation that led to them going outside.

Time for us to hit the road toward Canada, Yee Hah!

At the Chief Mountain border crossing, we were asked if

we had any weapons, guns, explosives, pepper spray, etc. We had decided to hide our pepper spray, but suddenly overcome with honesty, I decided to come clean and heard myself saying, "Yes," just as Cathy said, "No, I don't think so." We were forced to give it up. The border guards were young but not overly friendly and generally gave me the heebie-jeebies. We decided to eat a bite there while we were stopped, and we watched them go through a camper for contraband with a fine-toothed comb. Cathy eventually forgave me for making her the liar.

Just inside Canada we stopped at the Waterton Lakes National Park overlook display. The overlook at 5,250 feet offers a splendid view of Waterton Village some twenty miles north, off in the distance. The display had information on the two adjoining parks, Glacier National Park (US) and Waterton Lakes National Park (Canada). In 1932, the two parks became the world's first International Peace Park. A half century later the two parks are designated a Biosphere Reserve by UNESCO. The plaque reads:

"It is the mandate of national parks to protect; the mandate of all mankind to use wisely. Here the two come together as park managers and surrounding ranchers participate in UNESCO's Man and Biosphere program."

Another plaque gives the intent of a biosphere reserve:

"Biosphere reserves such as this park are found in over 65 countries throughout the world. Each provides an opportunity for study and comparison—between lands used by man and lands where our impact is kept to a minimum. Each biosphere reserve helps us towards a deeper understanding of the life and health of the planet we all share."

Three flags were flying prominently over this display— Canadian, American and the United Nations. Having just spent two weeks in Glacier National Park in the US, this is the first I had heard of the Peace Park or the Man and Biosphere reserve designation of these two parks. We also saw no UN flags. I said to Cathy, "You would never see the United Nations flag flying in Montana or anywhere else in the US besides outside the UN in New York." Seeing those three flags, all proudly displayed, only a few miles into Canada saddened me and reminded me of the US's two-billion-dollar debt to the United Nations.

8 p.m., Waterton Village Campground, Waterton, Canada. Waterton is a quaint village along Waterton Lake, a glacial moraine lake tucked into the Canadian Rockies. Vimy Peak, across the lake to the southeast, rises to an elevation of 8,000 feet. Deer and bighorn sheep roam through the village. A good portion of the lake area is a public campground. We are situated in the walk-in area, which has the best sites. A bike group of American kids is camped here; a couple with two kids is beside us and two Canadian guys just biked in from Cardston.

After dinner and showers, we walked to the amphitheater for a presentation on predator birds. The naturalist gave a fine talk and slide show. Her performance ended with her sitting by and placing sweet grass on the small fire she had lit, while the slide show clicked through a series of awesome park scenes accompanied by Buffy Saint-Marie singing "Skywalker", a traditional, modern blend of Native American music.

Her message was that we still have work to do to help protect the habitat of native animals in wilderness and to preserve places people (we) can go to learn. The last slide lingered on an injured owl in a cage, looking through the mesh grid to the outside.

She said National Parks first began as the playground for the rich, surrounded by wilderness. Now they are the only wilderness, surrounded by civilization. We need to preserve our parks, keep them wild and enlarge them.

She said the Blackfeet   still pursue their vision quests on Chief Mountain, fasting for three days and nights. A spirit comes to them in the form of an animal, becoming the person's totem for life. If the totem happens to be a predator bird—bald eagle, golden eagle, or hawk—it is considered an especially good totem because they fly closest to God. These birds are at the top of the food chain. By studying them, observing the health and prosperity of the predators, we can draw conclusions about the ecosystem in which they live. Likewise, we are mammals at the top of the food chain. The lessons learned from the predator birds may be applicable to our health and prosperity.

She said the Swainson's hawk flies from the park to winter in Brazil. This winter, 20,000 hawks died due to their eating pesticide-contaminated grasshoppers there. The United States and Canada sell these pesticides to third world countries because they are now banned from use at home. It is a small world.

She said these two National Parks contain the last natural habitat for the four major predators in North America— grizzly bear, black bear, mountain lion, and wolf. Wilderness is very important and is dwindling. We can start helping by first experiencing the wilderness ourselves in a quiet reflective way, thus learning something about living in harmony with nature.

Monday, July 22, 1996

11:00 p.m. We are in the tent. We just got through cleaning up after a late dinner of Tuna Helper, two batches of quesadillas, and Tang. We've had a long day.

This morning, we got up around 8:30 and got things together to climb Vimy Peak. We stopped in the village and had coffee and bagels, got some film, etc. Waterton is a relaxing village with a small, human scale. It was a beautiful morning with a nice mellow pace to life, the air clean, temperature perfect. Our bikes without their loads sweetly drifted along the streets.

We set out about 11:45 and got to the trailhead about 12:30. The four miles of single-track bike trail between the highway and the trailhead was slow going and hard riding, taking much concentration. This bike trail is not maintained and is occasionally used by horses. The grass was elbow high and the track narrow. We put the bikes through the test, and they answered the call. We forded a creek on a log with our bikes in the water as support. The fast-moving water was 18 inches deep in some places.

We locked the bikes at the trailhead and hiked four miles up to the peak. This again was an unmaintained trail. On the lower portion, we again passed through waist-high brush, before finally emerging into an upper spruce and fir forest, traipsing by beautiful flower-strewn meadows. The last five-hundred feet to the top was nearly an all-fours scramble through loose scree, well above the tree line. The peak is an arête, a narrow sharp ridge, two to three feet wide on top.

The vistas were incredible. To the NE, we were looking into the immense, undulating Canadian Plains. To the south, cradled in a high glacial hanging valley, was Crypt Lake, its overflow a wispy vale against the sheer rock cliffs. The US / Canadian border crosses the backside of the lake, running east-west. To the west and north lay the spectacularly rugged Canadian Rockies. Down below nestled Waterton Village looking like a toy train scene from our lofty viewpoint. We sat on the peak beside the rock cairn and ate a power bar and sipped some of our last water. We breathed deeply the energy and tranquility that encompassed us. On the way down, we came upon a spring flooding out of the ground. We drank lavishly the sweet water welling up by an old stump surrounded by a carpet of wildflowers.

Tuesday, July 23, 1996

Up this morning at 8 a.m. We talked with Leigh and Allen from Ontario, fellow campers, and parents of two great kids. We talked for an hour or more. Subjects meandered but centered on their experience as parents and Canadians living beside the most consumptive and powerful country in the world.

Leigh is a teacher, and she talked of how hard it is to raise their children out of this commercial culture. She said McDonald's distributes "Fun Day" coupons to the children through the schools, and on that day the teachers are asked to volunteer to work at McDonald's as the children come in to redeem their coupons. By doing this, the school receives 15% of sales, and in this time of budget woes, she had to go along.

Leigh said 90% of the kids in her class have visited Disney World. Disney has bought the rights to use the image of the Royal Canadian Mounties. Now in Canada, Mickey Mouse appears in the Royal Canadian Mounted Police uniform. Their struggle is to raise their kids outside of this commercialization of culture and traditions by replacing those values with their own. I wished them luck as we exchanged addresses and then bode them farewell.

Yesterday's outing was so "Canadian." This Park is much less bear-hysterical than its counterpart in Montana. Here we aren't coddled and overprotected. Cathy wanted to scoff at the Ranger in Glacier who tried to discourage us from taking any lengthy hikes as he considered them too strenuous without boots. Whereas here, we are responsible for our own activities, and the park matter-of-factly offers any hike.

Vimy Peak, its jagged summit and 4-foot-high cairn of stacked rocks looks to the east over the vast yawning plains of another country. Dots of cumulus clouds lie along the horizon. To the west, lie shattered towering mountains, ice patches, distant filmy waterfalls like pearl ribbons laced across vertical rocks, the sun glinting off the mists. On the rock where I sit the sunlight reveals an inner terrain of neon green fungus colonies, each colony outlined by a flat black fungus in some symbiotic lightshow—a barren crust of life. Lower, before the loose scree scramble of shale and rock, plant communities of 20 to 40 individuals nest in a crevice; tiny purple phlox, iridescent against the flat gray rocks, beckon me to kneel close, fill my face. My skin is tinted purple, the scent is of dusty stone, laced with the soft green moist coveted atmosphere that envelopes the haven.

Further down, the glacier lily dances in the sunlight near snow fields now reduced to north facing patches. Its bulbs nest in the soft moist soil lumpy from the cycles of winter's ice and spring's thaws. Patches of scraped and clawed earth are evidence of the grizzly's fancy for the bulb, the bear's claws adapted for digging and lifting stones, but unable to climb a tree like a black bear.

The mule deer, a buck and doe pair, aware of our approach, glide across the sloped rocky land as if moved by a smooth magnet. They drift across, heads erect, in a cantor that humbles me when, upon reaching this ground they so effortlessly traversed, I am panting, picking my footing on each step, hunched over into that same magnet.

Stopping, I realize this is where I am now. The force pulls and exerts itself on the ancient stem of my brain. This landscape moves me to center, to old bones, to recognition of periphery, to tones without color, but with so much information accessed through the core. My heart is here, beating the rhythm of the breathers, in harmony with the rooted kin.

We pause often, listen, look, breathe deeply through moist nostrils, exhale, feeling the leaving of damp air out of our souls. It is this exhaust that our larynx and vocal cords shape and form into sounds of language. My sighs speak to the core, honoring the coherent light of the hidden glade, glistening with wildflowers, grasses edged by the soft larch, the only conifer here which drops its needles each fall to meet the winter bare-limbed. Joy is in this breath, enveloping the subatomic roar of the rock, this frigid water of glaciers that I suck as it wells up out of the dark earth.

We are visitors here, beings with tremendous egos which focus energy on power and control of a fragmented existence, away from the breathing hearts and rooted clans, the soaring birds, the stone, the earth, the sky.

I sit here in the campground; mosquitoes smell my warm blood and dance its currents. I am surrounded by mountains; the glacial lake nearby extends beyond sight through mountain bends, across political boundaries, nations lying on its shores. White cumulus clouds drift quietly in from the west, rolling back the vivid turquoise morning sky, nodding farewell to Canada. Within hours they will drift above the great plains of Montana.

We talked with friends of this country. We felt the common bond of like values and culture, yet we are separated by the knife edge running east-west, of political entities which amass such complexity of culture and dreams.

Allen told of how he was at Arches National Park in Utah and the Ranger was talking to a group about the annual operating budget for the park being reduced to $900,000. "About one-half day's operational cost of an aircraft carrier," Allen thought to himself. The Ranger asked them if they had any ideas to help.

Allen decided not to mention the military budget but chose what he, as a Canadian, saw as an obvious solution. He piped up, "Your gas prices are so cheap, you could increase them one cent a gallon and raise millions." He said the other people instantly objected to that idea with emotional fervor that surprised him.

So, what are our priorities as a nation? Wilderness? Habitat protection? Biodiversity?

The attitude expressed by the West Wind Cafe owner

and millions of others in America seems to be that the pie is shrinking; the dream to seek your fortune is unattainable. There is a large industry in America (right wing talk-shows, the Christian Right, etc.) that target these people for financial gain, creating a dizzying mental, political and cultural landscape of black and white, us versus them. It's a landscape purposefully devoid of nature, because theirs are not the lessons of nature and harmony but of greed and division.

Nighttime in the tent. The sound of Cameron Falls, humming like a steady wind, envelopes the tent, soaks the core, soothes the temples behind the eyes and sets the pace for the village. Its rhythm is of the seasons.

Time blended with geography enables heart breathing, induces core thinking. I am in a bit of paradise with my companion for life, sharing, being. How fortunate I am, how I learn in the quick of a moment in these days.

There are several bikers in the campground tonight, a group of four with Adventure Cycling who started in Whitefish and are going up to Calgary, I think, and a French couple that I haven't talked to yet.

Today was a restful day, talking, writing, a short lazy ride into the village and a lunch of shepherd's pies and lemonade then back to the tent to read and nap. Then another drifting ride to the Lodge for coffee and talk.

Prince of Wales Lodge sits on a knoll overlooking the village and lakes. It is neat and comfortable with its huge wood beams, high ceilings and spectacular views out the massive windows. The waiters wear kilts and they have broken their rule and put a TV out in the main room so people can watch the Olympics. In the gift shop, we bought a wildflower book, and a book called *A Good Medicine Collection*—good reading for these parts.

Five bighorn sheep, all rams, visited the campground at dinner. Cathy eased up close to take pictures. Their huge curling horns are a cornucopia of testosterone realized, a code from the testicles in their furry sacks which they always seem to turn to the camera's eye. They lay down in the short grass, kneeling first like a horse or deer, their front hooves turned back under, then settling down, calm and secure to begin the process of reworking the contents of their first stomach. The cud is chewed, the lower mandible grinding in a sideways motion, like a man chews beef jerky.

Wednesday, July 24, 1996

8 a.m. Coffee is made. Cathy is grilling like a mad woman—blueberry pancakes and log cabin syrup. We sit and eat while talking, watching the rest of the campers rise and take down their tents.

We are in a shaded back corner of the campground. The five-acre field for camping has built-up rounded grassy berms to give privacy. It provides a green backdrop to the array of brightly colored tents. A couple nearby in their late sixties, who must be the last of the natty tenters, resisting the RV call, and having a good time of it, are packing up. They are living light on the earth, with a red and white checked tablecloth and pleasant smiling demeanors. The woman reminded Cathy of my sweet Aunt Marion.

We're packing up breakfast things, getting ready for a day outing of biking and hiking.

At a latte stop. Cathy rode back to get her glasses at the camp. It is another crystal blue-sky day; several guys in a pristine 1961 Bel Air from Saskatchewan cruise by, followed by a showy magpie.

Cathy, now with glasses on, returns and slips off again, this time to Welch's Chocolate Shop, just opposite me on this small patio. The few trees in Welch's otherwise red gravel landscaping are fenced by wire mesh to discourage the big horn sheep who wander silently through the village. They have a taste for antifreeze and often stop by the car garage to see if any might have spilled on the ground. Across the street from the chocolate shop are the village playground and tennis courts. Both these facilities seem to be well used every time we pass.

We plot our course for the day, up the Akamina Parkway, past the Discovery Well historic site (this used to be an oil boom town called Oil City) then up to Cameron Lake. All this is subject to change. The last sip of coffee is down, we're off!

8:20 p.m. Our fine dinner of spaghetti, chili beans and corn is done. We have hot cider and cocoa in our mugs.

Today we ended up riding to Cameron Lake, then we went off-road for two miles over to Crandell Lake and Crandell Campground, followed by a jaunt up to Red Rock Canyon and back into Waterton—thirty-five miles total. The highlight was coming across a young grizzly bear at Rowe Creek. We stopped our bikes as he crossed the road. We could see him moving through the woods within thirty feet from us. An impressive animal. We were excited to see him, and part of us wanted to get closer, but on the other hand...

Thursday, July 25, 1996

It was raining this morning; it's the first rain Waterton has had in three weeks which explains the miles of hose and elaborate sprinkler system used in the campground. It rains twice as much around Cameron Lake as it does at the park entrance; the distance between the two is about 14 miles. In the winter, the park is the warmest area in Alberta. Native peoples knew this from observing the animals.

We gathered our food supplies and walked over to a picnic shelter. Jerry from Winnipeg and his family were there. He insisted on getting a fire going in the heater (wood stove), and with ax in hand, he did! I cooked up a batch of French toast from the dozen eggs we bought last night. This is a luxury.

There was an American semi-retired man and his wife in the shelter also. They are on a motorcycle and happy to wait the rain out. Another Canadian in his 50s, ponytail, and tie-died shirt, came into the shelter with his wife and daughter. He joked with Jerry about showing us Americans how Canadians always have wood fires and live in shelters.

The Western Great Plains

Friday, July 26, 1996

Today we leave Waterton. We were up at 7:30 to blue skies and sunshine. We packed up and cooked egg sandwiches. Now I'm having a double latte at the coffee shop, looking up at the Canadian Rockies, veined with light green streaks where avalanches occur regularly. Fir and spruce trees line the corridors.

To this topography we have enjoyed, climbed, and sweated over, this great thrusting of ancient seabeds to the sky, we say good-bye. Your erratic rims, arêtes, cirques, scree banks, V-shaped valleys will forever be to our backs. Ahead, to the east, lies vastness on another scale, the Great Plains. Family, friends, and home lie along this eastward course. The heavens rise in our face. We cherish your staggering power, Rockies. Godspeed in your struggle to preserve your wilderness. Nature herself is the source of our hope and healing. It is 10:30 a.m. in Waterton, Alberta. Our bikes are resting on the fence rail, calling. So long Waterton.

3:12 p.m., Cardston, Alberta (pop. 3,467, wheat, grains, and cattle production). We stopped at the Fay Wray fountain in honor of Cardston's famous princess. In 1962, the hundredth anniversary of Cardston, Fay Wray, star of the 1933 film *King Kong*, came to visit and was made an honorary Blood Indian Princess by the Bloods. They gave her the name Beaver Woman.

We were in the Information Center and realized there was a road (Rt. 501) to Del Bonita that had just been paved. It would save us from going north to Magrath as we had planned, before dropping down to the border—a thirty-mile shortcut, so to speak. That sunk in, and we decided to camp here in Cardston City Park and ride the eighty miles to Cut Bank, Montana tomorrow. This was extra cool because a huge storm had been rising from the north, an anvil-headed storm, eighty to a hundred miles across.

The storm missed us to the northeast around dinnertime. We were just sitting down to steaks smothered with sautéed onions and garlic, green beans, and potato salad when a rush of cool wind blew in from the storm, the edge of which was passing ten miles away. The winds had been sucking into that baby all afternoon, giving us an unusual headwind instead of the tailwind we expected. Had we gone on to Magrath, we would have been right in the middle of it.

After dinner, we walked out to an adjoining field and watched the storm. It covered the whole eastern horizon. Its clouds, several miles high, caught the setting sunlight. It seemed alive, an independent being, a force beyond imagination moving across the Canadian Plains.

Today was a fun ride into the Plains through rolling hills and rangeland, past sporadic homesteads. We had an interesting event around noon; Cathy's chain broke. Fortunately, we had the tools, extra links, and hyper-glide pins to do the repairs. We were back on the road in half an hour. Man, that felt good to be prepared and be able to do the repair. Otherwise, we are days from a bike shop.

The land flattened as we neared Cardston. We passed by Leavitt, named for John Leavitt I, who in 1897 saw this land and said, "This is where I want my children to live." The catch is, he was a Mormon and with the aid of three wives, he sired twenty-six kids, twenty of whom settled in Leavitt. This roadside marker was our first indicator of Mormon country.

Then we noticed huge churches, one in Leavitt, four or five in Cardston. Cardston is 80% Mormon according to the BYU college student running the tourist info building. Cardston is home to the Alberta Temple, a huge Mormon shrine of stone on top of the main hill in town, all white and shiny, its grounds manicured, its guard-gated entrance closed to non-Mormons. The temple looks out toward the SW. On the distant western horizon rises Chief Mountain, the holy place of the Blackfeet Nation and other tribes of their confederacy. The Mormon temple pales in comparison to the majesty and power of this monolith rising for all to see and experience.

Saturday, July 27, 1996

6 p.m., in Cut Bank, Montana ("The coldest place in the nation"). We are at Maxie's, having a supreme pizza, beer, and water.

We left Cardston by 8:15 a.m. on an overcast morning, rain curtains to the west. We bagged BOB in plastic and headed out. Secondary 501 was a great road. In thirty miles, only a handful of cars passed us in either direction. The two-lane road rolled over the rich Southern Alberta Plains. Homesites were few and far between, just hay, wheat, and cattle. It was a wet area with lots of little ponds, ducks in each sweet spot. At one point Cathy had to stop to take off her jacket. It happened to be near a farm, and a black and white kitten ran out meowing and yowling for us. It followed me and BOB, and I led it away from Cathy, down the road; it was raising a heart-rending ruckus. When Cathy was ready, I told her to gun it so we could escape quickly. It was weird how that kitty latched on to me and BOB.

We rolled into Cut Bank (pop. 3,324) around 4 p.m. and found the Riverside Campground. For the two of us it was seven dollars, showers included. We set up camp by some sandstone hoodoos, then took showers. We were both bushed from the day's ride in the blazing sun.

We decided to ride downtown to the Lewis and Clark

Days Festival that was happening this weekend. Unfortunately, it was closing as we got there. A band of older musicians was sawing away at some Tex-Mex music from a corner stage in the blazing sun. It sounded like the radio in the old Buick my family owned when I was a kid, distant and thin. Even when I saw them playing, it took a while to put the sound I was hearing together with them. They were on their last song, and I couldn't blame them for calling it quits. The afternoon sun was ruthless. We asked some folks where we could eat, and that is how we ended up here, eating pizza at Maxie's.

Retrace 2022

September 8-10, 2022
St. Mary, MT to Waterton Lakes, Alberta, Canada

After three nights at Glacier Campground, we packed up and drove the Going-to-the-Sun Road again. The air was clearer and the temperature much colder. We did not stop at Logan Pass this time. Descending to St. Mary we saw the area around St. Mary Lake that had burned in the Reynolds Creek fire in 2015.

At Johnson's Campground, we set up camp and realized there was time to drive up to Many Glacier, so we did. We stopped at Many Glacier Campground. Only campers were allowed to drive through, but the host permitted us access after hearing our story. (I think it was the honeymoon part that convinced her.) We circled around a few times, but we could not recognize the site where we camped 26 years ago. With Jetta in tow, we walked to the trailhead signs for Ptarmigan Lake and Iceberg Lake and looked up the path, longing to venture further but knowing that dogs weren't allowed.

When we returned to Johnson's the temperature had dropped. We heated dinner inside our tent's large vestibule. We wore several layers of clothes to bed, including our down coats. We covered Jetta with towels and sweatshirts. That night it snowed on the mountain peaks. The morning was cold and foggy. We had planned to have breakfast at Johnson's Restaurant and were surprised it was closed. In fact, very few establishments were open since it was past the summer season. Luckily, we discovered the restaurant at the St. Mary Village motel. Due to Covid, it was serving takeout breakfast only. Ironically, we were allowed to take our order into the dining room to eat.

The sky began clearing as we drove back up to Many Glacier. The mountains were beautiful with the fresh snow, and the air was sparklingly clear under the lingering low clouds. We left Jetta in the car while we hiked the Swiftcurrent Nature Trail around the lake and back to Many Glacier Lodge. I went inside to write while Cathy meandered outside with Jetta. It was a perfectly clear day, and we breathed in the beauty.

We left Many Glacier in time to make our way to the now closed Chief Mountain border crossing. It was a gorgeous drive as we approached Chief Mountain with its fresh dusting of snow. At the crossing where we had forfeited our bear spray, we came to a line of orange cones arrayed across the road. Two cones supported a hand painted sign, "Border Closed". No one was present in the guard house. This simple hand lettered sign, adjoining the two largest countries in the Western Hemisphere, was at once endearing and quizzical. We stopped in the road in front of the sign, staring across at the highway that had once led us into Canada.

Overnight on the second night at Johnson's it got down to 28 degrees. The morning was frosty but clear. We bought pastries and coffee at the motel coffee shop in St. Mary's Village. Then we headed to Waterton via the Carway Border Crossing with our ArriveCan App prepared for entry. At Cardston we gave the town a quick spin, checking out the campground and the Fay Wray Memorial Fountain, generally trying to wake up our memories, but more wanting to continue to Waterton.

In Waterton Village, an impressive new visitor center had been built in the center of the still quaint town. Cathy bought some fudge at Welch's Chocolate Shop, spending way too much on stale late season candy.

The Waterton Village Campground had changed radically. The tent camping area was much smaller, and the berms were gone. RVs dominated the scene. We took a short blustery walk along the lake shore.

The most obvious difference here was due to historical wildfires that had ravaged the area in September 2017. The once evergreen mountain slopes now held the charred trunks of the dead trees. We drove for miles through the devastation to Cameron Lake. At the lake's edge, a few small groves of trees remained alive. We found a table and ate our lunch in silence, digesting what we were seeing, along with our food.

But these wildfires are part of a natural cycle. It helped to accept the ravaging damage as we read several educational displays like this one, explaining this natural cycle:

Forests Need Fire:

Fire destroys, but it also renews.

Periodic fires control the spread of harmful insects and disease in stands of whitebark pine. Fire also keeps meadows open, providing habitat for grazing animals and space for whitebark pine seedlings.

Whitebark pine is a keystone species, which means that many species rely on it for food and shelter and without it the ecosystem would be out of balance. Because white bark pine is endangered, Parks Canada uses multiple strategies to ensure its survival.

In Waterton Lakes National Park, everything is connected— pines, jays, bears, fire, and people. Yes, you are part of this ecosystem too.

Before we returned to our campsite in St. Mary, we stopped in the Prince of Wales Hotel to gaze from its enormous glass-walled lobby across Waterton Lake and up Vimy Peak. Then afterwards, we climbed Bear Hump trail for a higher, practically aerial view of the town and surrounding mountains. The view was unobstructed as we ascended the burned-out forest.

On the third morning at Johnson's, after packing the car, we headed straight to Cut Bank. We were sorry that we were not able to follow our original route into and out of Canada, due to the crossing being closed. But our new route took us on an interesting ride through Browning, MT and to the Camp Disappointment monument which commemorates the northern most point of the Lewis and Clark expedition.

Arriving there, we walked a quarter mile up the rutted gravel road to the 28-foot-tall stone monolith. This scene was disturbing. The monument was covered with angry graffiti, and it had been shot with high powered guns, each bullet blasting a golf ball-sized hole (I counted 28). We walked quietly back to our car, seeing a great deal of trash discarded in the scrubby prairie field, including broken up toilets and liquor bottles. This scene became more desperate when we came upon five used hypodermic needles scattered in the gravel of the road. We fell silent in Camp Disappointment.

Opposite Camp Disappointment along the asphalt highway we'd traversed from St. Mary, we were thrilled to see a herd of buffalo gathering. We stopped to shoot a video and take in the beauty of the herd running across the plains right in front of us, then stopping to kick up dust and roll in what looked like their favorite wallow. Their wildness, their fun and joy, touched our hearts. We needed that joy.

We arrived in Cut Bank around noon, grabbed sandwiches at the Subway and sat in the town park to eat next to the stage. We couldn't confirm that this was the same park where we had caught the last of the Lewis and Clark Days festivities. Our memories were foggy here. We did drive into the campground where we had stayed, now called Sunset RV Park. The hoodoos, that in our memories were large and awe inspiring, were less impressive to us now. We paused for some pictures in this weathered landscape. The gazebo that had served as a common kitchen area still stood but as a seating area.

101

Sunday, July 28, 1996

4 p.m. We're sitting in the shade of a round bale of hay out on the Great Plains. We're on our way to Choteau, Montana. Instead of going over to Highway 89, which we were told is narrow, curvy, and hilly with lots of traffic, we took this "short cut" from Valier. The clerk in Valier Gas, Food and Laundry, told us about this route and we decided to take it even though a good part of the route is gravel. We've been on marginal gravel for eighteen miles, about three hours of riding, and we're finally in sight of the asphalt road.

It has been an intense, inspiring, out-of-body experience, passing through vast fields of barley and hay, dropping down into little outcroppings in the coulees, some with farmsteads. At one point, a couple of vehicles approached us, then stopped, the wife in the lead car with two kids, the father behind in an old Ford F150 pulling a camper. They were going home, "just over that hill," the short, friendly dad in a ball cap with a fertilizer logo said. He farms wheat and barley and does some cattle ranching. "How is farming?" I asked. "It's OK, we need rain. It hasn't rained a drop this month," he answered. I wished him luck. One kid, the oldest, was out with his dad. "I caught a big fish!" he exclaimed spontaneously, then flinched at his exuberance. Exuberance is not a Montana thing to do.

We were stopped in the road, and there, in the middle of nowhere, an Air Force Security Patrol 4x4 came over the rise and signaled for us to move on. The farmer's truck started rolling slowly, getting enough speed on the gravel to jump start, then they were off into the distant horizon. At four corners, they turned to the east toward home.

When we finally got to that distant turnoff, we stopped to ponder the intersection—four corners of spring barley and plowed fields. I was pointing out to Cathy the distinctive veined and weathered wood of the closest telephone pole when she noticed a cat crouched on the crosspiece twenty-five feet in the air. It was a puzzling sight. Was it stranded up there in the middle of nowhere? Was it hunting the wayward bird? It didn't respond to one of Cathy's best "meows." It just stared down from its isolated, sun-strafed perch. "Let's go before this gets too heart-wrenching," Cathy sighed and off we started, scratching and spitting across the dusty gravel.

The mountains to the west seem to be getting closer as we head south and the Teton Range swings east. They are an obstinate reminder of how little we have traveled eastward. It's like our Plains ramble will not begin until the last distant peak descends below the western horizon. With its sinking, we will lose the last vestige of these mountains where we have measured our souls against the towering ice-draped peaks.

To reach home, we must sever our ties to this uplifting giant, and readjust to the shelter of the coulee, the whisper of the prairie grasses, the mystery unfolding. Far is not the focus, it is too scattered. We will create our own vision to see ourselves around and within these plains.

Overhead, five large birds soar on thermals, little white dots in formations that mimic the rising currents. They are gone when I return my gaze from a shade-induced daydream. This roll of hay, mechanically bound with orange polypropylene twine, is our shelter for this restful moment in our lives. A good place to close our eyes.

Monday, July 29, 1996

We are in the Choteau City Park (free camping), in the shade by a small stream at a picnic table. We got here last evening about 7:00, after seven hours of actual pedaling, clocking seventy-five miles. Choteau is in a broad valley. As we approached last evening, it was hidden from view; in the seeming flatness, we wondered where the town was. Then, like a western Shangri-La, we descended into this green shaded oasis. We stopped at the KOA one mile out of town and paid four dollars for showers. Feeling reborn, yet exhausted, we drifted into town to the city park. After setting up camp, we rode over to Main Street and found the Log Cabin Cafe, a great place with great prices. We ate luxuriously, ice water by the gallon, salads, seafood chowder, one half fried chicken, and on and on. We drifted back to our sweet nomadic home under a nearly full moon, the air much cooler, and after massages all around we slept the sleep of angels.

This morning we breakfasted at the same Log Cabin Cafe with the Great Falls newspaper and plenty of coffee. After breakfast we rode around town exploring. Choteau is a quiet western town, old western facades, second-hand stores out-numbering lawyers' offices—comfortable and friendly. Main Street parallels the railroad tracks and the six or so grain silos lining them. This region produces wheat, barley, and hay, but the feeling of the town is one of borderline stability. There is very little new construction evident in town.

We visited the Choteau Museum which featured exhibits of dinosaur remains from a major archeological dig about twenty miles out of town. They also had personal and business artifacts from the early days of Choteau. The skeleton of an unlucky individual slain by Indians was prominently displayed. It still had several arrowheads lodged in its vertebrae, and its skull was cracked several times. The skeleton was crudely held together with copper wire. The legend on its case implied the person must have been a bad character because the Indians buried the body in a shallow grave, a sign of disrespect.

We met a nice fellow, Brad. He and his wife used to have a B&B near Portland, Oregon. They are building another B&B ten miles south of here. He has been a longshoreman and an English teacher among other things. He told us about needle and thread grass, an invader of stressed areas. Sheep graze the grass when it is young, but as it matures and dries you must keep sheep away from it because the seeds have corkscrew-like tails that burrow into the sheep's skin causing sores and the possibility of infection.

We called our friend Mary and found out that the Baby Taylor guitar I ordered before we left has arrived in Roanoke! Cathryn will bring it out along with Cathy's violin. What great news, we'll have instruments in five days.

It has been a nice laid-back day of rest. This afternoon we pulled our bed into the shade on the grass and read and napped. We then took a leisurely bike ride, got groceries, cooked dinner, cleaned up. Now we are doing some reading.

Camped near us, a woman with two children and two scrawny kittens seems a tad on the desperate side. Her kids are crying, and the kittens are tied to stakes. I feel she is doing as proper a job as she can under the circumstances.

Tuesday, July 30, 1996

7:45 a.m. We're at the Log Cabin Cafe loading up on breakfast and coffee. Our bikes are out leaning on the fence, ready to go. It rained a bit last night; now it is a cool 66 degrees with grey overcast skies. We're on our way to Great Falls, 55 miles away. The State Fair is underway there. It started Sunday; Cathy bought a newspaper because there's a two-dollar coupon inside.

11:15 a.m., Fairfield, Montana, "Malt Barley Capital of the World". The ride from Choteau to Fairfield was nice, winding through ranchland, some of it irrigated. Grain and cattle trucks kept us company on the flat pavement. We rode by Freezeout

Lake and the Freezeout Lake Wildlife Management Area. The natural lake, fed by the Rocky Mountains to the west and covering thousands of acres, is edged by the brown Montana plains. It is a popular watering spot for thousands of migrating waterfowl. Several birdwatching platforms are perched along the shallow lake.

We are in the Corner Café, sharing a chocolate shake. Folks are friendly. One couple paused to talk. They had been to the rodeo at the State Fair in Great Falls last night. "It was good, especially the clown. He was great," said the wife. Kevin Craftsman and his wife (I missed her name) were a sweet couple, seemingly happy with their lot. They both wore jeans and boots and had identical large oval silver belt buckles which made me want to study the engraving, but I couldn't sit there staring at the woman's stomach for long and still be welcome in Fairfield. They ranch cattle and grow malt barley and canola, a tiny plant that gets to shoulder height and turns the fields into a sea of yellow. The pod is like a small pea pod and the canola seed is about the size of mustard seed. We learned this while sipping our shake and smiling with them. They have some irrigated land and some dry. He said the rain's too late for some of his crop. "It needed to rain two weeks ago, now everything is dried up, lost." The wife echoed this and added, "But that's the way it is in this game. You take your chances." Something told me they are happy with the big chances they have taken in life. We wished each other good luck and they left.

Another group came in, a threesome, father, daughter, and son-in-law. They had seen us in Choteau at breakfast. The father has a nephew in Omaha that bike tours the world over. His bike was recently stolen after 30,000 miles. He asked a lot of questions and seemed to enjoy our trip vicariously. His brothers farm in Gordon, Nebraska, and he went to high school there before going in the Air Force.

On the way out of town, past grain silos lining the railroad, there was a ranch that had a high fenced paddock of double-humped camels, four adults and a youngster. We stopped and stared. Their humps seemed so exaggerated, straight out of the *Far Side*.

We made great time, averaging 13 mph, and got to Great Falls by 4 p.m. We called the Montana River Outfitters with whom we have booked our canoe trip in a few days, but they were no help on suggesting any camping spots, so we stopped by the tourist information center. Two retired gentlemen were on duty, one deferred to the other, who reminded me of Floyd from Mayberry. They were helpful with their maps.

We headed out a mile or so along the Missouri River to the Missouri Meadows Campground. As we were looking at the only site left that had a shade cover on the table, a truck rolled up to the adjoining campsite. A Saint Bernard lumbered in the back; a dude in an old black cowboy hat, sheathed knife on his cowboy belt and spidery blue faded tattoos on his arms disappearing under his shirt sleeve, sauntered out of the passenger's side. "If y'all are thinking of campin' here, this here road is noisy at night." He motions to the Lower River Road, twenty yards over the chain-link fence. "We couldn't sleep a damn," he swore. "We're moving over there." He points to the blistery dry field with warped tables hunkered down under that big sky sun. It's almost too much to even look over there. He proceeds to sit down in a busted lounge chair in the partial shade of the truck, while a nice-looking woman in denim shorts and halter top, bare feet, and bronze-dry tan, starts to pick up a few things laying around the disheveled campsite.

Her sunglasses mask her emotions, but her body says she's tense, especially when it becomes clear that it is she who is going to move the tent and stuff over into the hazy hot field while he sits in the shade drinking beer. As she starts this, muttering something, Cathy and I look at each other; we're still on our bikes, surveying the territory from our modern mounts.

We simultaneously start our bikes rolling, turning to leave. "So long," I say, watching the woman with wonder and curiosity from behind my sunglasses. As we passed by on the river road, she was dragging a sleeping bag out of the tent and across the ground to throw in the back of their truck—a desperate scene. A modern-day Bonnie and Clyde? Nah. He said they were from Manhattan, Montana and he was working a week around here.

We rode back toward town, over the river to Dave's RV park.

Wednesday, July 31, 1996

9 a.m. We're at the Daily Grind coffee house on First Avenue in downtown Great Falls. Dave's RV park is marginal on several fronts: no shade during the day; traffic noise from a highway adjacent to the camping area; night lighting that you could almost read by. But it's still much better than Missouri Meadows. We made the best of it and slept well. The ride downtown was very pleasant, about 2.5 miles along the Missouri River. We have much to do today—library, bookstore, shoe repair to sew Cathy's front pannier, office supply, bike shop, and a free concert at lunch within a block of here.

Last night we talked to Cathy's parents, Ron and Betty. They are doing great. Her dad's retirement party is scheduled for the tenth of August. A big day for them.

Montana: Big sky in the East; Big mountains in the West. A state with a burr under its saddle. The rights of the individual, independence, and freedom are the centripetal forces at work here. This evolves in many encounters into an "us versus them" dichotomy. Perhaps the huge "far-ness" of the plains, where the speed limit doesn't matter (going faster to nowhere), and its boundlessness mates with the myth of the "rugged individual," is creating the ideal conditions for constructing internal boundaries that are projected onto the land.

This state is more in the pocket of Uncle Sam than most other states; the military dole easily fits into the rugged cowboy, macho, us/them scenario. Then there's the almost whining refrain, "The East controls the West." East in this case includes the government, environmentalists, and academics. Joining these disdainful "easterners" are Californians, especially movie stars. The myth of the old west, a fantasy that most white kids are raised on, is the crutch on which this crippled land leans.

Noon on the plaza of the First National Bank Building on Central Avenue in Great Falls. We're listening to Eric "Fingers" Ray, a one-man band who plays the walking blues. He croons out Leadbelly songs and "The Midnight Special" to a small group of folks by the sun-drenched city street. Eric's from Conroy, "up on the highline," and has a good solo act.

Cathy and I located cheap haircuts at Dahl's Beauty School. Nina, my trainee, has been cutting at the school since November. She's from a small town in northeastern Montana, Scotia (pop. 1,600). This is the closest beauty school to her home, an eight-hour drive away. She's not going back home to live now that she's out of high school and living here. Her latest boyfriend was an Air Force lad who got called off to Korea. She's not going for the military guys anymore. "They're always going to leave," she says as she shyly snips my hair.

Thursday, August 1, 1996

Eleven a.m. We're at the Daily Grind having a late breakfast
and coffee. We got up at 7:00 and got down to the laundromat
at Dave's RV. Then we rode into town to the Knicker Biker Bike
Shop, dropped off Cathy's bike for a tune-up, and walked ten
blocks through town to here. It's another clear blue-sky day; it
will be in the nineties. Word has it there is a cooling spell on the
way, that this will be the last "hot" day of the year.

Yesterday, we rode twenty-one miles around town, taking
Cathy's pannier to a shoe repair shop, book hunting where I
ordered *Great Plains* by Ian Frazier, buying film, and visiting
the library. We had dinner at El Comedero; its cheap and funky
interior hadn't been cleaned in years. We rode around the historic
district. The community band was playing a concert at the town
band shell. We stopped for a few tunes.

The concert was well attended. Folks brought their lawn
chairs; some sat on the grass, others stayed in their cars. Kids
played in the adjoining playground. The band shell was a tall
brick structure with five arched rows of band seating in front
of the director's podium. The interior of the concave shell was
stucco-ed and painted with a huge mural of the Great Falls.

The scene was like a huge diorama with the orchestra
super-imposed over the Great Falls mural. Out front to stage
right, on a short flagpole, Old Glory was glowing in the evening's
golden rays. This was Americana that I haven't seen in recent
memory—so sweet. The crowd was mostly older. The conductor
was obviously featuring a returned officer and tuba player from
the Air Force band. He was clean cut and wore the Community
Band uniform of khakis and navy-blue polo shirt. We were treated
to four or five pieces adapted for tuba! Of course, we heard the
"Beer Barrel Polka", "Bill Bailey" and "Tea for Tubas". After each
piece, we all applauded, and the folks watching from their cars

honked their horns. The kids playing on the nearby jungle gym went about their business unperturbed.

Tomorrow, Shakespeare's Julius Caesar, set in the 1930s, will be performed in the band shell. Next week, a George Bernard Shaw play will run through the week.

We rode out on the bike path along the river, which passed by an old Girl Scout Cabin and its horseshoe pitching pits. Across the river and over Sacagawea Island with its colonies of Canadian geese and sea gulls, the Missouri's waters are slowed by the Rainbow Dam, built at the head of the falls. On the opposite shore, a loudspeaker barks from the rodeo at the Montana State Fair.

Today, there is little to see of the Great Falls that Lewis and Clark encountered in 1805. The Missouri River was dammed several times, obliterating the natural falls. The dams were used to generate electricity for a copper mine and then for the town of Great Falls, also known as Electric City.

The city of Great Falls seems to be alive and well. The library was open and functioning in a fine facility, its front entrance a series of flowering beds created by the Great Falls Flower Society. The librarian I talked to said they are funded by county and city real estate taxes, about $190,000. The library was built in 1982 and has since been refurbished.

Certainly, Great Falls benefits from the Malstrom Air Force Base and a couple small colleges nearby as sources of steady soft money to help advance the city.

While riding around the historic district, which was the first area to be built in this city planned by the architect Paris Gibson in the 1880s, it struck me—our house is about the same age as these houses. In fact, this looks a little like the Old Southwest neighborhood in Roanoke.

Although the streets are gridded and numbered—Avenues run East-West, Streets run North-South—this planned city feels homey and mellow, warmed by human activity through time. The city center is going through many changes and gentrification of old buildings into shops and coffeehouses.

We ate lunch at Tracy's, a long-established restaurant and bar. It still had fifty-year-old Formica tabletops and brown short-napped carpet on the floor, continuing three feet up the wall. It was relatively clean considering the many years of use. The patrons around the wooden bar stared into space, silently, as if there was nothing in the world to do. The waitress, a long-time veteran, thin and wrinkled with make-up galore, was all business and tough as a coot.

We're now in the Purple Perk having iced mochas. We're working our way east to pick up our bikes, walking another half mile up Central Avenue. We called Mary from the library. Everything sounds great in her life. It's fun talking with her and hearing what our friends are up to. There is no way to convey over the phone what we are experiencing. We called Cathryn also. She is ready to come out in two more days with the Baby Taylor guitar.

7 p.m. A storm just blew through while we were in K-Mart getting slide film, socks, and some bungie cords to strap down the guitar and violin when they get here.

It is so strange. One day we are out in the middle of the plains on a gravel road, miles from nothing, another day we are in a daze strolling the aisles of K-Mart surrounded by *stuff* of Anywhere USA. Yet, out there on the plains, in the yawning vastness of wheat and barley lifting to the horizon, there is the tangible feeling of place, a connectedness. We feel a calming peace from needing nothing in this place that is removed from everything.

We picked up Cathy's bike and had a good talk with the

shop owner and his helper about Great Falls, the bike path, and things in general. The helper mentioned what he called "rednecks" being a problem in Great Falls. If this is so, then it is a different breed of redneck than I am used to.

10:45 p.m., in the tent. Cathy's on her way to dreamland, although she did just pipe up with, "We should take a lunch with us tomorrow too." We're going to ride down to Giant Springs, then over to the Outfitters to talk with Mark about details for our river trip. If time permits, and I hope it does, we'll go to the library for some reading and resting. We also want to get a space blanket for the guitar and go to the Fair in the afternoon to catch the rodeo.

Sometimes I must pinch myself. Is this really happening? So fluidly and effortlessly we adapt to each new day. What love, what tenderness, what courage, strength, honesty, bravery, and adventure. We are lucky together. Now is a comfortable place for us. We can plan and scheme for the future and we do this, but our love is anchored in the Here and Now. Here and Now are what counts, where love matters, where touch and caresses live, where our souls can be together, resting, reflecting. Here and Now is where absurdity's edge lies, where laughter begins, where thunder rolls across our bodies after the electric tingle of the flash of lightning. Here and Now is where friendship is honored and stroked, revealing its soft underbelly. This is Cathy's joy—our joy—rambling together. Here and Now is where the best of a situation is made, where the winnow falls in time's breeze, where contact is made. Together, we are learning to see, to share, to help, to be helped. Love is a stream we are within. Here and Now, this is all we have, this is all we need, this is everything.

Friday, August 2, 1996

Noon at Purple Perk for coffee. We had a wild night. At 2:30, the campground's sprinklers came on, showering our tent from all sides. We got up and realized the tent was pitched on top of a spray head that was rising with the water pressure and spraying from below too.

This was just in time to watch a big lighting storm blow through. It rained only a little but had strong winds. Around 8 a.m. we got up and quickly ate granola and yogurt as the black sky to the SW menacingly approached. When it reached us, we retreated into the tent and Cathy held the windward side down as it blew and rained a fuss. Then the sun appeared, and we took everything out and turned the tent over to dry. We set up again, careful to avoid the sprinklers. Tonight will be our last night at Dave's RV. All right!

10 p.m., in the tent. We rode on the bike trail to Giant Springs, an amazing amount of water welling up out of the ground. Differently colored green masses of water cress flourished in the pool of clear water. The spring wells up 134,000 gallons of crystal-clear water per minute that spills out to the Missouri River.

We stopped by the Outfitters and looked things over. It is sort of a loose operation. From there we rode over to the State Fair, locked the bikes up, and paid the $5 entrance fee. We went through the livestock, poultry, and small animal buildings, and the farming and horticulture building. We each ate a burrito, and we split a coke. In the 4-H Pavilion we ate ice cream and watched the judging of sheep rams and winter rams. This was great fun.

We paid $6 each for the evening rodeo show. This was quite an amazing scene, smoothly run with good quality action. It rained a bit, and we moved under the overhang of the upper bleachers. It was interesting watching the animals. Leaving, we ran into Kevin Craftsman. We met him and his wife a few days back in Fairfield at the Corner Cafe—the couple with the belt buckles. He was with a friend and recognized us first, as we walked along the Midway, gawking. He said he likes the calf-roping and bronco-riding because they do that on the ranch still. "But riding bulls, you have to be crazy to do that," he said grinning.

Saturday, August 3, 1996

We got up early and were loaded onto the bikes by 9:00. We were able to get into our room at the Super 8 Motel around 11:00. We discovered that we could keep our bikes and gear in a locked motel storage room that seems relatively secure while we are on the river. That's much more convenient than leaving them with the outfitters.

We lounged around in our room, waiting for Cathryn and David. This is our first night indoors since we left Seattle. We went down to a Subway and brought back sandwiches and beer. We watched the Olympics on TV and relaxed. Cathryn called; she and David have been delayed in Minneapolis and should get in around 1 or 2 a.m.

I called Dad and Annah Lee. They are doing well and his report from the urologist was good. He sounded good and said he was relieved to hear from us. Dad was raised in Oklahoma and Texas, and I told him about seeing the rodeo. He said he likes to watch rodeo; he still has some of the West in his bones. I told him meeting some of these farmers made me think of him. I want to get to know better that side of Dad, the Oklahoma side, and to hear what he's thinking and remembering. I'll take him on an outing when we get back. He's a retired Baptist minister but he'll be preaching tomorrow at Cambria, helping to keep the church going and growing.

Sunday, August 4-8, 1996

Cathryn and David got in around 1 a.m. We got up at 8:15, after sleeping in a real bed for the first time in 45 days. The four of us had breakfast and composed our grocery list for the next five days, then we hit the grocery store with two carts in operation and steady hands. We rang up $218 in groceries and beer, ice included.

Mark, the driver for the outfitters, was at the Super 8 at 11:00, and soon we were on our way north on Highway 87 to Coal Banks Landing, an hour and a half drive away.

We passed Fort Benton lying green and picturesque in the valley along the Missouri River. In the mid-1800s, Fort Benton was the most western terminus for steamboats on the Missouri, and the closest to the region's gold rush. Goods brought in by steamboat to Fort Benton fanned out by wagon or horseback to various gold strike towns in Montana's desolate plains. When the railroad came, it bled commerce out and away from the bustling river town.

We launched into the Missouri River around 12:30, our two canoes loaded down with one big cooler each, tents, gear, clothing, and the Baby Taylor my new guitar. What followed were four leisurely days of canoeing the Missouri with old friends. Often the situation would call for a round of grog to celebrate a new campsite, or a good fire amended with sage. At night, I played my guitar as we watched the river flow, and David danced with the fire as many a soul before.

This was sacred time, to be with friends and relax with the flowing Missouri River. At the end of this river trip, the outfitters transported us back to the Super 8.

Retrace 2022

Even though we had decided to avoid our previous shortcut between Cut Bank and Choteau, we found ourselves kicking up dust as Google led us on gravel roads through vast fields, giving us much of the feel of our original cycling trip.

As we entered Choteau, at the site of the town's little museum, the local high school senior class was having a fundraising car wash. After our dusty travels this was more than welcome, and we lined up and paid for a much-needed wash. Well, five dollars doesn't get you much, but at least some of the grime was washed away, and we felt like we had contributed in a small way the community.

It wasn't hard to find the Choteau City Park. Our imaginations helped us see our little tent in the shade on the banks of the creek, but the camping area had really grown up. It has become a very popular stopover for RVers.

While we were in Choteau, we stopped in the Log Cabin Restaurant. Cathy waited with Jetta on the patio while I went inside for milkshakes. I asked if anyone knew of Kevin Craftsman and was delighted when the waitress shared his phone number. Apparently, he is a frequent and well-liked customer at the Log Cabin. I returned to the patio with our shakes and gave Kevin a call. I knew it would be a call from out of the blue. Kevin answered and I told him who I was and some of the details of our meeting. I could tell he couldn't remember me, which was very understandable. But he was friendly and happy to talk with me.

Fully satiated from the milkshakes and the fun of my conversation with Kevin over the phone, we headed to Great Falls, where we checked into the Midtown Motel downtown, with Perkins Restaurant attached. Perkins is an excellent restaurant and we enjoyed great breakfasts, lunches, and dinners.

We stayed two nights here, giving us much-needed rest and time to catch up with laundry, and stocking up on our food supplies. We even took the opportunity to have Jetta bathed at PetSmart. This was her first professional bath ever and when we picked her up, she looked supremely proud with her flowy puffed fur and new bandana. She looked so loveable that it was hard to stop touching her. She enjoyed all the attention and according to the people around her, they enjoyed her too.

We found Great Falls to be a very walkable experience. We passed many colorful murals when we walked to the nearby Mighty Mo Brewing Company for dinner at a sidewalk table. In the expansive Great Falls Park, we found the bandshell where concerts are played, although it was silent at that moment and the mural had been painted over, sky blue. Adjacent to this park was the Great Falls Library. I went in and met Jane, a research librarian. We had a good conversation about Great Falls and its layout, designed by Paris Gibson in 1886 when about a thousand people lived there.

We visited Giant Springs, watching the clear spring water well up and flow 200 feet into the Missouri River. This runoff, 156 million gallons per day, makes up the entire Roe River, the shortest river in the world, connecting Giant Springs to the Missouri River.

Driving around Great Falls, we found where we camped 26 years ago. We got a chuckle remembering when the park sprinkler system came on, gushing from the sprinkler head under our tent.

Friday, August 9, 1996

Back at Super 8, last night we talked with David and Cathryn about the course we've set through the rest of Montana. We should cross the border into Wyoming, leaving the third largest state in six or seven days. This leg of our trip will be different as new memories collect and connect. One physical difference is the guitar and violin. The fit of the instruments onto BOB is an untried affair, but I am confident things will be fine and the space blanket will protect the guitar from the heat and sun. I picked up the book *Great Plains* this evening from B. Dalton. The stage is set. Cathy and I are ready to cross the plains, one day at a time, one hour at a time. We will have to watch our coins also.

Saturday, August 10, 1996

We had one last meal together with our friends this morning. It's great to be with friends who value nature. We only need to place ourselves in her arms.

Cathy and I had our panniers loaded and were ready to ride onward into the unknown. We haven't ridden any distance in a couple weeks. In some ways, I feel this is a new beginning, heading across the Great Plains. The next few days are supposed to be hot, in the high nineties and sunny. We're looking at a ninety-mile ride today.

Sunday, August 11, 1996

Up at 7 A.M. It's chilly outside (46 degrees). We are camped at Aspen Campground, a wooded park four and a half miles north of Neihart. We got here around 7 p.m. And what are we doing in a forest in the mountains? Well...

Yesterday we started out of Great Falls on Highways 87/89/200 for about 23 miles of winter wheat, grasshoppers, combines, and sun. It was nice rolling terrain, Belt Creek having done some contour work for eons. Coming into Belt, we pulled into a rest area. The Montana Chapter of the Christian Motorcyclists Association ("Riding with The Son") had set up a break area for some of the 200,000 motorcyclists returning this way from the rally in Sturgis, SD. They had ice water, grape juice, coffee, and cookies. They invited us over for snacks and we gladly accepted, the temperature sitting at ninety-five. In our chatting, which ranged around travel (ours), motorcycles (theirs), and pedaling versus motoring, our route plans came up. This debate was presented as the flat Judith Gap route, which we were on, versus the Kings Hill Pass route (elevation 7,363 feet). They were certain that we'd like the mountain route better. "Caution!" I thought, "Motor people, they don't know contour, traffic, or road shoulders." But the Plains are numbing in their consistent flatness and heat, and the call was for SW winds, meaning the headwinds through Judith Gap would be extra rough. Also, there are more campsites along this Route 89, which is a National Forest Scenic Byway. Enough said!

We are flexible. And boy, what a difference a right turn makes. We immediately started a gradual climb up into a highland farming region. Then we dropped down into the Little Belt Mountains National Forest with lodge pole pine, ponderosa pine and fir trees. We rode along Belt Creek, a brisk mountain stream flowing through metamorphic and granite boulders.

Aspen campground wasn't much, but we were exhausted and happy to throw up our home and cook beans and rice. Cathy finally got out the violin and found a sweet note from David and Carroll our friends back home who also had included some fiddle tune music and a twenty-dollar bill. It was great hearing her play while I jigged and stirred the pot. I got the guitar out also. We ate into the dark, took cold sponge baths, and retired to the comfort of hugs and kisses.

It feels great to be riding again. The instruments ride well, no problem. We have eight miles of climbing to get to the pass this morning and then some downhill!

2 p.m. We're over the other side of King Hill, some 31 miles down the road. It's hot out and we need to rest. Though we are still going gradually downhill, we have picked up a medium headwind. The land is becoming drier again, sage brush and hay.

This morning, at the little grocery store in Niehart (pop. 43), a former silver mining town, we had a cup of coffee and some doughnuts on the wood bench out front. A young lad puttered up on a small dirt bike, waving and smiling, got a bag of ice in his backpack, and smiled and waved again as he motored off happy as a lark.

The climb to Kings Hill Pass was steep but not bad. We stopped at the campground a mile from the top and snacked. We had expected water there—But no! The smoky haze from a wildfire downwind of here smelled sweet of sage, pine, and grass, but the haze, along with the blazing sun, created a feeling of oppressive heat. There was a view to the south, but the distant details were washed out.

Out of nowhere appeared a Coca-Cola sign, a couple buildings in the glare, a gravel parking lot with three pickup trucks and a sedan. We pulled in and got off the bikes, our legs wobbling. The sun blanketed everything from just past its nadir. I parked my rig against the building in a two-foot-wide strip of shade, grabbed the handlebar bag, took off gloves and helmet, and looked to see how Cathy's docking was going. She had found some shade also. We walked in past the "This business is supported by Timber Dollars" sign and opened the inner door. It was cool and dark like a cave as our eyes started to dilate. There were six older folks, elbows up at the bar. Conversation stopped; heads turned. We voiced our greetings and we headed for a table. We split an order of BBQ and fries, three quarts of ice water, two cokes on ice, and after I made sure they had cream, one bottomless cup of coffee.

This is fantastic. The adventure, the unknown, just cruising through this with all the joys a guy can hope for. My wife, campanera, lover, conversationalist, protagonist, complete supporter, is the architect of my joy. We are traveling, seeing new sights, meeting people, feeling the terrain. We have a comfortable home and kitchen and I have a book that is interesting, a camera, a tape recorder, a guitar, and a violin. What else, I ask, could a guy want?

10 p.m., White Sulfur Springs, Montana. We rolled into town around 4:30 and headed straight for the Spa Hot Springs Motel due to a hot tip from a man and his wife at the Newlan Creek Bar. They are traveling on a motorcycle and live in Great Falls. He said he just got back from Virginia and liked it. He said he was in Charleston. (Well, actually, that's in West Virginia, but close enough for out here.)

For $12 we can camp in the motel's field, which is beside a picnic area where we can cook. We also can use the toilets and showers inside. But the main attraction is the hot springs. There are two pools, one large pool outside that is 96 degrees and a smaller pool inside that's 105 degrees.

The story of these hot springs epitomizes the history of European westward expansion. The mineral springs are said to be healing waters and for years they were, in a very tangible manner. The Native Americans called them Wampum waters, meaning good waters, and the springs were special to the Indigenous people of this region for centuries. Many tribes including the Blackfeet, Flathead, and Crow brought their sick and elderly to bathe, erecting their shelters near the steaming waters that flowed through the valley. The valley was known to be a neutral ground, the Valley of Peace, to these often-warring tribes. Conflict could occur on the other side of the Little Belt Mountains, but not here.

This continued until a Flathead Indian told a certain Mr. James Brewer around 1866 about the healing waters. Brewer became fascinated with the spring, moved to the valley, erected a cabin, and settled down. He built a bathhouse and began charging the Natives 75 cents for a bath. Whiskey was extra.

There goes the neighborhood! He named it Brewer's Spring, then sold out to a Dr. William Parberry who often prescribed the healing waters for a fee. He changed the name to White Sulphur Springs. Later, John Ringling of Ringling Brothers' Circus, bought the springs, but the depression ended his spa dreams.

Spa Hot Springs Motel is shabby on the exterior; inside the pools have a neat funky feel. The smell of sulfur is moderately strong. The son of the owner told us that two old ladies swear that if you add salt and pepper, it tastes exactly like chicken soup. Darn, and we've already had dinner!

After setting up camp, we swam in the large outdoor pool beneath an elaborate mural depicting the history and wildlife of the surrounding area. The water felt great to our tired bodies. It mystically turned my silver ring as golden as my wedding band. Three older sisters from Florida who are driving around the country seemed to enjoy the spa, and we talked as we bobbed together in the warm waters. They have a cousin that lives here and is a ranch hand, sells insurance, and whatever else he can do to turn a buck. He told them about horses having bicameral brains, but the sides don't communicate, so you must teach both sides. "Like kids," the youngest said, deadpanning. One sister claimed in the 30s she raced against cars, riding Indian ponies that her father brought back from the West to their home in North Carolina.

It is cooling down nicely. This evening the sky is purple from the haze of the smoke from two fires, one near Helena. It is incredible how much smoke is saturating this huge valley.

I've started making a song list and will need to go over the tunes. I want to have an hour or so of music together and throw in some of Cathy's violin and singing. Soon, I want to give it a try and pass the hat; a free meal would really help us financially.

Monday, August 12, 1996

1:30 in Harlowton. We're at a cafe ordering lunch and absorbing glasses of ice water. For the first time since we started, we had great tailwinds and averaged eighteen miles per hour for fifty-nine miles from White Sulfur Springs. The land is rolling and hilly, the hilltops sometimes capped with pine trees. About thirty miles back we crossed a divide into the headwaters of the North Fork of the Musselshell River. This river flows through Harlowton and is the source of a green swath through the valley, irrigation pipes hissing and spitting into the stark noon day.

It is ninety-six degrees, and the sun is blazing through the yellow haze caused by several forest and grass fires to the south in the Big Belt Mountains. The distant mountains are barely discernible, mere smoky images. Harlowton is baking in the sun. The burned-out theater on Main Street and the tired faded signs on the buildings give the appearance of a town barely avoiding boarding up their town hall. Its lifeline is Highway 12 and the fact that there is nothing else within a sixty-mile radius. So many of these small towns seem tired, as if it is they who are bicycling across this hot barren land. All one's effort is to just get by, to do just enough. Sometimes they learn how little just enough is, and they stretch that. With hunting and fishing being the highest aspiration of many folks here, the concept of quality is not often exercised.

The lack of quality of the Montana River Outfitters was phenomenal. They had no maps for us, did not tell us about the excellent Bureau of Land Management booklet about the geology and history of the river that other paddlers had shown us, and when I told the outfitter that I wished we had known, there was no response. They don't care. I'd like to see some heart here.

Tuesday, August 13, 1996

9 a.m. After ten miles we're at the Ryegate Cafe splitting an order of pancakes and coffees.

Yesterday was a record day—81 miles, and we averaged 18 MPH. The great tailwinds continued until we got to Deadman's Basin at 5:30. The reservoir and camping was up a one-mile gravel road. We got there, found a shady camping spot by some olive bushes, put our bathing suits on, and headed to the water a hundred yards away. This is a dry, barren land, and the sight of the blue water of the lake, with no trees around it, is incongruous. The muddy dirt around the lake reveals how much the lake has receded, and the muck in the lake was thick. But in we went. Man, it felt great in the 96-degree heat, wind, and sun.

There were two guys and a girl playing on Skidoos. They came up from Billings, 75 miles away, to ride those things around in this pond in a desert.

A lengthy search for drinking water came up dry, even though the current Montana Tour Guide says it's here. We boiled lake water to cook spaghetti and used our membrane filter to purify water for drinking. The filter really saved us; we were miles from anything and bushed. After dinner, Cathy got out the fiddle, and I plunked on the Taylor. Our little Bedouin camp in the shady draw, and music drifting out over the hills was sweet. We worked on "The Night they Drove Ole Dixie Down" and some fiddle tunes. I'm keeping my gig list in the top of my handlebar bag under the clear plastic top so I can read and sing each song as I ride.

Well, we're off toward Billings. Cathy wants to spend two days there, a little R&R. Sounds like time to play music, write, and read.

7 p.m., Billings, Montana KOA. We rolled in here about 5:30. We had gone to another campground, but it was more expensive, and this was a quarter mile away. This is the first KOA we have camped in. It is like white bread, but the showers are nice, and we have a shady spot by the cottonwood-lined Yellowstone River. We are pooped.

We rode 76 miles, pedaling for 6 hours and 12 minutes, most of this was with moderate headwinds, so we worked to get here. Route 3 was great with wide shoulders and not much traffic, so we could ride beside each other and talk. This changed radically entering the town of Broadview when the road narrowed for 30 miles through Comanche Basin, a barren alkaline flat, a no-man's land. Ponds here have evaporated, leaving eerie white crystal ghost ponds. Ponds which still held some water were ringed by an alkali crust, and here swam ducks. Black ibis and sandpipers waded in the shallows.

I wonder if they are aware that their life-giving domain is dwindling by the moment in this dry sunbaked brown basin between the Yellowstone River 20 miles to the south and the Musselshell River 30 miles to the north.

Hastening this process, a Montana DOT water truck, its yellow light flashing, was backed down beside the road, sucking up scarce water into its monstrous tank. It passed us, lumbering along up the road, yellow light winking out of sight. Later, we came upon a worksite with graders planing the parched earth flat, and there the tanker truck slowly moved along the fresh cut earth, leaking the pond's juices to momentarily settle the dust.

We stopped at the Broadview Cafe and Bar, a broken-down fading structure in a dismal fading town. The ghostly stand of grain elevators beside the single railroad track hinted to the *raison de vivre* of this town along the lonely stretch of scorched pavement.

The cafe was dankly dark in a way that offered no relief from the heat of the flat chaparral and wheat fields outside. We felt we were biding time in a nowhere consciousness in the middle of nowhere. The walls were lined with 5 cent, 25 cent, and one $1 video gambling machines—video crack. A woman blandly stood on one foot before one of the blinking altars, her other foot crossed, the toes fidgeting with its flopping flip flop sandal. She was silhouetted against an exposed window, its numbing light barely streaming past her body. Long fingers of her right hand touched the screen deftly, knowingly, unconsciously, as if blessing it with the laying on of hands. After a while she returned to the bar, gathered her purse, said something to the barmaid, and turned to leave. By the door, as if on a whim—yet this is something deeper—she paused, her bag slung over her shoulder. She inserted a coin, the screen responded, awakening from its repetitious blinking, and a series of card images appeared. Her touch was swift, almost careless, her middle finger stroked a line of images which darkened to her wanton touch. She moved to leave even before the machine revealed its tragic decree—almost, maybe, next time for sure.

I asked the barmaid, alone except for us aliens, about the machines, "How much do you make off a machine in a year?" Immediately, I sensed her disgust at such a question. Don't I know these machines are for touching the glowing screen? Otherwise, they are just furniture, or nothing more than the 3'x5' color poster of the posterior of a Perfect 10 holding a Perfect 6 of Rainier. This is Rainier country after all, no questions asked.

At the point where Highway 3 loses its shoulder and becomes a builder of character, I rehearsed with Cathy what I would yell from my aft position if we must ditch ourselves off the road. "Get off!" is what my numbed mind came up with. "Sounds painful," Cathy replied, looking at the prickly roadside.

At some point we stopped on a wide asphalt apron used as a construction staging area and got out rolls, cheese, mustard, M&M's, and water, and sat on our jackets, our backs against our prone bikes. This was very good and comfortable, like snatching a bit of joy from the gates of hell.

It was at this lunch that I realized that anyone from out of Montana who has bought land in Central or Eastern Montana has not ridden a bicycle through Montana. In a car, you can go fast enough to miss the places between the cities. They even eliminated the daytime speed limit. But on a bicycle, we're like proctologists, spreading the nether regions of the decaying towns and the deteriorating homes. And we go slowly, so slowly. Conversely, and more to the point, if you ride a bicycle across Montana, you likely won't be buying any of its Hollywood star-inflated land.

As I write this, Cathy sleeps. It is pleasant tonight. Earlier, after a walk over to the Yellowstone to touch its waters, we got in the tent and I played guitar and we sang for forty-five minutes—quietly, because the tent has great acoustics. Though my body is tired, I am energized by the effort, the learning, the trust, the earth.

We have developed a few rules as we bike along. The rules are born from the realm of cause and effect, drawn from a small survey—our trip, and spiced with superstition. One rule that now seems so obvious, but was painful to learn, is that under no circumstances, no matter how long it has been, should one utter a statement acknowledging how good the tires are doing. Enough said on that one. Another rule, more an advisory, is that the pleasantness of the tailwind should not be admitted to; same goes for the "good road." Another obvious rule is do not believe any automobile driver about road conditions and levelness. They have no idea.

Wednesday, August 14, 1996

We had a good night's sleep and breakfasted on pancakes and drip coffee in the shade of the cottonwoods. I read to Cathy some of what I wrote last night while flipping cakes. We chuckled at the fun of it and talked more of what we've experienced in Montana. This is our thirty-third day within Montana's borders, the nineteenth day east of the Rockies.

6:30 p.m., back at our campsite. We rode into Billings around 10:30 a.m., stopping first at the information center to inquire about local museums, and to look up things in the Yellow Pages—art supply stores, food co-ops, etc. We found a nice natural food store and got several days' supply of dried food—chili mix, veggie burger mix, hummus, tabouli, refried beans, couscous, powdered milk, a couple kinds of trail mix, tea, and dried vegetable protein. We continued up Grand Avenue to the Montana Arts and Crafts store where I found a nice journal of rugged quality that fits in my handlebar bag. The woman working there was an art student at the Rocky Mountain College in Billings. She is also a belly dancer, violist, and bagpiper. I asked her where Cathy and I might be able to play music for a meal or just an appreciative audience. She said she belly dances at the Art Space Coffee House downtown on Main Street, and they love it.

She said she would stop in this evening to check us out.

Well, Cathy balked at playing any violin in public but agreed to sing a couple songs. I think the thought of it scares her, and she hasn't been able to play much violin in the last six months. We found the coffee house after stopping at Cafe Jones, which was a cool spot but not inclined to live music. I told the cook there I wanted to play some guitar, and I asked him where the Art Space Coffee House was. He gave me directions, and then he said, "It's a 'smoker' place."

I brushed that comment aside, and we rode a few blocks to the Art Space. Cathy waited outside with our bikes. From five feet in front of the door, the stench of tobacco greeted us, not just the smell of tobacco smoke, but tobacco film—greasy. I entered, my hopes dwindling as I passed each table; folks were French inhaling, "James Deaning" a tube, or holding a cig inches from their face, elbow propped on the table. Up toward the bar, a leaflet advertised Saturday night as "Cigars and Guitars" night. I still groped forward, scanning through the haze for a person in charge. I still really wanted to play. I glanced to the right at two young people, being too hip, both their cigs dangling straight down from their talking mouths, flipping with each consonant. I gave up and retreated to the sidewalk and fresh air. I kept moving; my clothes seeped smoke for ten minutes. I thought of my new guitar, the new smell of its spruce top and oil finish, and I remembered the many bar gigs, especially in the late 70s when my Bozo' guitar reeked of smoke each time the case was cracked open. Times change, I change. I told Cathy, to her great relief, "Nope, this isn't the place," and we rode away.

We found the Western Heritage Museum, which dealt in a pre-modern way with the early history of white men in the Yellowstone River Basin. The facility was highly slanted to the white settlers' perspective—that the Indian presence was a hindrance to the march of civilization. At one time, there were sixty million bison. Then from 1871-1883 the population was reduced to about 200 bison.

One exhibit featured a Macintosh computer with a touchscreen display of a series of HyperCard stacks produced by local high school students, using audio and video cards. Each stack was the history of a particular landmark or town like the Crazy Mountains or the Crow Indian Reservation. We touched the screen to see and hear a selection. One series, by a Native American boy, gave the history of a town by explaining that in 1884, the US Army had to come to protect the homesteaders from Indian attackers. I was struck by the ease at which you were enticed to touch the screen and was reminded of the video lotto machines. Interestingly, today's *Billings Herald* had a front-page headline about twelve more states starting Lotto games and there is concern about the addictive nature of it.

We ate lunch at South Park. We noticed several Native American men sitting on the tables, their bicycles nearby, hanging out. This is considered the ethnic side of town.

On our way back to camp, we stopped and bought four ears of sweet corn from a farmer. Then we jumped into the pool. It felt great. We shared the hot tub with a couple of RV-ers from Las Vegas. They were friendly and asked questions about life off the interstate.

Cathy's doing the laundry. We have a good meal planned for this evening. In the early morning we're hitting the road for Little Bighorn. A SE wind has started up off the Yellowstone, and I feel like strumming the guitar.

Retrace 2022

September 13-14, 2022
Little Belt Mountains to Billings, MT

At this point in our journey, the distance lengthened between our camping sites from 26 years ago. This reflected how we had gotten in shape and were able to ride farther. Even though we were in the plains now, the terrain remained hilly. At the rest stop where we had met the motorcycle club, we turned south to follow our route into the Little Belt Mountains. Although smoky skies lingered, the mountains were beautiful. We stopped several times to look up the canyon-like valleys. At Aspen Campground, we had lunch at one of the sites in a big meadow. Only two sites were occupied. We did not have vivid visual memories, but we certainly enjoyed the scenery as we rode through the mountains.

After lunch we continued down the highway, searching for other landmarks that I had recorded in my journal. We were unable to pick anything out until we got to the town of Hot Springs. Although Spa Hot Springs Motel had been expanded and improved, we could still see the area where we had been allowed to camp. Considering Jetta on this hot day, we decided to forgo a visit to the pool. From outside, above the privacy fence, we could see the well-maintained mural high on the wall of the motel.

From White Sulphur Springs, we continued on the open road through Montana and finally came to the turnoff for Deadman's Basin. We followed the road to the reservoir. When it transformed into a rutted gravel obstacle course, we decided going further was too risky for Evee's low clearance. From the barren hillside above, we could look out over the desolate lake. Few other people were in sight. After a quick stretch of our legs and a rest stop for Jetta, we headed on towards

Billings where our site awaited us at the KOA.

As we approached Billings on MT Highway 3, we stopped at a pull-off to look down on the city. The smoky haze, which had cloaked us since St. Mary, masked the panoramic view, but we could make out the downtown and the Yellowstone River curving across the landscape. At the overlook, elaborate makeshift memorials had been assembled, cobbled together with all sorts of items. In addition to artificial flowers, people had contributed shoes, sunglasses, toy cars, stuffed animals, earbuds, pens, rocks, t-shirts, and other items whose significance escaped us.

We stayed at the same Billings KOA as on our bike trip. It boasts being the world's first KOA, opened in 1962. It is a destination itself with a pool, mini golf, fenced dog park, and large playground. The family restrooms are immaculate with private stalls providing shower and toilet facilities. Although Pistol Pete's is gone, Whole Hog provides 20-hour a day food service from a 30-foot Jayco trailer.

Since our bike trip, the sites had been rearranged following a major flood of the Yellowstone. We followed a short path that crossed over the block levee wall erected between the grassy tent campsites and the river. The river was low, but wide, and on several visits, we walked along the edge filling our pockets with a diverse sample of its stones. Once, a flock of white pelicans flew low over the water, silently and majestically passing us.

Our neighbor in the tent area was a young woman, Bronte, from Eugene, OR spending some time touring the country. We shared stories of places we all had been including Hopkins, Belize. She was heading toward Many Glacier in Glacier National Park. Since she didn't already have a reservation, and the campground would likely be full, we recommended Johnson's in St. Mary.

With Jetta in tow, downtown Billings was not as accessible or enticing. It was too hot to leave her in the car, so we drove the streets to look for any familiar landmarks. The businesses had changed, and the city had evolved. We were bushed that day and headed back to

KOA. The pool was closed for the season, so we settled for a leisurely but competitive game of mini golf. I beat Cathy by one stroke.

Exactly one month earlier, as we were driving west toward Seattle, we passed Billings. Although we didn't stop in town on that leg of our trip, we did visit nearby Pompey's Pillar National Monument, 25 miles to the northeast. The 150' sandstone butte is named for Sacagawea's son Pomp. The restrictions against dogs on the trails prevented us from hiking up to see Native American petroglyphs and William Clark's carved signature from 1806, but we took quick turns in the Visitor Center, lunched at a picnic table with a great view of the pillar, and felt satisfied with our visit.

Thursday, August 15, 1996

8:30. We've finished breakfast at Pistol Pete's Bar-B-Q at the KOA, talking with folks from the Saint Louis area. We're completely packed, our rigs leaning against a rail fence. Cathy is mailing some postcards and getting the address for the Billings AAA. We need some maps of South Dakota, and this might be our last chance. South Dakota, we imagine, is four or five days away through barren territory.

While we cooked dinner last night, Cathy got out her violin and played while I grinned and stirred. Later we played guitar and violin together. There is nothing like stringed music drifting though the campsite.

7:20 p.m., Little Bighorn Campground. We set up camp and showered in the funky cinder block cube; water barely trickled out of the shower head, but it felt great! Spaghetti is underway, the stove roaring. The sun is down behind a row of linden and cottonwood trees, and the cooler evening air flows out of the shady spots.

Today, we rode 70 miles from Billings to here in about five hours of riding time. It was a hot sunny day, but we did OK. Highway 87 to Hardin was beautiful—very little traffic. The two-lane blacktop weaved and rolled through the ridges and valleys, for a time tangent to the meandering East Fork of Pryor Creek making its way to the Yellowstone. Then we climbed a gentle contour over the divide where creeks drain eastward to the Bighorn River. It joins the Yellowstone here at Little Bighorn.

We saw a golden eagle perched on the topmost point of a pine. As we drew nearer, it jumped into a glide, swooping out along a ravine, its black shadow the only visible evidence as it blended into the backdrop of brown grasses and olive blue sages. We both slowed to a wobble trying to see it again, and there for

135

an instant, its slanted wings could be seen, then away. We turned back to our pedaling, concurring on what we'd seen on this hushed highway.

I felt a wobble in my legs and realized I needed food. I also wanted shade. There was none, so we rode on. I ate a Power bar on the roll. It was absorbed before it ever reached my stomach, as did the ambient temperature water in my water bottle. Water bottle tea we call it. Survival is the name of the game.

We rode a few more miles in the noon sun, hoping the next curve or rise would bring something—anything—that cast a shadow. We were nearly ready to stop and create shade with our space blanket, when ahead in the shimmering distance I saw them. "Trees," I yelled, and we pedaled apace, sizing the scene with the nearing moments.

The two big cottonwood trees were at the bottom of a steep embankment along a barbed wire fence. In their shade lounged a russet-colored bull, big as a barn door—though this fellow hadn't seen a barn, much less a door in years. He hadn't seen people either, or leastways, ones looking like us in spandex shorts, helmets, and provisions under our arms. One bundle was the silver-side-out space blanket still wrapped around my guitar. The bull got up as we started down the bank, me acting silly and bantering to him loudly, "Why I oughta..." and other inanities. Cathy, a tad more afraid of the big ole curly-naped bovine, just plain yelled, "Get on out of here, Bull."

We both were wonking by then and forgot to leave our helmets with the bikes laying by the road. Wonking is the word that describes our mental condition and lack of physical capabilities when we have been riding for a while and have depleted our energy reserves. It is analogous to a computer freezing up; you can see the screen but just can't do anything with it.

Lunch was luxurious. The space blanket, turned picnic cloth and napping pallet, served wonderfully. We had lots of food goodies, water, and a big ole swath of shade. The ambiance may have been a bit earthy, but a finer spot could not be found on Highway 87 between Billings and Hardin.

In Hardin, we stopped at the visitor's center and history museum to ask directions and to eat and drink again. The folks were friendly and helpful. The grounds offered several large cottonwoods and mown grass that we lay around on in our bare feet, munching and drinking till we'd regained the energy needed for the last push of 15 miles to Crow Agency and Little Bighorn.

This road was a nice, paved frontage road adjacent to Interstate 90 on our left. On our right the Northern Pacific rail line stretched from horizon to horizon. We made good time rolling along between 14 and 20 mph. Of course, I-90 roared, whined, bumped, and hissed a continuous stream of all that the world's automotive manufacturers can muster in a half century. I felt sorry for those travelers, sitting over there, with cramped and aching butts, bored of the monotonous straight and wide highway where no speed is fast enough.

How many of those dazed people happened to glance up and see the bizarre scene of two bikers, panniers bulging, one pulling a trailer with a silver mummified guitar and flying a large triangular neon-yellow banner? Were they grinning or grimacing? The sunlight was too bright to tell. They must have been thinking we were crazy as loons. Who's to say?

I thought back to the little towns we rode through in this blistering landscape—Broadview, Hardin, Dunmore, and others—with their decaying buildings bearing vacant eyes of broken windows, some patched with faded plywood.

Now, instead of the quiet lonesome main streets, we hear the incessant strangling noise of automotive freedom seekers fleeing these disregarded places, seeking the landscape of the colorful brochures that spew the new myth—keno, gambling, and the high life. It's much like in the mid to late 1800s when the territories of the Great Plains, along with private companies (the Northern Pacific Railroad for one) pamphleted the eastern United States and Europe with Eden-promising advertisements.

As we neared Crow Agency, a few more structures appeared along the road, most in disrepair, all achingly dismal and struggling, nested on dry parcels of land cordoned off by rusted 3-strand barbed wire hanging along rotted posts. We passed a sign pointing up a dirt road toward the re-enactment site for Custer's Last Stand. Looking out over this tired land, I thought about those 200 Cavalry soldiers, young kids mostly, poor, army-welfare dependents. There they were, lying in little depressions scratched into the hard ground, grasshoppers scattering, looking out over this barren land at 2,000 Indians amassed and seeking revenge for the White Man's invasion and string of broken promises. Did they look around and think, "What the hell am I doing here?"

As we ride silently through this landscape, am I not looking at the remnant of an era that necessarily had to end in this land of broken dreams? Have we learned from the history of this land enough to instill hope of a coming regeneration, a positive conscious way of living on and with the earth and its multitude of people of differing means and cultures? Or is this idea diluted into palpable jelly, the spoon-fed gruel of the numbed, KOA, Disney, Sacred Mountain Pow Wow Water Slide, Bear USA, RV Drive-Through, Wilderness TV Land, touch-screen video-blessed masses, thus ensuring a continuum of greed and excess that so marks this land through which we are riding?

In our campsite this evening, an old fellow with a collar-adjusting twitch stopped by, trying to sell us some "authentic, genuine silver Indian jewelry" out of a cardboard box. Our noodles were boiling, and he understood, finally, that we weren't buying. Now, his attention shifted to our bicycles. He sincerely asked, "Tell me, why are you doing it?" I answered simply, "This is our honeymoon." It seemed an unsatisfyingly short explanation to him, but as he left, he offered his wisdom—Be good. Go to the church of your choice. Life is short.

The Crow Indian Pow Wow is thrumming in the fairgrounds a mile or so away. I hear the announcer on the loudspeaker system above the "dum dum dum" rhythm of drums and chants of the dancers. Superimposed over this is the wail of tractor-trailers on I-90, two hundred yards away. A train passing (and one is coming now), just 30 yards behind our tent, is the ultimate sound effect. Camping in the "Wild West!" Good night.

Friday, August 16, 1996

7:30 a.m., Sagebrush Cafe, Little Bighorn, Montana. Riding out of the campground in the dawn orange sunlight, we see an elderly Crow woman, in a gingham dress and sweater, speaking Crow into the phone at the booth. In the restaurant, the music plays on a looping tape out of a boom box—"Sinking of the Bismarck," "Custer's Last Survivor," "North to Alaska," "In 1814 took a little trip..."—snare drum music for breakfast.

We're contemplating trying to make it to Broadus today, 106 miles. It depends on the terrain, winds, and our legs. There isn't a cloud in the sky, and we got a good night's rest. Out the cafe window, I can see the knoll up ahead. A dozen trees cap the ridge. A lone flag waves atop its pole marking the Battle of Little Bighorn.

"Know the Power that is Peace" — Black Elk, Little Bighorn National Monument. We can't afford the entrance fee so we won't be entering the monument, but on the way to the hilltop is a huge prairie dog settlement. Cathy's trying to photograph them, but they've chirped the alarm and are hiding out in their holes.

Saturday, August 17, 1996

8:30 a.m., Red Shale Campground, Ashland. Yesterday, boy what a day! We rode 72 miles in 6 hours of actually pumping the pedals.

Leaving Little Bighorn on Highway 212, the highway rolled and climbed out of the Little Bighorn River basin, over the divide to Busby and Rosebud Creek, out of the Crow Reservation, and into the Northern Cheyenne Indian Reservation. We stopped at Custer's Last Camp, a gas and food stop; its cinderblock building offered a bit of shade. Inside, we asked for water, but they can't drink the water from their well due to a leaking gas tank. We bought a huge Pepsi on ice, chips, and cookies, and ate some of our trail mix. The place was run down but friendly, several Indians speaking to us. Two old duffers on Goldwings, wandering around after Sturgis, looked our rigs over in admiration and wonder. "How can y'all ride in this heat?" asked one of the vested, button-wearing men, sweating. (It is in the upper nineties.) Cathy gave them a map of Montana, and off we rode over more hills and down to Lame Deer. The Goldwings passed tooting and waving.

The landscape on the reservation was more wooded with pine trees, and hilly with small valleys associated with creek drainages. It was somewhat greener, especially in the bottoms.

We pulled into Lame Deer around 2:30 in the blazing sun. The town was stretched along a main street. We turned up this street, looking for shade and something cold to drink. Lame Deer is the seat of the Northern Cheyenne Reservation, and the street and sidewalks were abuzz with activity. A Native American police officer was talking to a group of distraught women and children on one side of the street, while another larger group of young people were gathered across the street in front of the Catholic church, paying close attention to the policeman's moves. Obviously, trouble.

We were about as conspicuous as you can get, two touring bikes loaded for bear, one pulling a big trailer, one of the riders is a woman, and we are white. Several blocks went by, but nowhere worth stopping. Finally, we settled for a drab convenience store, its black asphalt parking lot edged on one side by a row of struggling linden trees. We parked the bikes in their shade, and I went in for some cold Power-aid drinks. We carried a pallet over and proceeded to sit in the shade and chill out. Some boys, 6th graders, cruised over on their small bikes, curious as to what we were doing in Lame Deer and on bikes to boot. At first, they were quiet, but then they warmed to us, especially after we learned they needed air in one of their tires, and I got our pump and promptly filled 'er up.

From them we learned that everyone was in town getting their "per cap" checks from the reservation, and that this was the first year Crows got more than Cheyenne. These are monthly checks each member of the tribe receives from the tribal council, around $150 each for the boys.

An eighteen- or nineteen-year-old girl and her younger brother rode up on their bikes. They stopped eight feet away, paused for a full minute as if we weren't there, and then started talking, asking us questions. She has a two-year-old girl that her mom has taken to South Dakota for a visit and to give her a break from mothering. She doesn't like life on the reservation. She doesn't mention the father of her daughter. She's thinking of going to the college in Lame Deer, but her goals are unclear. She goes out to fight fires for $9.50 per hour, but her kid sometimes interferes with being able to go. Her older brother is out now on the big fire in Oregon.

She drew her "per cap" today. She also gets a welfare check from the county, drawn on a US Government check. She is good at math, but not so good at reading. She said the current leader of their Cheyenne tribal council is a crook and that, "He can't even read." He has someone he pays to read things for him. He signed a check to her aunt for, "No dollars and no cents. That just proves he can't read." She continued, her disdain rising, "He and his relatives have taken money from the tribe. Now the tribe is poor. We don't even have a decent school. The school is just a bunch of trailers." She pointed down to a field across the street. Between two buildings, there was a white trailer in the blazing sun. She rocked her bike back and forth, looking out across the asphalt, at the people buying gas, the road. I got the feeling her gaze didn't know where to stop. "They're trying to get him out. I don't know why they can't," she blurted and then, as if frustrated by it all, she fell silent. Soon she and her quiet little brother rode off.

I went back inside for a monster gulp of lemonade, and we hit our food stuffs some more, readying to go. A woman in her thirties came across the lot saying, "I've just got to find out what you two are doing." She had some road advice for us, offered us a ride to Ashland (we declined), and then told us that there would be a lot of "drunk Indians" on the road this weekend, "cause they got their checks," and we should be careful and keep out of sight. "Because they will hassle you 'cause you are white." We said thanks and got on our bikes to ride back through town and eastward on Highway 212 to Ashland.

The climb up to the divide was about ten miles and steep, the road narrow with bad shoulders, but we hung in on it and crossed the divide in good time. At the top the landscape changed. There had been a big fire eight years ago that burned off the eastern side of the range. The trees disappeared even down into the bottom lands.

In Ashland we stopped at the mom-and-pop grocery for supplies. I asked a guy our age about the Red Shale Campground. He said it was nice, and he was pretty sure it had drinking water. He had passed us on the climb earlier and said we looked fresh, considering. His name is Dennis, and he does some biking also. I told him to come out later to the campground, bring some beer, and we'd pay. He said he might, though he and his wife and two kids had just gotten back from vacation, and he probably should stay and help with the kids. "We're all beat," he said.

When we got to the campground, we were beat and wonking after 70-plus miles in the 96 degree heat. The first thing we searched for was water, and we discovered a sign, "The water has been closed down, you can get water at the National Forest Service office in Ashland." Great! The place seemed perfect, no one around, ponderosa pines, picnic tables, Johnny houses, but no blankety-blank water.

With our two exhausted minds, we decided to unload our stuff, then I would ride out to a house we saw on the highway a few miles back and fill up all the water containers. Just as I was gathering all our empty water containers to put in the now empty BOB trailer, a one-ton pick-up truck with an all-terrain vehicle in back came around the campground loop. I went out and asked the driver if he was camping and had water or if he knew where we could get water. "I know where there's well water, good drinking water too," he drawled, a pinch of Copenhagen helping the words out.

All right! I got the bottles, empty water bag, and empty Platypus bag and threw them in the cab. When I opened the cab door, a coke can rattled to the ground; the cab was a mess. Off we went, straight out across the loop road and down a ravine, bushwhacking it. I could tell he loved this. He and his family own eighty-five thousand acres overall, some adjoining the camping area. We found a wire "gate"; he opened it, and then we were bumping across rough pastureland, staring back at cows staring at us.

We talked easily. "Oh, about five thousand head now," he said to my question. "We ranch the old way, with horses. We

143

let them make a living; we just watch after things." By then we drove up to a hull of a shack, overgrown by weeds, with an iron pipe sticking out over a ten-foot diameter galvanized tank. The tank was half full of water and green algae. "Ben's my name," he offered. He started poking around an electrical box to get the pump going. "There," he said and a few seconds later a fine stream of water came flowing out the end of the crusty pipe. I let it run a few moments to get the bigger chunks of crud out and then bent over for a taste. Cold, that's a good start, pretty irony tasting but not bad, especially in this situation. I filled up our bottles and we talked. I liked this tough barrel-chested Montanan rancher.

One of the first things he told me about himself was that he used to work for the National Forest Service. "Oh yeah?" I said, interested but still wonked, as he gave a good pause, bumping and creaking back toward the campground. "I was a smoke jumper," he revealed, pride busting out of that wide chest, though he tried to hide it. I had read *Young Men and Fire* by Norman Maclean, a book about the Mann Gulch Fire disaster in Montana in which twenty-three smoke jumpers perished. The book was first and foremost an ode to smoke jumpers, the elite group of wild men who fall from the sky to fire. I read it as preparation for Montana.

His eyes danced a little when I told him this, showing my awareness of the guts, the risk, and the rush of being a smoke jumper. Ben has jumped on two hundred and fifty fires. "Never broke a bone," he added, deadpanning, "but sprained an ankle now and then." He's jumped thirty-five rescue jumps, landed in trees—soft landing, according to him—and was burned on the legs once by a flare-up—"bad situation," he said. By now I knew I had a master deadpan artist driving. He joined up at eighteen and went to smoke jumper's school. Out of forty in his freshman class, ten made it, "All ranchers' boys. You had to run one and a half miles in eleven minutes. I ran it in nine and a half. I was in good shape then."

When we got back to camp, Cathy had the tent up and things looking good. I invited Ben to meet my wife (it still is strange saying that) and visit some. He liked what we're doing, I could tell, though bicycles were not his thing. "You know, it's good that it takes all kinds in this world, like you two," he confessed. He can't believe we're riding bicycles across the US carrying what we have, and I allowed it's a little crazy. He sat sidesaddle on the picnic table, one foot on the ground and watched us prepare dinner. He liked Cathy, and I had him repeat his smoke jumping statistics to her, which he enjoyed. I started a fire after gathering a few branches from around the site.

He said he'd eaten and wasn't too sure about couscous and vegetables anyway. "I'm a steak man," he said. They butcher one cow a month, share it with his sister and her husband, who I could tell Ben's not too fond of. He got a kick out of me telling him about the time I made Cathy mad, asking her to go faster. "I can't!" she had said, then proceeded to pedal off so fast I couldn't catch her.

Ben grinned and dropped his face down for a moment, a motion he makes when he's about to laugh or enjoy something so much he could kick a cow pie. Ben's never been married, but he clearly had a keen interest in our new marriage and said he didn't know if he'd ever get married. When Cathy told him that I had told my mom, way back, that I wouldn't get married until I found a woman who'd ride bicycles across the US with me, he looked down again with a grin. "Yeah, mine would have to do it on a horse," he concluded.

While talking with Ben, a Montana Highway Patrol car cruised by us and around the loop twice. This is the first Montana Highway Patrol Cathy and I have seen in forty-five days of being in Montana. Ben sensed our wonder and added, "Oh he's just meeting his girlfriend up here on the sly. She's a highway patrol too. They're both married. They meet up here." Sure enough, in drove another highway patrol car with a woman at the wheel. "She don't like me much," Ben says. Cathy is glad Ben's here to enlighten us, "I wouldn't be able to sleep, thinking there was an escaped convict or something going on."

About this time, another vehicle drove up. It was Dennis from the grocery store bringing some beers and a couple bottles of drinking water. "I got to thinking there might not be water up here," he said. He wanted to talk about our trip. Turned out the two men knew each other, mainly from seeing each other around. There was some instantaneous communication between the two of them, and I sensed a little unease. Ben left soon after Dennis arrived. Dennis told us he didn't know Ben well, that he used to have a problem with the bottle, but he's trying to kick it, and seems to be successful.

Dennis is a photographer and used to be with the *Indianapolis Star*. He is married to a teacher at the reservation school in Ashland. They have a two-year-old and a newborn. The school hired him with grant monies to be the photographer for a photo book, "sort of a day in the life of the reservation," he explained. "It's due out soon." Dennis always wanted to do what we're doing. It was somewhat sad when he said he'd never be able to, now that he has a wife and two kids; his wife isn't the type to want to do it. We told him we'd heard of families biking across, even with youngsters on the back of Dad's tandem. We talked for a while as Cathy and I ate. He was very careful not to be imposing on us, which couldn't have been farther from the truth. We enjoyed talking with him—with anybody! After a while (and a beer), he left, giving us his address and accepting our well wishes.

After dinner, I stoked the fire. We took bottle baths on the table by firelight, and then I played thirty minutes or so on the guitar with the fire flickering, enjoying the pine-sweet smell and a blanket of Montana stars.

Breakfast this morning is leftover couscous, fruit cocktail, granola, and coffee. It's a pretty morning, partly cloudy; Cathy read yesterday that it wasn't going to be as hot today. We have a short ride ahead to Broadus, about thirty-five miles, so we aren't in a big rush this morning.

9:30 p.m., Town and Country RV Park, Broadus. This morning around ten, as we were packing, Ben stopped by. He had a cold 32oz. Powerade for us. He was on his way to the "Big City" (Miles City) to do some roping—just practicing with some friends. He'd been up since 4:30 this morning. He and three others moved two hundred cattle to another field, with horses. When I asked did they move them around in fenced fields so as not to over-graze, he said the environmentalists would get mad if he didn't, though he claimed the cattle didn't harm a pasture. "You just reseed it."

Today's ride was the pits—headwinds, hilly, we both had low energy, and it was hot. We had psyched ourselves into thinking it was going to be an easy day. This is like playing with dynamite, this kind of thinking. Broadus is only thirty-nine miles from Red Shale Campground, but it took us three and a half riding hours to get here through dry, barren, heat-shattered land with no trees.

We stopped at an abandoned roofless house and located some shade around back in an attached garage. It was open to the elements and home to critters, old beer bottles, a hollow TV shell with a bullet hole through the screen, and a couple of decayed couches. Cliff swallows had built mud nests on the walls at the ceiling; a young swallow's head bobbed into view in one of the nests. The place was desolate, but we gratefully accepted its shade.

We're camped at the Town and Country RV Park—"Tenters welcome." It has showers and laundry, both of which we used. There are five or six trailers in the park; most of them belong to men who are working on a road construction project around here. They travel around from road job to road job. I talked to one guy in the laundry. He is married, lives up on the Highline near Route 2.

We ate at the Cashway Cafe coming into town. We drank pitchers of ice water and three glasses of lemonade, each. The sky was black to the west, but the storm just missed us. There's not much in Broadus; we ate at the same restaurant for dinner. Cathy's stomach is upset and we're both pooped. We went to bed around 9:30, and I wrote this.

Sunday, August 18, 1996

8:16 p.m., in Jumping Jacks Restaurant, Belle Fourche, South Dakota. We rode ninety-six miles today from Broadus. At dusk, we had four more miles to reach Belle Fourche, SD. Winds started blowing off the starboard beam, and we realized we were in a race with the violent storm we'd watched for the last hour off to the right. Cathy paused to cut her rear flasher on (it took at least 30 precious seconds), then we pedaled our hearts out, racing the storm. We could see lights off in the distance, the first evidence of people for forty miles. The heavy gusts of wind hit when we were a couple hundred feet from a business appearing from behind trees, a gas station for sure. The leading edge of the storm hit; dirt and litter blew horizontally in front of us. We turned in under an overhang by the door and in the lee of the building just as walls of driving rain hit. We made it!

As it turns out, the gas station also houses a good trucker's restaurant (Jumping Jacks) with friendly waitresses where we've just learned, to our delight, that there are motel rooms upstairs for twenty-five dollars. We're home!

Monday, August 19, 1996

We're down having coffee and breakfast in the restaurant. We slept great after showers and a bit of The Weather Channel on TV. I played some guitar while Cathy showered. The guitar sounds sweet and plays nice.

Yesterday we hit a milestone. About 8 miles before reaching Wyoming we passed 2,000 miles on the odometer, meaning that we had biked more than a thousand miles within Montana's borders.

US Highway 212 in southeastern Montana is a ribbon of asphalt charged by truckers using it as a shortcut to Rapid City. The roadside was strewn with decaying antelope carcasses and grasshoppers. Out here, grasshoppers eat smashed grasshoppers on the road, an activity that leads to star clusters of smashed grasshoppers dotting the black steamy surface.

Often, we would see a sign up ahead for a cafe, bar, or motel and think, "Oh, a shady place to take a break," only to find as we ride nearer that although its sign still looks good, the building is a hulk, a windowless boarded shell, crumbling. I especially remember the sign for the "20 Grand Bar and Cafe" twenty miles east of Broadus—nowhere in a vast stretch of prairie. We slowed, the perked coffee cup already in my mind's hand, when the blank-eyed, weed-fringed building appeared, collapsing into dust under the big Montana sky. Same with the double-wide beside it. But the sign still beckoned the wayward traveler. Could this be hell? Tantalizing signs on an endless highway through eastern Montana?

We rode into Alzada MT, a dustheap three miles from Wyoming. The Alzada Motel sign still looked OK, but the wooden building overgrown by weeds listed to port, and its roof was nearly gone. There was a lone guy up in the roof trusses with a crowbar, salvaging wood. There was not much new construction going on that we saw, especially in the country.

The Stoneville Cafe, the only functioning establishment in the town, advertised "Cheap Drinks, Lousy Food" and was an oasis of dreariness in a sea of tired scrubland pierced by Highway 212. We got lemonades, burgers, and fries. While there we called Cathy's parents, her brother Ken (his birthday), and our friend Mary (her birthday). It was great talking to everyone.

A woman in her early thirties with long brown hair streaked with blonde, sat at a table, smoking and studying pictures. She was the tattoo artist. Her thigh was a swirl of dull blue etchings displayed below her short cheerleader style skirt. Her midriff flashed as she sauntered toward the bar in the next room. Her handiwork was plastered on the longhaired, knife-holstered biker that works there.

Our waitress sullenly served us. She perked up some when we tried to talk with her. She is trapped here, working until two in the morning, the mental stimulation coming only from tattoo designs and bar talk. Our half-baked idea of camping there was out of the question, so we didn't ask. Even though it was nearing 4:00, we headed on in a headwind to Belle Fourche.

We cut through a corner of Wyoming on the way to South Dakota. (This was the first time Cathy had been to either state.) At the border into Wyoming, the landscape changed to a slightly lusher grassland range with tree-lined coulees in the distance. We scanned the roadsides for an impromptu campsite but found none with water.

We crossed into South Dakota. The horizon, in the twilight, hinted a varied terrain of buttes, hills, canyons, and rangeland. The effect was friendlier, less distraught. Once we made it to Jumping Jacks in Belle Fourche, we found it was a-bustle with people. It had that crossroads kind of feel, making it friendlier, more conversational, and less rigid than what we experienced in eastern Montana.

We're down the road in a comfortable antique shop with a coffee counter. I saw espressos and lattes on the menu board and was skeptical. The owner explained, "Oh, I'm from Seattle, so I know good coffee." I said, "All right!" and we slapped a low five. She came to Belle Fourche to get away from the big city. Cathy and I settled into writing notes to accompany the sage we're mailing off to friends back home. The sage smells great, and the coffee tastes good.

Spearfish Town Campground. This is a very nice, large campground with a clean creek and lots of trees. It is a beautiful, clear, fall-like day.

We played music after showers, until Cathy broke a "G" string (honest). Off we dashed to the only music store in town, but, alas, they were closed. Now, I'm cooking spaghetti, and Cathy's looking over the route for the coming week that will take us through the Black Hills.

In Belle Fourche and Spearfish, the scene is vibrant. Antiques are big here. The tourist dollar is important, and they pursue it with some class. Yes, the Cow Town signs are still around and cowboys and roundups, but it is tinged with a bit of humility, work, and a bit more diversity. In modern Montana the door seems closed to new ideas as if ideas are outsiders along with "Easterners" or, God forbid, "Environmentalists."

I wish I could have gotten an environmentalist and a rancher to sit down and talk. I think that this was the saddest thing about being in Montana; the chances of a dialogue seemed very slim. But this is exactly where dialogue is needed. I heard some real concerns of the ranchers about problems with regulations. Let's air it out, work on it. I also heard some loose-as-a-goose ecological statistics and facts bantered as gospel truth. Is there a way to de-politicize this environmental question? I wonder.

The symbols of the West—the cowboy, the rugged individual—have been co-opted by those who benefit from no regulations. They cry about Big Government and getting Government off their backs, yet they benefit from this same government. The farmer this morning in Belle Fourche had been to a meeting with Congressional people discussing aid to farmers whose crops were damaged by the drought and grasshoppers.

Retrace 2022

The drive out of Billings on Old 87 and into Montana's eastern plains surprised us with its beauty. Without the exertion of pedaling, we easily ascended and descended the rolling, broken hills. At car speed, the vast open landscape passed almost too quickly. The sun radiated its muted heat through the persistent smoky haze.

We found the site of the Little Bighorn campground by the railroad tracks. It was an abandoned shambles, thoroughly defaced with graffiti and shattered windows, the ground an ugly confusion of discarded 21st century artifacts (litter).

Nearby, lay the Little Bighorn Battlefield National Monument. With my senior pass in hand, we proceeded through the entrance station. Jetta was not allowed out of the car here, so that ruled out all activities except driving the four-and-a-half-mile tour road. We had not done this on our bikes, so this was a new experience. Passing the markers of fallen native Lakota Sioux, Northern Cheyenne, and Arapaho warriors, alongside U S soldiers and their Crow and Arikara scouts, we imagined the bloody battle and reflected on the significance of the history here.

Our tour of Little Big Horn took longer than we had planned, and we hurried down the road again. At Lame Deer, we turned off Highway 212 onto the relatively new road into the town center. Many new buildings and road improvements obscured our memories. We were happy to see an outwardly more prosperous town. A little farther along 212 we saw the Charging Horse Casino. Perhaps this was bringing in more prosperity for the residents of Lame Deer.

In Ashland, we were trying to find the mom-and-pop grocery

store from 26 years ago where we had met Dennis. We had pulled off the road in front of a small store to check it out. A Montana Highway Patrol car pulled in beside us and the officer offered help. He thought the store we were looking for was across the street. We went over and the folks working in the store agreed. We explained to them that we'd shopped there 26 years ago as we bicycled across America to our home in Virginia. This initiated a fine discussion of what we were experiencing as we traveled. We had my original journal, and this really helped as we read our experience to them. They were nice folk, and we felt buoyed by their wonder and support.

Red Shale Campground still had no water available, but we were prepared and had lunch at a shady picnic table close to where we had camped. The wooded rolling land matched our old memories of camping there, of Ben the Smoke Jumper and Dennis from the store. We noted only two sites were being used, still that's more than the last time we were here.

We tried to find the RV park in Broadus, knowing that if it still existed, it had probably changed names. We drove around a forsaken campground that may have been what we were looking for, but maybe not too. It didn't seem worthwhile to ponder it too long as we were anxious to put some miles behind us.

We drove through Alzada. Amazingly, the tired Stoneville Cafe was still there, its old barn wood siding barely hanging on. It was advertising Shirtless Wednesdays.

Entering Belle Fourche, we had no problem recognizing the building that had sheltered us from the storm. It was still a gas station, Mid-America Travel Plaza, and Jumping Jacks Restaurant was still there adjacent to the convenience store. The clerk inside was unimpressed as we excitedly shared our memories of the place. He informed us that the motel was no longer in service, mainly due to lack of staff, and he went back to studying his cell phone.

The Black Hills

Tuesday, August 20, 1996

Spearfish Campground. I talked with Ed who's retired and "bumming." He, his wife and two brothers had owned a chain of grocery stores in this area (Custer, Deadwood, Lead, Hot Springs, and Rapid City). They sold out to a corporation but stayed to help them. Ed explained that in the process, the president of the corporation "had taken up with my lady. It broke my heart." He added, "After that, I just pulled the pin and decided to do some bumming." One of his brothers died, and now Ed drives his 1976 Dodge Camper Van, in mint condition, out to these parts for most of the summer. From Thanksgiving to the first of June, he lives in Southern California. I asked if he was in touch with his ex-wife. "No, I treat it as a death. We had two sons. We all miss her, and I wish her the best," he said sincerely. Ed offered us an old fishing pole (we didn't take it) and a few small apples he'd picked (we accepted). I played him a few songs on the guitar. He wished he'd had some spoons to play along with and wanted to hear more. As we parted, he counseled us to take our time, to have fun (we are!).

Later, as we were ready to leave, Ed came over and got our address and took our picture with the bikes and gear. He delved deeper into the meaning of life. He said he gave too much to his job. "Let those others have those million-dollar mansions, you don't need it. All you need is a home you can sleep good in, and chicken and potatoes roasting in a pot. Don't give your life for money; just don't do it." Cathy said, "You're preaching to the choir there." I said, "Amen."

We're at the Latchstring Inn in Savoy, thirteen miles up Spearfish Canyon, taking a break from the climb, having a snack, writing, and looking off the shaded deck onto the canyon. Last night, we slept under oak trees, the first large oak trees we've seen since leaving Virginia. The ecosystem is very diverse here in the Black Hills—a meeting of Eastern Deciduous Forest, Northern Evergreen Forest, and Northern Great Plains vegetation. It is a joy to be climbing up into this canyon with its deciduous trees, firs, spruce, and pines, and wildflowers, many we haven't seen since Glacier Park a month ago.

Wednesday, August 21, 1996

We're at Horse Creek, a private campground near Sheridan Lake. We stayed last night at Hanna Campground. Leaving there this morning, we had a lot of climbing, especially two climbs, each about three miles long of steady 7% grades. We pedaled along at about four mph, enjoying what we slowly passed.

We came into Lead about 10:15, but there was not much going on, no place to get a cup of coffee. We ate some snacks by the Homestake Mine. It is the largest and most productive gold mine in the Northern Hemisphere and still operates both an open pit and an underground mine. Clearly, this is the heart and soul of Lead's economy and probably the whole of the Black Hills.

We rode by huge metal buildings, dusty and rumbling, where stone is crushed so the gold can be extracted. The buildings are connected by conveyor belts that traverse everywhere, over the road and up the hillsides. The terrain is steeply hilly. The town's main street descends at an angle; side roads drop down from it. Homes are built on poles, and steel beams are needed to create level areas to live and park.

The sloping nature of this town is a hindrance to tourism. I had envisioned doing some sidewalk guitar playing with the hat out, but the place was otherwise dead. We rode on.

At Pactola Lake we stopped at the Forest Service Museum and Information facility. Cathy bought a great book, *Tallgrass Prairie* published by the Nature Conservancy. Outside, as we mounted our steeds, I realized my front tire was flat, so back in the shade we went and took care of business.

The day was clear and cool. It was quite breezy, but most of the time as we wound through the mountains, the wind was at our backs. We never got an overall view of the Black Hills, just glimpses. We passed several ski resorts and the Mickelson Memorial Trail which has about half of its planned 260-mile bicycling/hiking path open. We saw our first buffalo in a paddock. In the adjoining field a man slowly gathered bales of hay into his pickup truck.

Horse Creek Campground is in a little valley with a small stream bisecting the large grassy field. A small pine-covered cliff is to our backs with its grey rocks jutting out from the tree cover.

This area is an interesting mix of vegetation and topography. It is hard to imagine that we rode bikes for days and days across the barren Montana plains, then in one day we are in this hilly, mountainous geography with streams stocked with brown and brook trout, birch groves, oak stands, spruce, fir, red-stemmed dogwood, and wildflowers. We saw three ospreys flying near the Pactola Reservoir calling to us with a shriek. We hadn't seen osprey since the far western Montana rivers, some thirteen-hundred biking miles in the past.

Tonight, after hot showers, we played some music. Cathy put her new G string on her violin and a couple with two kids complimented her playing.

Thursday, August 22, 1996

11 a.m., Keystone, South Dakota. It was 41 degrees at 7:00 when we arose. The tent was dripping inside with our condensed breath. Outside, it was damp from a heavy dew. We packed and moved the tent into the morning sun. While waiting for it to dry, we had coffee. I played guitar.

We discussed our day's destination, extracted from a stack of information: the AAA Campgrounds of South Dakota brochure generally shows private campgrounds that have paid to be included; the National Forest Service brochure which only lists their facilities; the South Dakota State Park brochure which offers the info on state park campgrounds. Cathy skillfully dissects this maze of information each evening and morning.

While we planned our day, an eight-year-old lad came out across the field cradling his latest crafted paper boat—a double-fin keeled, double-ender—which he hoped would make it down the stream 50 feet past the large rock in the middle that divided the flow into treacherous rapids (at the scale of the paper boat). He squatted at stream's edge, happy for witnesses, and launched his dream into the flowing stream. It listed to port then righted itself and bobbed along. At the moment of truth, it veered to the left and shot the rapids straight on. The boy, following apace on the bank, jubilantly announced to us, "It made it!"

We had a sweet 13-mile ride this morning. Here, at the table in this Keystone courtyard, one eats the offerings of the faux western restaurants, such as Indian Tacos or Buffalo Burgers. Playing over the loud-speaker system is music from the 1960s like "The Man Who Shot Liberty Valence" and "Respect."

On the sidewalk, Paha Ska, a Dakota Sioux man dressed in ceremonial headgear, sits by his sign: Picture Yes, for a Tip. Thank you. He paints faces for a fee and sells other paintings too.

I gave Paha Ska a dollar and asked if he'd write his name

in my book. His name translates as "White Hills". "In winter not all is black," he said. When he added that he was from Pine Ridge, I asked him if he was there during the latest uprising with Leonard Peltier. He said he was in the Black Hills. I asked him what he thought of AIM (American Indian Movement). He said a lot of Indians don't agree. He has children that are blonde and blue-eyed, and he would have to feel bad toward his own kin. His wife is blonde and blue-eyed from Toledo, Ohio. His sons have Irish and Swedish wives. As for the Black Hills, he said they would always be here. He offered his big open hand to shake; his disjointed thumb made his hand feel even larger. I wished him good luck.

This morning, Cathy expressed that she sometimes fears missing some amazing places, maybe just a mile off our path. But this trip is about acknowledging and succumbing to the beauty before us. We will always be one mile away from an infinite set of places and possibilities. The challenge is to be present where we are. To this end we endeavor and have many moments of joy daily. Here is where the journey lies.

And now, we're off to Mt. Rushmore.

The ride from Keystone to the top of Mt. Rushmore, where the monument can be viewed, was the hardest climb we've encountered—8%-plus grade for two miles. We were down to 3 mph, sometimes having to stand to pedal. Cathy called it hard; I say challenging! But we made it and felt pretty good at the top.

Mt. Rushmore was worth the climb, an awesome endeavor—the scale immense, yet at a distance, very human. It struck me as a very audacious memorial, very male—altering the face of a mountain with caricatures of four men (US presidents). Very much like diverting streams, leveling mountains, and all those other male-type big picture enterprises.

This monument is a sore spot with the Sioux. In the mid-

1800s, they signed a treaty with the US. They submitted to the loss of much of their lands, but the Black Hills would always be theirs. Then, in 1876 gold was found and overnight an endless stream of white men, prospectors mainly, flooded into the Black Hills. The Army weakly attempted to stop them but to no avail, and whites have occupied the Black Hills since. About twelve miles from Mt. Rushmore, the Crazy Horse Memorial is underway, another carved granite mountain top, this time with a horse.

We ate at Mt. Rushmore and toured the grounds. The place was packed with tourists, like us. It was the most people we have been around at one time since Seattle.

We left, headed for Sylvan Lake, a campground in Custer State Park. We had two big climbs; the last was a six-mile pull that went through beautiful pine forests, the road switching back four or five times and at one point going through a one-lane tunnel through a huge granite boulder. When we reached the top, we were informed at the entrance that the campground was full, had no bike sites, and we should have called two days ago to make reservations. No one had told us about that, not even the State Park information brochure.

We were at the top of a mountain at that point, so nothing to do but continue down to the town of Custer. We found the Campground of American Presidents which had showers and laundry. We ate a mountain of spaghetti with pesto sauce. After everything was cleaned up, I played into the dark. A half-moon cast shadows over the campground.

Friday, August 23, 1996

I'm on pancake duty for breakfast, a chore I relish. We have developed efficient systems for several categories of meals and accoutrements, pancakes being one we have down to a T. Coffee is another highly developed art form here in camp—drip coffee, with that white stuff that we try to remember to pick up when we are in restaurants. Today we have an excellent route planned through the Norbeck Wildlife Preserve and around the scenic Wildlife Loop in Custer State Park. We hope to see buffalo on our way to Wind Cave.

10:24 a.m. We've ridden up a lonely side road to the cabin called the Badger Hole built by South Dakota's poet laureate, Badger Clark. He lived here his last thirty years until his death in 1957 (1883-1957). He built the cabin along with a carpenter friend, and in this secluded home he wrote of the Black Hills, the West, and cowboy life. He never married but was engaged twice to the same woman from Deadwood. The home is "exactly" as he left it when he entered the hospital in Rapid City and died of lung cancer.

Badger liked to dress with a military flair. In his bedroom, the wall is lined with ten pairs of Cavalry-style riding boots. An old Spanish-style guitar with lots of gaudy inlay rested in a corner by his writing table. One wall-sized bookcase was filled with his father's books. Badger's collection of 78 rpm records was almost exclusively John Philip Sousa marches. A friend gave him a radio, but Badger returned it claiming it was a noisy intrusion. He had no horse or car, no running water, and no electricity. A beautiful wood cook stove occupied much of his small kitchen. He kept a box of DDT for fleas, silverfish, mice, and roaches. A photograph of a young buck staring into his window suggested that he was feeding the deer.

We walked the one-mile loop trail around the Badger Hole, reading excerpts of his poetry from a brochure. This is surely a sweet place. I was surprised and thankful that we took this side trip to Badger's cabin. His lifestyle energized me and lifted my spirits. Music, poetry, friends, and love are natural consequences of living simply with nature on this earth.

On the Wildlife Loop Road, the herd of bison was making the crossing, maybe 500 cows and calves together in pairs. The bulls crossed alone whenever they pleased. We dropped out of the Black Hills, touched in on a short flat stretch of prairie grassland and then rode back into the foothills, seeing more bison, wild donkeys, and prairie dog towns. The hills were steep and tiring, like running a series of 220-yard dashes in 98-degree heat.

Retrace 2022

Black Hills to Wind Cave National Park, SD

We camped overnight at Spearfish City Park. From there, our drive to Sylvan Lake took us by the Latchstring Inn and to Hanna Campground, both still lovely. Autumn colors were beginning to show, mixed in with the fall wildflowers. At Pactola Lake, we had lunch at a table in front of the closed visitor center.

Horse Creek Campground had become Bearded Buffalo Resort. New cabins lined the banks of the small stream and on that day no toy boats floated into sight. At Keystone, we passed through the tourist trap without bothering to stop.

Entering the Black Hills, as the views opened up, we realized that we had finally outdistanced the smoke that had followed us from the Rockies. Months prior, Cathy intent on staying at Sylvan Lake had made reservations for three nights. She felt an odd satisfaction camping there, finally, after having been turned away 26 years ago.

It was a pleasant campground, but its real value was its location. A short, wooded hike took us to the stunningly beautiful Sylvan Lake. Granite spires surround its mirrorlike surface. Rock climbers, fisherman, and hikers enjoyed the sunny weekend while we walked Jetta around the lake. But the most magical time was after dark. No artificial lighting interrupted the deep darkness. Unlike the crowded days, at night we found ourselves alone at the lake shore, mesmerized between the Milky Way and its reflection shimmering on the surface.

Since we had a car, we were able to take advantage of the wonderful scenic drives in Custer State Park. Completed in 1922, the roads were designed by South Dakota Governor, Peter Norbeck, to meander through the granite formations, including tunnels that frame the faces on Mount Rushmore. We left the park to visit the Crazy Horse Monument—we had skipped it when we had been on our bikes because it was out of our way. Although we made the effort this time, we balked at the $30 entrance fee. From the parking area, we could see the massive undertaking, still under construction.

We drove past Mount Rushmore several times, but we did not stop to tour. Instead, we chose to take short hikes with Jetta within the state park. We spotted big horn sheep and mountain goats along the park roads. On the Wildlife Loop, our hike through the mixed grass prairie was captivating, and we delighted in sightings of prairie dogs and bison. We took time to return to The Badger Hole and were disappointed to find it closed for the season. We made mental notes regarding touring after Labor Day. Are places closed because there are fewer people, or are there fewer people because so much is closed?

After three enjoyable days and nights at Sylvan Lake, we headed into a less scheduled segment of our retrace trip. Cathy had left several nights open with no reservations as we made our way out of South Dakota and across Nebraska. We decided to only travel as far as Wind Cave National Park. We were hoping to have time to take turns visiting the cave, but the tours were completely booked. Instead, at our campsite, we erected our tarp to provide shade during the afternoon heat. That evening we attended a successful park program to listen to the bugling elk. There were about two dozen participants. At dusk, in our individual cars, we followed our ranger guide to a nearby overlook. We parked and silently waited in the darkness. Soon we could hear the high whistle of the male elk, bugling to his harem, a magical flute blowing across the prairie.

Journey: Middle

The Eastern Great Plains

Saturday, August 24, 1996

8:30 a.m. We're in Hot Springs, a small friendly town, at the Family Restaurant looking at maps and scheming. We rolled away from Wind Cave at 7:00. After a couple miles, we came upon a herd of several hundred buffalo beside the road. The males were snorting and rumbling, a sound that shook the ground. I recorded them a bit, and Cathy took photos. It was an awesome sight. At the edge of the herd, a cow chased off a lone coyote that had gotten too close. It disappeared over a rise, maybe to be more successful in its hunt for breakfast, possibly a wiggly prairie dog. Buffalo graze prairie grasses short, helping prairie dogs detect stalking coyotes from atop their mounds.

After breakfast, we toured the *in situ* mammoth site in Hot Springs. It was an incredible place, a 26,000-year-old sinkhole that had filled with warm artesian waters, trapping hundreds of animals. They still have 50 feet more depth to excavate. To date they have found 52 male mammoths. Most of the remains were of the woolly mammoth that stood six feet at the shoulders, but remains of the rare Colombian mammoth also were found. They had ten-foot-long tusks and stood thirteen feet at the shoulder. They also found bones of camel and the rare Short-faced Bear (only ten in the world), 30% bigger than the biggest grizzly. This place is such a capsule of time, just a wink in geologic time, yet what a find.

3:45 in Oelrichs, South Dakota. We stopped here at a gas station/convenience store in the blazing sun; "100 degrees," says the rotund manager. When pulling into the station, a woman was on the phone at the corner of Highway 18 and Highway 385. When the man with her, Gary, asked us where we were coming from, a conversation ensued. They are independent filmmakers, cameramen by profession, out from California trying to put together a film depicting the problems of the American Indian from their perspective, "so that the US government might better understand the wrongs that continue to the present." We told them about the division we have felt from many, the Us versus Them syndrome. Gary picked up on this and said he thought the fragmentation of people into different interest groups was the most challenging condition in America's environmental wellbeing.

Gary reminded me of an old friend. His pleasant eyes and smile revealed his child-self having fun. People who have fun naturally, like falling off a log, tend to involve themselves in thoughtful, serious endeavors. I think I'm like that.

We carried on with heartfelt conversation in the pall of heat, sensing a special moment and seizing it. Oh, had there been a nice cafe with iced mochas, fresh baked goodies, and fruit. Yet, no matter, I am thankful to have met them, my sights were lifted once again.

Inside the store, we bought a Mountain Dew, a Coke, and a bag of popcorn, borrowed two folding chairs, and retreated to the shade of an elm and some cottonwoods. We were surrounded by the detritus and paraphernalia of a service station. A transmission and gearshift lay almost hidden in the shoots of an elm stump. An old shed with grayed German wood-siding held nine racks of mule and white-tailed deer and three horned cow skulls. A '58 Chevy Impala rested nearby, dappled with rust, its goofy grill smiling at us.

The water here is the worst we have tasted on the trip. Cathy says a stalactite is forming on the faucet in the women's restroom. Rather than refilling, I will drink the water bottle tea we are carrying.

We have about forty miles to go through this heat. The winds that play in our faces seem to be dying down. Maybe it's time we roll on.

9:30 p.m., Chadron, Nebraska. From Oelrichs, we rode through Buffalo Gap National Grasslands where only cattle (no buffalo) can be seen now. After thirty miles of rolling grasslands and rangeland, and one flat tire, we dropped into the White River Valley where we stopped to pick more sage. In exceptionally strong headwinds we had to pedal downhill as the sun nestled into the Nebraska plains. We rolled into Chadron at dusk, drained.

As we dropped into town, we saw a sign for "R&L RV Drive Thru and Camping." This was great. The only camping we knew of was nine miles further on Rt. 20. We pulled in. No one was in the office, so we found the tent area and began to set up. There was already one tent there. We were immediately beset by droves of mosquitoes. It was too dark to see them, but we could feel them all over. We set up in record time, got our clean clothes and toiletries, and hit the showers. The mosquitoes canceled our dinner plans of cooking out, so wearing head lamps we rode our bikes down the dark road to McDonald's. It was a tolerable meal, though it was still McDonald's.

Sunday, August 25, 1996

8 a.m., We're in Helen's Restaurant, in Chadron, Nebraska. Today is Sunday; lots of families are out for breakfast. Today, we begin the 430-mile crossing of Nebraska to Omaha on Highway 20. The day is sunny and so are we.

We made it through last night despite the 1:30 a.m. arrival of Frank and a lady friend who drove him to his tent from the Days Inn Lounge. They were both very loud, no attempt to

168

moderate their voices. Hers was very adolescent, giggly; his was nearly unintelligible, Neanderthal grunts and hums. She gave a loud play-by-play. Apparently, he never wears underwear and got naked immediately. After a series of grunts reminiscent of the bison we'd heard earlier in the day, she finally had hers removed. We were the forced auditory audience to this primal floundering. Surprisingly, Frank must have fumbled, because the tone of her voice changed from birdlike murmurs to a deeper, edgier sound. Then the car door opened to the dinging of the key-in-ignition warning, and the engine kicked to a roar (a big old Buick, I imagined), and off she drove. Silence descended once again save for a few last grunts from Frank. This morning Cathy saw Frank walking off about 6:15. He wore jeans, boots, cowboy hat, and was shirtless, swatting the mosquitoes as he rounded the office building in the dazzling daybreak sun. The thought of him roaming the land with only four hours of sleep is a scary one.

This morning, we passed the site of the Bordeaux Trading Post that had its heyday in the fur trade from 1846 to 1872. They traded with Native Americans and white trappers who exchanged buffalo robes, furs, and ponies for guns, powder, beads, blankets, and whiskey. The present building was built on the same site as the original, but it still seemed almost as remote as when they were operating 125 years ago. The gravel parking area was empty and the place rundown, a historical tourist trap.

We stopped at the Chadron Visitors information building for Nebraska campground guides. We didn't know that Fred was working there at 9:30 this Sunday morning. He talked for an hour about local history, right on up to Wounded Knee II in 1976. Things he said: 25% of South Dakota is reservations. The Pine Ridge Reservation comprises the poorest county in the US. The Sioux were nomadic people and could not adapt to reservation life. The Sioux were given poor quality land in Pine Ridge; they were screwed on that deal. Russell Means and Dennis Banks (AIM) just stirred up trouble and accomplished nothing except got some people shot and burned up a nice church. For a couple years after Wounded Knee II there were skirmishes with Indians and whites on Highway 20. The Indians wanted Sitting Bull's artifacts that are on display at Fort Robinson in Crawford, Nebraska. It set back relations with the Indians 100 years; things are just getting back to normal. The average life expectancy of a Sioux Indian male is 45; cirrhosis of the liver is the main cause of death. White Clay, just across the Border from Pine Ridge sells the most beer and wine per capita in Nebraska. Sioux walk across the border from Pine Ridge with their checks to buy booze. When they buy a truckload of booze (they prefer beer), a party ensues; relatives and friends come over, and they drink all night. In the morning, Indians are passed out on the lawns, wherever. That is Fred's eyewitness account, as he had Indians move in across the street.

Fred's dislike of Russell Means was obvious, as he painted him as a "troublemaker" who was "stirring up trouble for no good." It is an irony that these very words, I'm sure, were used to describe Sitting Bull in the 1870s. Yet now, Fred and most current residents of this land view Sitting Bull as an honorable, brave chief who fought for his people's lands. One of the goals of modern "troublemakers" like Russell Means and the American Indian Movement is to regain the Black Hills for the Sioux, which Fred sees as an impossible concept. "You can't go back," is how he said it. This was exactly the rationale for taking the Black Hills from the Sioux in the first place. Already too many white settlers and prospectors who were wild for gold had come to the Black Hills. Thus, despite treaties they took it from the Sioux.

In fact, this was a foregone deed when Sitting Bull was fighting the losing battle for his land. At what point, was the deed "done"? I'd say Custer knew exactly what he was doing when he brought along two prospectors in his expedition into the Black Hills. When they found gold, as they certainly knew they would, and broadcast this find, they knew the flood of people would overwhelm the Indians.

Evidence of the impact of gold fever was well known—the flood of people, the towns springing up overnight. The California gold rush in 1849 and the gold rush to Montana and western Washington in the 1860s were testaments to this phenomenon. White man's reaction to gold was well known and predictable. With that nugget of gold found by Horatio Nelson Ross, with Custer in 1874, Sitting Bull's struggle was doomed, just as Russell Means' objective appears to be today.

Monday, August 26, 1996

8 a.m. We're eating at JJ's Restaurant in Gordon. The clique of old women has now begun talking to us; they had exhausted their other topics—shopping, electric bills, and home repair.

We stayed last night in Winship Park in Gordon, bivouacked near a small stage and some spruce, about thirty feet from the bathrooms. We bathed under the spigot in the women's room—felt great. We had to cover the side of the tent with the space blanket to block the orange lights flooding the park. This worked great and we slept well.

Today we face headwinds. It's cloudy and 59 degrees. We roll on now.

Historical marker, eleven miles east of Gordon, Nebraska in the Sand Hills: "One of the first ranches in this area was set up on the Niobrara River five miles south of here in 1877 by E. S. Newman on the edges of the Sand Hills. He, as did other ranchers that followed him to this area, thought the Sand Hills to be inhospitable to humans and cattle alike. He ranched cattle to sell to the government for delivery to the Indians of Pine Ridge Agency twenty miles to the north.

"The winter of 1879 was very severe. He and other ranchers, searching for hundreds of lost cows, searched the Sand Hills south of the Niobrara River and found hundreds of healthy cattle in the well-watered Sand Hills. The Sand Hills have since become one of the most productive cattle raising regions in the world."

Ole E. S. Newman settled here in a giant cosmic/ ecological/human screw up. He latched onto the government's tit in an ironic articulation. First, to suppress the Native Indians and get them onto reservations where they wouldn't bother settlers, the government supervised and condoned the annihilation of millions of bison, on which those people depended for food, tools, and shelter. At this, they were very successful, reducing the numbers of bison from millions to only 200. By 1878, all the Indians were on reservations. At that point, the government had to drive Texas Longhorn cattle up here to feed them because most of the reservation land was worthless.

The towns we pass through have museums run by their historical societies. We try to stop in. History, in most of the museums, begins around the early 1800s. Anything before that is a preamble. Yet these Plains are home to the first humans to cross the Bering land bridge 14,000 years ago. They hunted mammoth, short-faced bear, camel, and deer.

As Highway 20 enters the Sand Hills region, the change is gradual. The Sand Hills are the largest tract of sand dunes in the Western Hemisphere. The landscape becomes hillier; the grass and sage-covered hills are small and dune-shaped. Some hills show bare sand in steep points where grass cannot hold.

Ten miles east of Gordon, we entered Cherry County, the

largest county in Nebraska, covering an area larger than the state of Connecticut. Ninety-eight percent of Cherry County is in the Sand Hills.

When we crested a small rise and looked three miles in the distance to Merriman (pop.183), the scene was sobering in its remoteness. Here, Highway 20's pavement visually narrows as it nears the stands of cottonwood on both sides of the highway—a pleasing dark green in contrast to the yellow olive green of the surrounding vista. One lone structure hints at community; a sixty-foot stark white grain elevator stands out above the trees.

As we get nearer, more details emerge—buildings, homes, and trailers. Merriman's only intersection is at Rt. 61, a bleak highway that crosses 67 miles of Sand Hill country before coming to anything with a name. But the intersection is the center of town. The Post Office, Sand Bar, Sand Cafe, farm equipment store, and the grain elevator are all within a stone's throw of it.

We stop at the Sand Cafe, the only eatery in town. It is lunchtime, and the place is packed with cowboy hat-wearing older men and their wives and a few younger people. A lone waitress struggles with the rush, but there is a current *Omaha Daily News* and cold water, so we are content to wait and rest and read and enjoy this place. People in Nebraska are friendly. They speak to us; they wave from their cars; they chat. Food prices are very reasonable, and the water is good.

Cathy wrote postcards, and after an hour and a half lunch we stopped by the Post Office. I photographed a quaintly crafted sign displaying about 20 cattle brands of the Sand Hills.

We rode a mile east out of town to a sand and gravel road that traverses a mile south to Cottonwood Lake State Recreation Area. This lake is an example of the many small lakes associated with the Ogallala Aquifer that lay under us and dotted the Sand Hills. We were alone here. Cottonwoods rimmed the lake and were scattered about the camping area. We set up, then went for a swim and bathed in the lake, came back and lounged in the shade, played music, and read.

It is now 5:30 p.m. An older couple has arrived from Custer, SD in a 5th-wheel trailer. It is huge, pulled by a 2-ton diesel pickup. They speak with us. He wears a cowboy hat, and she's sporting culottes. They're having fun. We say we were in Custer four days ago. She refers to our bikes as motorcycles. Just now a car arrives pulling a boat. I suspect fishing is a big function for the lake.

The sound of the RV's generator cast a stale hum over this beautiful setting. RVs are changing the face of America's outdoors. Gone are the quiet evenings around the campfire. Now it's the satellite TV dish and generators humming. We asked if they ran the generator all night. They said, "No, just charging up the camcorder batteries."

The man told us about crossing the Canadian border and Canadian Customs asking if he had any guns. "Not with me," he told them. "Then they proceeded to tear the trailer apart looking for them." His pants were riding on his hips at pubic level. His cowboy shirt with snaps and embroidered wagon wheels above each pointed pocket must have had extra-long tails to still be tucked in as it strained at his pride. "They never did find them," he boasted.

After dinner, we walked up on a sand hill ridge and stood staring out over soft olive-green dunes in the purple evening light. "I'm glad we're going slow," I thought. Off to the NW rose the grain elevator above the town-shrouding cottonwoods. The nearly full moon was rising over the lake, the purple light playing devilishly on the yellow sunflowers and the grasses with their stalks holding forth filaments of silk to the heavens.

Retrace 2022

September 20, 2022
Chadron, NE to Badlands National Park, SD

In a way, we were happy to be travelling now at 60 mph, past Oelrichs and into Chadron. Grinning from our seats, we noted the old motel we had camped behind, remembering Frank and his lady. We saw the McDonald's was still there, but we missed the Visitor Information Center as we looped quickly through town. And suddenly, Chadron was behind us.

At Gordon, we found Winship Park, recognizable with its gazebo stage. There were several folks who were hanging out, looking rather aimless. We said hello, then found a table for our lunch, as they drifted away. The irrigated lawn seemed ridiculously lush and green to our dusty prairie-adapted eyes. Camping didn't seem to be tolerated now, and I'm not sure we would have felt as safe.

We had been looking forward to being back at the campground at Cottonwood Lake Recreation Area. We planned to stay two nights. This would give us time to drive an hour to visit Badlands National Park, then return to our tent at Cottonwood Lake.

However, Merriman had changed. The businesses were closed and shabby. At Cottonwood Lake, we drove past where we had camped on our bike trip and were surprised by the expanse of the wetlands. Several small lakes extended beyond the area we had remembered. Not another soul was around. As we explored, our unease began to grow. The small lakes were thick with algae. The facilities were not well kept. Bird droppings had accumulated in piles on the covered picnic tables. The pit toilets were just downright nasty. We did not feel good about staying here for the night, much less leaving our things alone the next day to travel up to Badlands.

We decided we should change plans and head on up to Badlands for the night. Cathy called the park concessionaire at Cedar Pass campground. There were two first come sites left, but the desk clerk said they would probably be filled before we could get there. However, there was one reservable site open for one night where someone had just cancelled. Would we like that? Well yes, please.

And so, we headed north across the Nebraska plains back into South Dakota. The drive was beautiful, drifting through undulating hillsides and wide-open sky. Our site was the best in the campground. Rather than being wedged in between large RVs, our site was alone on a bluff at the edge of the loop, overlooking the jagged badlands. We set up the tent and poured some wine just in time to exhale the day and enjoy a front row seat for the rich red sunset. The stars appeared, then the whole Milky Way, as the night sky blackened. We knew we had made the right decision to come here.

The next morning the sky was overcast. We packed up, bought coffee at the park's restaurant, checked out the Visitor Center, and followed the black asphalt scenic road as it snaked into the Badlands. Since it was cooler, we were able to leave Jetta in the car while we explored a few short hikes. The hills were rich shades of grey with golden grasses in the valleys. Bighorn sheep grazed by the side of the road. We drove as far as Yellow Mounds Overlook where the chalky grey hills transformed to rainbows of intense yellow, maroon, pink, and blue-green. We hiked up a steep hillside and were awestruck at the vivid panorama.

Tuesday, August 27, 1996

We got an early start, and rolled out of camp at 7 a.m. We're eating $2 pancakes at the Sand Cafe and looking over maps. The night was cool and occasionally punctuated by the call of loons out on the lake. In the center of the Great Plains, there are waterways for water birds to survive. I think of this as being so far from water, especially the loon's habitat.

10:20 a.m. Cody, (pop. 177), "The little town that refuses to die." We are at the Double D Cafe having chocolate malts. About eight miles back, we were passed by a car that slowed and pulled over up ahead. The driver got out and stood behind his car, wringing his hands, and waiting for us. We were still ten yards away when he started talking—fast. Turns out he sells "RELIV" health products. His name is Winston, and he appears to have had several of his high-energy drinks already this morning. The trunk comes up, and Winston is digging around for his card, brochure, and his $40 distributors kit. He talks rapidly in that nasal tone of the Midwest. Winston's from Elgin, Illinois, and he is furiously mixing us a cup of orange "RELIV INNERGIZE." He mixes another. His wife gets out, a little embarrassed. His hand shakes as he pours the brew. He talks in the AMWAY way of talking, in which he asks simple questions like: Do you drink nutritional drinks? (Sure.) Do you exercise a lot? (Obviously, yes.) The idea is to involve you and to get you in a "yes mood" so that you think, "Well, by gosh, I think I will try that." We did enjoy the drinks; after two hours of riding over these Sand Hills you like anything that is cold.

The folks from the campground with the RV generator passed us, tooting. They run a wintertime campground in Arizona. He said he never sees any Nebraska or Kansas license plates. He thinks they are up here working, putting up hay or feeding cattle—no time to go anywhere. This morning he came over to observe our final packing and rolling off. He wished us well, as did we. They are heading for Virginia Beach and Myrtle Beach.

7:30 p.m. We're in a laundromat in Valentine. We cruised into Valentine in good time. It was a fun day crossing the Sand Hills. The winds were on our starboard most of the way, which didn't slow us too much. Highway 20 meandered up and down and over the hills with gradual sweeping curves. I felt like an albatross, gracefully gliding in the troughs of ocean swells.

We passed through several small, struggling towns today. Nenzel (pop. 138) is basically an intersection with a nice grassy shady picnic area by the road. There was a church and parsonage of 1950s vintage, a couple of empty buildings, and no one about. Nothing was open, just some trucks moving farm equipment, coming to the T-intersection with Rt. 20, then turning, roaring, and groaning off over the hills. We lay in the grass resting. Cathy trimmed my mustache and beard with the Swiss Army knife scissors. I relaxed as if this were a posh health spa, watching the play of dappled sunlight through the maple leaves projecting their orange sherbet glow onto my closed eyelids. I groaned in contentment.

Eight miles along the black ribbon, we rode into Kilgore, "The Gateway to the Rosebud Reservation." Three miles east of Kilgore we crossed time zones, leaving behind Mountain Time which had the sun rising at 5:45 a.m. and setting at 8 p.m.

The town of Crookston (pop. 89) was heartrending in its decay and desolation. The galvanized-sided grain elevator with many of its tin sheets curling and hanging off, stood forlornly by the abandoned railroad line, its tracks pulled, undoubtedly cut into cattle guard crossings. A girl of eight or nine walked through the rubble in the scorched grasses and sand by the elevator. A man walked to a truck and drove away. A white dog sauntered down Highway 20. Nothing else moved.

Valentine (pop. 2800, elevation 2590') is "The Heart of the Sand Hills". Cattle ranching is the economic engine of this region. Valentine also benefits from the Niobrara River which crosses Highway 20 five miles to the east. There are five canoe and innertube outfitters in town and a new bike shop. The bike shop's manager, Nora, says the people of Valentine and surrounding areas are "taking a liking to biking," mainly mountain bikes. While we were talking with her, a man from Gordon came in to pick up his bike that was in for repairs. He had seen us passing through two days ago.

We set up camp behind the Valentine Motel. The old fellow at the desk was very kind. He owned the motel, and he showed us through his attached home. His wife's collection of about 300 dolls was displayed all over the place. He was as proud of them as his wife. She said, "I always loved dolls." They celebrated their 69th wedding anniversary and 90th birthdays this year.

Wednesday, August 28, 1996

7:45 a.m. We're in a cafe having breakfast. We're packed up and ready to roll down to Ainsworth where we will meet up with Roanoke friends, Jim and Lisa.

Eight out of ten of the people eating breakfast here look to be either drivers or ranchers. Two men in their forties are dressed in ties, the first ties we have seen in a long time. Mostly, the men wear ball caps, though one big man sports an Irish-green cowboy hat and matching green John Deere suspenders.

We talked last evening over a banana split and milkshake about Valentine, which is in the heart of cattle country. The cattle trucks with double-decked cattle cages roll through town constantly. When we rode in yesterday from the west, a huge cattle yard with paddocks of cows and mud generated a stomach wrenching acrid smell. I wonder, what is it like to live in a town whose economic heartbeat echoes the cows'?

There are few areas where the rancher can exercise some control. The rancher must put up enough hay to last the winter and keep a good healthy stock. He must be able financially to wait out the market if prices are not favorable, as is the case now according to ranchers in Montana. Otherwise, forces outside of the marketplace control the rancher's profit line—the cost of fuel, transportation, and the price offered per pound by the powerful consortium of meat packers and other market entities.

Noon. We stopped at the Hitching Post Cafe in Wood Lake (pop. 59). I had a burger and coke; Cathy had peach pie and chocolate milk. A handmade sign on the wall by the cash register said in bold letters: EAT BEEF. THE ONLY MAD COW WE KNOW IS OPRAH.

In the parking lot, we talked to the first highway patrolman we have seen in Nebraska. No wonder. He drives 1,200 miles a week patrolling his area. He characterized Nebraskans as "nice people, just not many of them." He said the Ogallala Aquifer is rising. In the last two years lakes have been reappearing that have been dry basins for decades. He said they have had unprecedented rainfall in the last four or five years. The water at the Hitching Post was great sweet water. He said this water was from a well around 150 feet deep. In some areas around here, you can hit water in six feet, but you must go deeper to get to good water. The water at last night's campground was from a hand pump and couldn't have been very deep. It tasted of iron and sulfur.

We are now in Johnstown (pop. 48), named for John Barry who donated the land the town is on and was a right-of-way scout when the railroad came through. Johnstown was the site of the CBS movie *O Pioneers!*, the town's claim to fame, though neither Cathy nor I have heard of it (this doesn't mean much though). We are in the park by the House of Plants and Gifts with "a variety of YOU NAME IT under one roof" and across main street from the L-Bow Room Bar and Pool.

We stopped at the gas station when we pulled in here for a cold drink. The guy in the gas station/restaurant/convenience store owns both this and the L-Bow Room. His hat was cocked on his head, the bill launched skyward. He sat behind the counter which was holding him up. He looked like he'd been napping, his face and forehead pulpy pale. I commented that it must be nap time and he allowed that he needed one. He said, as if confessing, "I own the bar too, and last night I decided to drink, and now I'm paying for it." The confession continued, "I do this once a year to learn why I don't do it, and last night was this year's." I said I hoped he had fun. "Last night yes, today no," he groaned, already starting to slump back onto the countertop, cradled in his big beefy arms.

Across the street in the little town park, it appeared that somebody had recently smashed their vehicle into a concrete picnic table under the cottonwood shade tree, breaking it into a heap of concrete and re-bar chunks. Two women getting into separate cars paused and looked over at the crumpled table. "Oh my," one of them gasped. They lamented some more, then got in their cars and drove off.

As I stood waiting for Cathy on the front porch of the House of Plants, the owner's husband came out and explained the table's demise. "They drank too much over at the bar last night and one of 'em got mad and pushed the table with his pick-up truck." He said a family was camping near it when it happened. Sounds like they had a night to remember in Johnstown.

This man farms corn. He says this is his best corn yet. They will harvest in October and November. Corn prices are $4 per bushel (56 pounds), up from $2.60 per bushel two years ago. This is great news for him, and he can barely contain his excitement. He says cattle ranchers are having a hard time though. In two years, the price they get on the hoof has dropped from $1.20 per pound to 62 cents per pound, yet the price of a cut of beef at the store remains the same.

4:40 p.m. We are at the Pizza Hut in Ainsworth (pop. 1,870). Ainsworth is "The Country Music Capital of Nebraska." They have a festival in June called the "Middle of Nowhere Celebration." How's that for class and a sense of humor? We are waiting for Jim and Lisa to pick us up.

We had a fine time talking about Cathy's college days at William and Mary. Like an old tree with its deep taproot, this trip (each new day, each hard mile, each place we circle to lie down in) sends the tap root deeper inside my being.

We have made arrangements with Rusty and Thelma, owners of the Lazy A Motel, to store our bikes until tomorrow when we will come back and camp in the field behind the motel. We had a good conversation with them.

Rusty was a mate on a battleship at Pearl Harbor in December 1941. He was waiting on the ship for a launch to take him and others ashore. Rusty had a date lined up with his sweetheart, Thelma. The launch was on its way out, but never made it. The Japanese bombers struck. "And my wife is Japanese, you see," he said, explaining something about love.

Rusty worked in the engine room. It normally took the ship at anchor two hours to prepare to sail. "But we were underway in 17 minutes," he said, still proud. During the whole war they had a charmed ship. She never was hit. Rusty didn't see any of the action, just gauges and dials and the noise of the engine room.

Rusty believes the Navy knew the Japanese were going

to attack because they had moved the aircraft carriers to Hawaii and put battleships in their place, "which were of no real use to them," he said.

Today we passed out of Cherry County, named for a past officer at Fort Niobrara. The fort was built a few miles east of Valentine in 1876, a couple years after settlers urged the army to do so because they feared the Sioux Indians that had been corralled in the Rosebud Reservation just to the north. But there was no "Indian trouble"; the Ghost Dance of the 1880s was the last scare the settlers had. John Pershing, before becoming General Pershing of W.W.I fame, was an officer there.

Highway 20 passed twenty miles north of the location of the Lakeland Sod High School. A roadside marker tells us it was built in the 1920s by local farmers with sod walls and roof. The school housed the teacher and provided a shed for the horses of the children who rode many miles to the school. Thirty-three children attended the school up to the mid-1930s when it closed. I wonder what happened to the graduates of Sod High School. In the wind and sun of this late August day, as schools gear up to start throughout the US, this view of endless grass-covered sand hills makes me wonder what prospects of life went through those young minds. Was the vast expanse of empty horizons a catalyst of new possibilities?

Thursday, August 29, 1996

Jim and Lisa met us at Pizza Hut last evening. We stuffed our gear into their car and drove an hour to Smith Falls State Park on the Niobrara River where we camped overnight. Jim and I were up late jawin' and playing music.

Today, we floated down the Niobrara. We had arranged for Brewer's Canoers from Valentine to drop us off then pick us up 12 miles downriver. The water felt great, and we lounged and lolled about on the canvas decks of the big rented innertubes, totally relaxed.

Afterwards we drove back to Ainsworth, and we all set up camp behind the Lazy A Motel. Jim got out his bagpipes and we played together, while Cathy and Lisa talked.

Friday, August 30, 1996

We had a final breakfast with Jim and Lisa at the L L Cafe. Then itching to get on the road, we climbed on our bikes and headed east. Jim gave us a rousing bagpipe sendoff that brought tears to our eyes. A few miles down the road they passed us tooting and waving. Seeing our friends, we smiled again. Thirty-seven miles down the road in Stuart, "The Heart of Hay Country" we took a break in the shade before moving on.

Ten more miles down the road and we've stopped in the town park of Atkinson to mix some lemonade and stretch out in the shade. School is in session, and the West Holt Huskies football team is suited up on the practice field. Nebraska is big-time football country. We haven't seen any soccer playing here.

We are out of the Sand Hills and into the Plains. Gone are the rolling grassy dunes, the landscape is very flat. Cattle and hay are still the focus of activity in this region. Atkinson has a nice town park, as does every small town we've come across, with large cottonwood trees, silver maples, and catalpa trees. We have 18 more miles to go to O'Neill, the "Irish Capital of Nebraska."

10:20 p.m., Carney Park, O'Neill (pop. 3,856). We got to O'Neill around 5:30 and cruised down Main Street looking at the bustling town. Several Irish pubs lined the street. We bought groceries including a locally grown watermelon. We found the town park easily and set up camp.

Just as we'd set up, a 67-year-old fellow walked up and started talking. He's a contractor supervisor working on a school project. He oversees the carpet, base, and finish trim on the school. He works for Warren Buffet out of Omaha who "is the second richest man in the world. He's worth five times as much as Ross Perot," he claims. He retired but couldn't handle being around the house and "housecleaning" and started back up with Buffet's organization. He says he is away all the time now, which seems to suit him. He talked for a while, seemed lonely, and by the time he left we had to get dinner underway—rice, green beans and two top sirloin steaks.

After dinner, we took our watermelon over to a set of bleachers overlooking the park's rodeo ring. The lights were on, and about ten young people were practicing roping three calves, a horned steer, and a goat. It was a 4-H club Friday night, and it looked like fun. They would release a calf from the gate, and the roper on horseback would chase it down the ring, sometimes roping it, most times not.

They also practiced racing out to the center of the ring where they would jump off their horse, grab and flip a goat on its side, tie up three of its legs in a flurry of arm movements while the goat bleated woefully. The goat was being held on a short rope in the center of the ring by little Rudy, the youngest member of the group and the daredevil. His right hand was wrapped in a big bandage, yet he was out riding his pony like a madman. Once, a young boy rode helter-skelter out to where Rudy held the goat. He got off awkwardly and ran to the goat then pulled up short and just danced around. I heard him say "We'll wait," and Cathy laughed. After a few moments he energetically grabbed and threw the bawling goat down in an attempt to resurrect his slow time. Cathy, still laughing, explained the goat was peeing when the lad first approached, thus the delay!

At one point Rudy whispered to a teenage girl, Jackie, who was good with the rope and horse. She pointed to the back of the ring and offhandedly said, "Just go back there." Well, Rudy walked about twenty feet back, and still in the bright lights of the ring started peeing a long arc as several girls yelled, "No. Not there!" But too late, and they all laughed, galloping their horses in the opposite direction.

It was a mellow group of young people. An adult man was there at the release gate, quietly in charge. We had a good time watching them, eating watermelon, and talking to a father and daughter who were on their way to the Badlands and the Black Hills for the Labor Day weekend. He is a butcher down in St. Paul, butchering and freezing beef for local folks. He talked about the beef and corn markets, the futures market, and how the beef people are investigating the slaughterhouses, who set the price of beef, for monopolistic activity. He didn't doubt they had a case.

Retrace 2022

September 21, 2022
Valentine to O'Neill, NE

Our detour to the Badlands took us off our bike route and we did not catch up to it again until Valentine, missing the small Nebraska towns we had passed 26 years earlier. In Valentine, we could not find the old Valentine Motel with the campground behind. Progress had ushered in other buildings and businesses. Not much was familiar to us.

We stopped in Johnstown and found little had changed. O Pioneers! had left an indelible mark with the board sidewalk and old West facades. I went into the L Bow Room Bar and found it still alive but under different management while Cathy waited with Jetta in the town's renovated roadside park.

We quickly covered the miles to Ainsworth. Rusty and Thelma's Lazy A appeared to have been closed for quite a while. Before we left town we made a quick stop at the L L, now called the D&B Cafe.

We crossed into Central Time and lost an hour the day we got to O'Neill. The city park was much the same. A few RVs were parked, and we set up next to a young man's tent. He seemed to have been living there for a while. We sat on the rodeo bleachers and though no one was riding that night, we still felt nostalgic thinking of Rudy and the other kids. The arena had been named since we had been there to honor long time rodeo advocate, Carrol McKay who had died in 2011.

<<<<< >>>>>

The Midwest

Saturday, August 31, 1996

At Woody's Café and Chevy Dealership, in O'Neill. We had a nice night's sleep, very damp this morning. We ate the rest of the watermelon this morning, packed and rode the two miles to here. Time for a Nebraska breakfast.

We are in a different region with more trees. This morning the sound of birds greeted us, the first we'd noticed in a long time. Also, the towns are getting closer together and more populace. We are leaving the West and entering the Midwest. I was getting used to the sparsely populated Sand Hills, but traveling is the vehicle of change and change we have.

There are six distinct topographic regions in Nebraska: Valleys; Rolling Hills; Plains; Dissected Plains; Sand Hills; and Valley-Side Slopes. We will have passed through all six regions when we cross the Missouri River out of Nebraska. By far, the largest region is the Sand Hills, taking up much of Nebraska's middle. I grew to like the Sand Hills region that we were in for six days. I liked the rolling grassy dunes, the small towns spread out along Highway 20 like a cheap string of Christmas lights. For the most part, the people were friendly and seemed content. Crime, or rather the lack of it, was one of their reasons for liking the Sand Hills. They were mostly ranchers or those in service to the ranchers.

12:30 p.m. We stopped in Ewing (pop. 449). Main Street was empty. We found a lad selling watermelons out of his pickup on the highway. We bought one for $1.50 and ate it in the shade of a silver maple by a closed gas station. It was a great watermelon.

They are just getting ripe in Nebraska according to a picture on the front page of the *Omaha News Herald*. We agree. I hadn't had a watermelon all summer until last night; now I've had two. There was a sign taped to the door of the gas station: Jerry in hospital, back in a day or two.

4 p.m., Shirley's Cafe, Neligh (pop. 1,735). We're on top of our first hill in over 105 miles. We've left the plains region of Nebraska and are into the dissected plains region.

6:10 Riverside Park, Neligh. We set up camp in this nice town park; the showers were great. Cathy's in the tent reading. I made some drip coffee to go with the apple I cut up. We're by the banks of the Elkhorn River that we have been riding along today. The Elkhorn is a shallow silty river, its banks lined with cottonwood, box elder, silver maple, and a host of brushy vegetation. The park, being by the river, is down off the hill.

Tonight, the park is a-buzz with kids and people playing horseshoes. We commented on the fact we hadn't heard anyone raise their voice at kids in a while. These parks are a testament to a certain appreciation of the outdoors, a place to relax and be together, a common ground open to all—travelers, locals, kids, and retirees in RVs—really little jewels each town offers.

Our tent is pitched between two spreading silver maples forming an arch of shade, blocking the night lights which seem to afflict all these sweet town parks. I've taken to scanning the near horizon, looking for where the night lights will be before we place our tent.

The sky is dark and hazy to the southeast, and it was all day as we rode toward the dingy horizon. My Virginia weather instincts caution "Storm soon," but the old fellows in Shirley's Cafe don't think anything will happen. I figure they have seen this sky before, and their experience tells them not to worry.

I am reminded of the sign we read on the side of the Youth Services building in O'Neill—Learn to say, 'So what?' and mean it. Preceding this musing was—This Too Will Pass. I thought about that and wondered if this is the key to understanding Nebraskans. Are these the hard lessons learned from farming and ranching? Certainly, many of the forces important in their lives are natural, beyond economic forces and the realm of human gerrymandering. "You play the game and take your chances," as one rancher put it.

Sunday, September 1, 1996

We were up and out by 7:30 a.m. We're at Daddy's Cafe for breakfast in downtown Neligh, a four-block street lined by a menagerie of stores. Out the window and across the wide street, which has pull-in parking on both sides, I see a 1930s-era building with fine details on its upper windows. Its street level has undergone changes; it has been sided recently with cedar shakes and now houses The Flower Shop. Next door The Village Shop occupies another 1930s-era building painted white with lavender trim. (They are having a Sale: Buy one sale item, get second sale item half-price.) Next to The Village Shop, a dark brown 1960s-era rehab building houses the Neligh Office Plaza with the Nebraska State Patrol Office and Antelope County Attorneys, Anten, Seth and Prus, P.C. Twice But Nice occupies the old bank space next door.

In the slumbering campground last night, a van towing a small trailer arrived around 10:15 p.m., and because we don't have a car in front of our tent site, they pulled in with us. We were almost asleep when three kids stampeded out. They were warned, "People are trying to sleep," but they knew the score. They played as if it were noon at Coney Island. A ball hit our tent

190

which got us both howling at the boy retriever. Still no change, especially when Mom gave them cookies and milk at 10:45! Dust finally settled sometime after 11:00. It was tempting early this morning to have Cathy play some scratchy violin while I packed up. Alas, we quietly rolled away, thankful to be away from those travelers.

The morning sky is hazy, the sunrise a deep red orange. We are in more humid climes, perhaps because we're nearing the confluence of the Elkhorn with the Platte and the Platte with the Missouri. There are many wetlands along the road, flatland. Today will be interesting as we go through dissected plains back to plains.

As we gulp last hits of coffee, the radio at Daddy's Cafe broadcasts a church service with full organ and piano choir. We can't hear what's being said. It sounds a little like Rush Limbaugh's delivery, but the organ music gives it away. It's Sunday.

4:15, Riverside Park, Wisner (pop. 1,535). We just rode into Wisner, the "Table Tennis Capital" of Nebraska. Corn, hay, and cattle are what is going on around Wisner. Being Sunday, the little town was vacant, except for the Dairy Keen and some traffic around the gas station. Today's winds were a sustained 15-20 mph and were either on our nose or our starboard quarter—hard riding.

We pulled into Norfolk around noon, just beating the church traffic. We took Rt. 275 Business into the city (pop. 12,000). Downtown was empty and rundown, its economic heart being drained by new malls out on the bypass. Instead, a different economy is seen—the Salvation Army thrift store, Scotty's guitar works, and many secondhand shops. When we stopped in the street to look at Marisela's Mexican Restaurant, Marisela came out on the sidewalk and beckoned us in. As she came out, a young white wino was asking us where we were going. We told him Virginia and then turned our attention toward Marisela and our stomachs. As we leaned our bikes against the restaurant, he yelled from the middle of the street, "Is that West Virginia or Virginia?" "Virginia," I yelled back. Befuddled by it all, he swore as he turned to walk on, responding with "West, by God, Virginia!"

There appeared to be a large Mexican population in Norfolk judging by the posters advertising the Gran Baile tomorrow with three Mexican Bands. Several Mexican folks came into the restaurant while we ate the Special of the Day, Chicken Mole, to the sounds of Mexican pop music.

We left Norfolk at 1:00 p.m. into heavy headwinds—slow. Norfolk is at the western edge of the Rolling Hills topographic region, and this is an apt description. It's like riding a very, very slow roller coaster. Fortunately, this continued for only about ten miles then leveled out somewhat, and we could make a little better time.

We just got through bathing—one of our more creative bathing productions. We are near the rodeo arena. There are two white 80-foot-long barns filled with stalls. On the outside wall of one of them is a series of spigots and a concrete pad where horses and livestock get bathed. We used our space blanket and rigged a small circular shower stall with one person holding the blanket out and the corners tied to the barn. It worked perfectly and felt wonderful.

There is very little activity in the park tonight. There are nice restrooms, many shade trees, and a ballfield with lights. The Elkhorn River passes to the south and one family is fishing along the bank by their pickup truck. Cathy is practicing the "Swallowtail Jig". I'm going to get dinner together.

Monday, September 2, 1996

We woke this morning to the din of the grain elevator in Wisner, a mile away. On the banks of the Elkhorn, where we pitched our tent under oaks and silver maples, the mosquitoes were horrendous. Last evening when they started feeding, we quickly pitched the tent and retreated to its sanctuary. We played some guitar and sang songs for a while, then drifted to sleep to the raucous sound of peepers and crickets. This morning knowing the mosquitoes were bad, we did as much packing in the tent as we could. I had to pee bad. I finally got out in a cloud of mosquitoes and stepped behind a tree away from the one RV camper that was a hundred yards away. Feeling discreet, I commenced peeing while swatting with one hand. Suddenly, I realized I was right in front of two women who were powerwalking with their miniature poodles about 20 yards away. Nothing to do to change that!

In the mosquito haze, we had the fastest takedown, load-up, and ride-away yet. We followed the grain elevator's rumble into town and stopped at the convenience store for coffee and the bathroom.

We got to talking with the clerk and a customer named Matt. Matt drives a cattle truck for one of the local feed yards. The feed yards buy cattle in Canada (now because the US dollar is strong) bringing them down to Wisner. There they feed them corn and hay, bulking them up 900 pounds. This takes about four months in the feedlot. Then they are sold to the slaughterhouses.

Matt drives for an outfit which runs seven lots. Six of them are full now with about 18,000 head of cattle. He said prices are better for beef than they were a couple of months ago and added, with a confidential, understated air, that "they are making some money now."

Matt explained that the whole town of Wisner is employed in the stocking and feeding of cattle. He started talking about the grain elevator and the corn-flaker. I remarked that I'd like to see what was making all this racket. They laughed, and Matt said he'd go down with us and that Jeff, the manager there, would love to give us a tour.

Done deal! We rode the two blocks back to the roaring elevator. Matt introduced us to Jeff, a big, gentle, smiling Nebraskan who gathered some earplugs for us and enthusiastically took us into the boiler room. Basically, they clean the corn of old cobs and stuff, steam the corn kernels to 190 degrees in four big cookers, then smash these hot kernels with big rollers, producing a flaked corn. This is then sucked up to the top of the elevator where proteins, vitamins, and minerals are added. The flaked corn feed is augured to bins that the feed trucks drive underneath, onto scales. They get a load of corn feed and out to the feedlots it goes. It is fed to the cattle that day, because after a few days it would get moldy. The elevator cooks up feed for four feedlots that inform them each morning how much corn to process. They want the corn early because they feed in the mornings.

Jeff showed us all around. I recorded him, but I doubt it will come out over the noise. We climbed to the top of the elevator to a small room where they control the mixture being added to the flaked corn. Another man was in the room, wearing safety goggles and earplugs, turning knobs. The roar was deafening. The control panel was straight out of a B-grade science fiction scene with old glowing lights on a huge steel-grey control panel. I expected to see a sliding gurney that delivers the next victim (probably a vegetarian) into the transmogrifying chamber to produce another John Madden look-a-like carnivore.

We go outside, and he weighs us and our bikes on the road scales—500 pounds. Jeff commented on how they just have a "quiet, simple life. Cattle, corn, and football," he said grinning. He asks where we're from. We might as well say "the far side of the moon," as far as feeling he has any mental image of Virginia.

Nobody out here has been to Virginia. West Virginia has some recognition, probably from John Denver's "Country Roads."

We left the elevator rumbling. I am flabbergasted by the picture I'm getting of Nebraska—cattle and corn. Corn in Nebraska is grown to feed cattle that are trucked in from Canada to be fattened for the American market. The extent of the natural resources, the number of lives and livelihoods interwoven with the cut of beef on the grill in Everywhere, USA is staggering. I think back to the sign in the restaurant in central Nebraska, EAT BEEF. THE ONLY MAD COW WE KNOW IS OPRAH. "Eat beef," what a political, cultural, and economic statement.

Riding along, we soon passed two feedlots—smelly, unwholesome, scabs on the earth. Thousands of cows were lined up, their heads stuck through fences into vast concrete troughs. The troughs extended a quarter mile into the distance and recently had been stocked with feed by a freaky looking mechanical conveyor designed for that purpose only. I took a couple pictures. We imagined we were spies from the Vegetarian Revolution Command (back East). If apprehended, we would have had to eat my journals (with A-1 Sauce, of course).

Traffic began to increase as we approached Omaha. We rode sixteen miles down the road to West Point and had brunch in a cafe. Eating with us, were six Black people, the first I'd seen since Great Falls, Montana, and I thought about how white this part of the West is until we near a city or an army base.

About forty miles out of Omaha, we turned due east on Highway 31, a two-lane country road with no shoulders but less traffic. This is the way I want to leave Nebraska, on slow roads through rural countryside of endless cornfields and cattle.

We passed a girl mowing the yard as if keeping the adjacent cornfields away. She saw us bicycling by, our panniers, the trailer, the flag—travelers passing a Nebraska family home. Holding her gaze on us, a little smile curled her lips, and I wondered what she was thinking. And then we were gone. It is amazing how fast, how instantly, our bikes can transport us. We have entered and left thousands of worlds thus far, and the leaving is so instantly permanent. There is no reverse on our bicycles.

Today, in the countryside about three miles west of here, the road was closed. The detour sign pointed to the right up a dirt and gravel road. As we contemplated our options, a truck approached up the gravel road. The man and wife talked with us a little and told us our best way to go was to the left, the way they were coming from. The road wasn't too bad, some wash boarding, some deeper gravel, but that made even the slowest riding feel good, because that was the easiest way to move ourselves and belongings along through the countryside. We rode, chattering by farmhouses with barking dogs, pig barns, cattle sheds, and flower beds. I wondered, when does a detour become not a detour. This made me smile and the friendly corn waved, so did the occasional wild hemp plant in full bud waving beside the cornfields in Nebraska.

5 p.m., Tower of the Four Winds, Blair, Nebraska. We're 68 miles down the road at the Tower of the Four Winds, a tribute to Oglala Sioux holy man Black Elk (1863-1950), and to Nebraska poet laureate John G. Neihardt (1881-1973) who in his book *Black Elk Speaks* captured Black Elk's visions. These visions inspired Rev. F. W. Thomsen, professor emeritus at Dana College, to design the mosaic here.

"The universal Messiah with outstretched arms blessing all people stands within the tree of life. Around them is an ever-widening circle of light forming the hoop of the world, which holds all living things. Singing birds fly between the cottonwood leaves radiating from this sacred tree."

"Two roads cross this hoop of the world," Black Elk said. "The good road and the road of difficulties you have made to cross, and where they cross, that place is holy." Dedicated 27 June 1987.

We climbed up a very steep hill for half a mile to the top of a bluff where this Tower of the Four Winds stands. The bluff overlooks the rolling farmland of northeastern Nebraska and the town of Blair. The sun is setting behind the tower, its shadow providing cool shade. Behind the tower, as if part of it, in the same motif, stands a huge cast-concrete round edifice with a short-domed roof. At first, we thought it was some type of sanctuary, but no; it is the water tank for the town. The fence has been breached, and one side of the tank is sprayed with graffiti and swastikas. Indeed, this is a crossing of the two roads, right here, making this a holy place.

7 p.m., Bob Hardy RV Park, Blair. We are camping about a mile and a half from the Tower of the Four Winds. This RV Park is a grassy patch of land bordered by a residential community, a highway, and railroad tracks. I can see old buildings of downtown peeking above the raised tracks. We are about three miles from the Missouri River at this point, just at the edge of the Rolling Hills and Valleys terrain. We fixed tuna, tomato, and bagel sandwiches, grape Kool Aid, and mandarin oranges.

What a day! We are nearing a city, much more traffic, more roads, and faster driving.

Tuesday, September 3, 1996

Blair, Nebraska. We've stopped at the Maple Leaf Restaurant on Main Street. Locals use it as the morning watering hole, men at one table, women at another. I overheard a comment, "Grandpa always said, 'Make a plan and then work your plan.'" The walls here are hung with black and white photos of Blair in the 1880s-90s.

After breakfast, we stood out under the awning and watched the pouring rain and tremendous lightning. People stopped and talked, then ran to their cars. The morning light reflected a steely gray from the wet street. Shortly, it lifted enough for us to ride two blocks to a laundromat. No one else was there. We had it to ourselves, which was perfect. The rain returned, even darker. We watched through the big plate glass window as sheets of water pushed down Main Street. Inside the laundromat, we were wearing very little, washing everything we could. The machines purred quietly. I played my guitar and sang. Cathy read. The rain cascaded.

Retrace 2022

From O'Neill, we drove on without stopping for the next 100 miles or so, passing through Neligh and the Riverside Park, and on through Norfolk. At Wisner, we drove into the camping area of the fairgrounds for a picnic lunch. The fairgrounds are near the grain elevator where we met Jeff twenty-six years ago. After lunch, we stopped there, and I found Jeff inside. He had a hard time remembering us, but when I told him we had stopped by the grain elevators with our bicycles twenty-six years ago and he weighed us, this clicked in his memory. He explained they were processing the corn differently now, no longer flaking or using additives. I read him my entries from our visit so long ago, and we laughed. I think he really enjoyed being remembered by us. I took a picture of Jeff smiling, and we left smiling too.

We camped one night at Bob Hardy Park in Blair with several RVs. We visited the Tower of the Four Winds. It had really been developed into a nice park, Black Elk-Neihardt Park, with paved walking trails. We walked the extensive grounds with Jetta enjoying the autumn wildflowers. Downtown, we had breakfast at the Maple Leaf which is now called Billy's. The old laundromat was gone, but we found The Wash Tub laundromat nearby and washed our clothes.

Wednesday, September 4, 1996

We stayed at a Ramada Inn in Council Bluffs, IA last night. What a day yesterday was! After washing our clothes in Blair, we waterproofed our bags and instruments even though it had stopped raining, then rolled cleanly out of town. We crossed the Missouri River at 11:30, took a photo from the bridge, and rode into Iowa.

We rode about six miles out to the DeSoto Wildlife Refuge and the wreck of the steam paddle wheeler, the *Bertrand* . The 178-foot, 251-ton mountain steamboat was on its way to Fort Benton, Montana in 1865 when it hit a snag in DeSoto Bend and sank. The *Bertrand* was quickly buried in silt, which didn't allow oxygen to rot the goods. It stayed buried until the late 1960s when it was found and excavated.

The visitor center was excellent in design and function. We looked through the salvaged stores of the *Bertrand,* kept in the controlled environment of a glassed-in display area. Out of its 10,000 cubic foot hold was salvaged, among other items, hundreds of planes, wrenches, shovels, plows, picks, saws, carpenter's tools, blacksmith tools, china, glasses, lamps, irons, shoes, hats, mirrors, clocks, frying pans, pitch forks, door knobs, pad locks, keys, leather-working tools, scales, pocket knives, harnesses, Schrodder's spice bitters, brandy from F&G Hibbert in London England, champagne, ale, wine, demijohns, canned tomatoes, peanuts, peaches, sardines, strawberries, oysters, lemonade mix, gooseberries, clay and wooden smoking pipes, rubber combs, green ink, pencils, honey, jellies, mustard, pepper sauce, cases of children's shoes, men's and women's hats, pants, shawls, buttons, and sewing supplies.

The *Bertrand* was built in 1864 in Wheeling, West Virginia. Like hundreds of paddle wheelers plowing the waters of America's great rivers during this era of westward expansion, the

Bertrand carried the seeds of change into the wild west, feeding the gold rush frenzy, pushing civilization further, with ax, pick, and plow for turning the prairie soil, draining wetlands, silting streams in the search for gold, changing the ecosystem for all time. It is apt that the *Bertrand* and the DeSoto Wildlife Refuge are joined here in a prophetic union. The *Bertrand* sank into the sand with the implements of environmental change that now requires the creation of wildlife refuges like this one to preserve vital ecosystems, wildlife, and diversity.

It was 1 or 2 p.m. when we left the refuge after lunching under a tree. We connected with Highway 183 in the town of Missouri Valley, a farming town newly attached economically to Interstate 29 via convenience stores, antique malls, and car dealerships. Route 183 is a two-lane country road with no shoulder, running down the eastern edge of the Missouri River Valley, through cornfields and more cornfields and some soybean fields thrown in for good measure.

This is the day after Labor Day, and people seem to be driving with an edge, a holiday hangover, or maybe we're just nearing more people.

In Crescent, we stopped for iced tea at a convenience store where we saw news of Iraqi/US confrontations controlled by computer-guided console monitors. Life goes on. People streamed in getting Lotto tickets. Out back, in the shade of cherry trees at the crusty edge of the parking lot, Cathy noticed small purplish leafhoppers sucking juice from the branches of a tree. They were lined up along the branch like a miniature rosary, and I wondered if anyone knew they were alive in their world, just thirty yards from the Lotto machines.

The clerk told us of camping at Big Lake, not more than 10 miles away. We started to leave—flat tire. Fixed it, then rolled on.

We had to cross two hills on gravel roads, tough climbs. Finally, we got to the lake. The clerk's information was bad because there was no camping and no water. We decided to ride into Council Bluffs and get a motel room since it was getting late.

We checked into the Ramada Inn, showered, lay on the bed, checked out the tube, then decided to get something to eat. The Ramada Inn's restaurant and lounge were deathly tired and sallow looking. The clerks offered to shuttle us across town, for free, to Harvey's *Kanesville Queen* riverboat gambling casino to eat at their famous buffet. We gorged ourselves on juicy cuts of prime rib, Mahi Mahi, chicken Cordon Bleu, and all the fixings.

Then we waddled out the gigantic gangway to the gambling boat. The walkway was trimmed along both sides with twelve hanging TV monitors, all playing the same images of gambling people, the fun, the sex, the excitement. The walkway, with mahogany base trim, carpet, mirrors, and enticing video images beckoned satiated bodies up to the "riverboat."

We wandered to each floor, and stood, mouths agape at the scene of all the gaming tables, the slot machines, lights flashing, and the sound, the primitive, blood-curdling screams of hundreds of machines, pumping out climactic sirens, warbles, and screeches in such a cacophony I have never experienced, working the now highly sexed, daring, strong, unencumbered Iowa tourist to the edge of ecstasy. Play more, play more! Drink from the offerings of the strolling barmaids, their short crepe skirts lifted on one side, exposing sheer nylon thighs and haunches up to their little waists, buttocks pouting with each step, the trilling, pulsing, throbbing music, the splashing allure of the exotic felted tables. Distance fades in this swirl. If you take the first step, you're in over your head, swimming giddily. We leave. The driver that returned us said the first two weeks Harvey's was open, they made 14 million dollars.

In one day, we rode from the ruins of the riverboat *Bertrand* to this modern riverboat, the *Kanesville Queen*. I wonder, what will the resulting refuges be like, spawned from the cargo hold of this riverboat?

Back in the room, we lay in the bed, full and exhausted, holding each other, then slept the sleep of travelers.

This morning we showered and packed out of the air-conditioned room and biked downtown to the Endless Trails Bike Shop where I got my crankcase lubed and tightened. I also got three new tubes and a rear tire. We ate across the street at a nice café and spent a good while talking to the owner and his helper. I called Adventure Cycling and ordered the three maps for the St. Louis to Yorktown, Virginia portion of their TransAmerica route. They are mailing them to the Post Office in Ottumwa, Iowa. We should get there this coming Sunday and pick them up on Monday.

After leaving the bike shop, we went to the Chamber of Commerce for Iowa camping information and maps. It is hot and we decided not to go far today, only about 10 miles to Lake Manawa State Park. The next closest camping after leaving Council Bluffs is forty-five miles away.

There does seem to be a change underway. The landscape has changed. We are out of the Great Plains and its solitude and into the Midwest and its farming, people, traffic, and a little bit of a new unknown. Also, the season is changing. We are seeing evidence of fall in the colors of the leaves, the shorter days, in the passing of Labor Day, in the school buses dropping off school kids, in the football practices after school. We are less than two thousand miles from home, and the intervening land is steeped in mystery and promise for us.

We pulled into the campground at Manawa Lake around 5:30. We set up beside Kay and Neil, a couple who are out for a week of camping in their van and riding Iowa's bike trails. They celebrated their twenty-fifth wedding anniversary on a supported trip riding from B&B to B&B in Wisconsin. They came over with some maps, and we swapped stories. Their advice about Iowa biking was to expect a lot of hills and few paved shoulders and watch out for farm equipment on the road—we are a little early; harvest is still two weeks or so away.

This campground overlooks Council Bluffs to the northwest. Council Bluffs is the snotty-nosed kid brother to the suave Omaha. Council Bluffs has a population of 63,000, yet the tallest structure in town is a grain elevator. A year ago, they began allowing riverboat gambling. Now there are three gambling outfits, each with its own schtick.

Council Bluffs used to be named Kanesville and was a hub of Mormon activity. Here Brigham Young was voted into leadership of the Church of the Latter-day Saints. The town had a population of around 12,000 in the 1890s. When the railroad came to town, Brigham Young decided to take the Mormons to Utah. Overnight, the city went from 12,000 to 3,000 people. Soon after, it was renamed Council Bluffs.

The city is sucked into riverboat promotion. Some development continues, but there is an air of stagnation about the city. The Chamber of Commerce was not a beehive of activity but another dead-end job receptacle. When we stopped by the Chamber, I asked if there was a good coffee shop in the city and was directed to one that just opened.

The coffee shop was in an old building. It was very warm inside and didn't seem to have air-conditioning. We asked the waitress, one of two partners, for what we considered to be a simple order for a coffee shop. She looked puzzled, turned, and asked the woman visible in the kitchen pass-through behind the bar, "Ilene, do we have iced mocha?" A long pause ensued. Finally, Ilene said she could *try* to make it (the emphasis on *try* was her own). I asked what they did have. Lattes were among the limited items. These we ordered, and we were served some hot milk drinks, the weirdest lattes we've ever tasted. Cathy deduced they didn't have any coffee in them, and I tend to agree. Still, we stayed in the stuffy little place, fanning ourselves, long enough to read the paper and study our maps.

Retrace 2022

September 23, 2022
DeSoto Wildlife Refuge to Council Bluffs, IA

We were drawn back to the DeSoto Wildlife Refuge, mainly to see the Bertrand *Exhibit. It was still astounding with the abundance and diversity of its preserved cargo. But we were just as delighted with Visitor Center's astonishing collection of flora and fauna preserved by expert taxidermists in an expansive educational display of ecology and wildlife.*

In the parking lot, dozens of migrating monarch butterflies rested in the pines. We drove out the gravel road to where the Bertrand *had been excavated, enjoying the tranquil scenery of this refuge graced with huge flocks of pelicans above tawny fall fields of wildflowers, berries, and fruits.*

We stayed at Microtel Inn and Suites in Council Bluffs. The Kanesville Queen *was gone, but we were a short drive to the huge* Ameristar Casino Hotel. *We walked in to see about finding a cheap meal. The casino was crowded and smoky. The slot machines required credit cards or some type of preliminary registration, so there was no casual dropping of a quarter or two. The past couple of years of Covid precautions left us feeling uncomfortable in the crowd, so we quickly left. The restaurants were upscale and expensive.*

The clerk at our motel suggested a takeout Chinese restaurant, so we called in an order before driving out to get it. It felt good to be in a motel, so we stayed in the room lounging around the rest of the evening.

Thursday, September 5, 1996

Got up and out on the road by 8:00 a.m. We rode six miles to the trailhead for the Wabash Trace Nature Trail. The trace was a packed cinder trail, once the Wabash Railroad Line. Norfolk and Western Railroad had owned it at one time. Much of the trail passed through a tunnel of trees. The smells, the light, the fallen leaves on the path, the drying feed corn, all felt autumnal, like a passing.

We rode the 22 miles down the Trace to Malvern then started heading due east on Highway 34. We had a milkshake at Pat's Place, sitting in the shade of a huge old silver maple. Malvern is a one street town. Main St. stretches three blocks, many of its buildings empty, many needing work. We're seeing a lot disabled folks, war veterans, people tucked away under this fold of society.

We're 50 miles down the road in Red Oak, "A Shade Better." The Subway "sandwich artist" says people here like to fish, hang out at bars, bowl, and go to Omaha (one hour away by car). Farming is the main occupation, feed corn and beans.

Friday, September 6, 1996

8 a.m., Viking Lake State Park. We're having peaches, granola, and coffee for breakfast. It's nice here, but there are no other tent campers. It's a cool evening amongst Osage Orange trees, Burr oaks, blue herons, downy woodpeckers, and dogwoods with white berries. Corn plants are brown and tufted on the stalks, fields and fields of these.

We stopped in Stanton yesterday to see the "World's Largest Swedish Coffee Pot," which turned out to be a dolled-up water tank done in honor of the town's most famous Swedish

Princess Virginia Christine—Mrs. Olson, the Folger's Coffee lady. The coffeepot is nearly 125 feet tall and is lighted at night.

We visited the Swedish Heritage Cultural Center housed in an old school building on a hill. We got there at 3:55 and the place closed at 4:00, but we were welcomed in and given a grand tour which included a locally produced video of the history of this Swedish colony.

Stanton was started by Rev. Brendt Halland. His original surname was Johansen, but he changed it when he emigrated from Sweden because there were already too many Johnsons here. He started an orphanage in what was then known as the Halland Settlement. He wanted to name the town for the capital of Halland County in Sweden, but the railroad insisted it be called Stanton, for Lincoln's War Secretary. In the video, at the point of this explanation, the fake-bearded portrayer of Rev. Halland, really shone forth with a very dry and cynical sneer, as he spit out, "Stanton!" This actor came into the room as the video wound down.

Iowa is a state of early (1860s-1910) immigrant colonies. In southern Iowa there are Swedish, Irish, French, German, and Danish Colonies. Don, our host at the Cultural Center, kindly served us fresh coffee (Folger's) as we watched the video, and he showed us around the museum.

Don says about 30% of Stanton is Swedish. The Swedes that visit, and quite a few do, always want to know, "Where are the cowboys and Indians?" He doesn't read the Swedish newspaper, but they sent a reporter to Nebraska to meet a "real Indian Chief face to face." The article had a pen and ink caricature of an "Indian Brave" with a tomahawk in hand. "They wouldn't like that," he says, referring to the real Native Americans.

Don listed the recent movies filmed in Iowa: *Field of Dreams, Twister,* and *Bridges of Madison County.* He chuckled at the illusions of movies and how different they are from reality.

He admitted, "Most people don't know the difference."

He told us of the town's bike shop, so we rode up to Wayne's. His shop is in his garage. He had a nice selection of mountain and road bikes, all displayed on his asphalt driveway. Wayne ran in and got his wife Mary, and we sat in his shop and told stories of the road. Wayne is quite the biker. He is 65 and looks very healthy and alive. He has well-coifed white hair, and his tanned skin and love of activity are a testament to exercise. A few weeks ago, he entered a nationally sanctioned 24-hour bike race. The course was a 15-mile loop. Wayne won his age bracket handily, riding 307 miles in 24 hours. We congratulated him on his fine accomplishment. He seemed to relish our trip and took pictures of us on our bikes making sure to get all our gear into the frame.

Wayne's shop is located a block north of the coffee pot in a quaint little neighborhood of houses. We walked down the street to photograph the coffee pot and met Myrna and Iva. ("Myrna's got several master's degrees, and she loves to talk," Mary told me.) I photographed them in Myrna's front yard with the coffee pot in the background. They loved it.

As I am writing this, I'm on my second good cup of coffee this morning. The sun is out, things are drying, and we're going to have another fine day of biking. We both are feeling great. We took a little walk this morning, looking at this new ecosystem. We're flooded with new and yet more familiar plants and animals. The undulating prairie that we are riding across, a riverine terrain, has been totally altered by the mechanized plow. We are seeing more gravel county roads and more state roads, indicating more people, more towns, more cars.

We're about 25 miles down the road. Just outside of Corning, we passed a building that housed Manifest Destiny, Inc. We pondered, for miles, what its purpose was. I asked a woman later in town about it. She explained that it is a business that boards, houses, and cares for disabled people. We have been seeing an unusual number of these folks since entering this state. I asked her if Iowa had a lot of businesses that take care of people who in the past had been institutionalized. She confirmed yes.

Nearby, we passed a historical marker describing the Icarian Colony. It was formed in France by Etienne Cabet. They surrendered all possessions to a common fund. They moved to New Orleans in 1848, then Dallas and Illinois. Finally, 235 members bought nine sections of land north of Corning in Adams County, Iowa. The Colony dissolved in 1895. The Icarians were noted for being well-educated. Today, much of their 2,000-volume library is retained at the University of Omaha.

We reached the town of Creston today at about 4:30 and went in a WalMart and bought fuel and film. We were thinking of cooking spaghetti tonight, so we found the HyVee grocery store, a large supermarket. We went in and were grabbed by the all-you-can-eat salad and soup bar. It looked delicious, lots of fruit, salad, pasta, and broiled chicken. We had a nice dinner in the cafe portion of the store, lots of other people eating, 90% of them appeared to be over 65.

9:30 p.m. Creston Cozy Campers Campground. We pulled in here around 6 p.m. It's a funky little privately run campground near town. The Cozy Campers are sort of a club of RVers that manage the campground and hangout here in the summer. One guy came walking down to our tent with a roll of toilet paper under his polo shirt explaining "We can't keep any in the johns," as he motions to the little red building at the bottom of the hill. He gave us the toilet paper to take along. He checked out our rigs and was impressed to the point of leaving. He was "forced" by the doctor to retire at 62. "Nervous breakdown," he said matter-of-factly. Now he winters in Texas and summers in Iowa.

We pulled off showers at the water pipe, using the space blanket as a curtain. After things were put away, it was dark, and we played some music together—"Old Joe Clark", "Off to California", and "Ashoken Farewell". The mosquitoes came out, so we retired to the tent.

Saturday, September 7, 1996

Noon. Last night, during the night, Cathy went out to pee. The wind had died to a whisper, but the wind direction had changed, and this whisper was coming from the nearby sewage treatment pond. As she got back into the tent, so did the stench. It was about as bad as the odor on the downwind side of a manure spreader we passed on the road. We almost fell over it was so bad. "Oh God, let's get out of here," Cathy said, thinking it was nearly dawn. But a hasty check of the clock revealed it was only 12:30 a.m., too early, by far, to pack out. We ducked our heads under the cover, moaning and yearning for morning when we could leave.

Now we are thirty-five miles down Highway 34 in Osceola at the Quilt Patch Restaurant looking at maps. The maps are becoming a mesh of highways—federal, state and county, four-lane, two-lane, asphalt or gravel. Many important factors are not readily available like terrain or traffic density. We try to overlay our needs (small routes, camping, water) in fifty- to eighty-mile dashes across the maps. The feeling of movement is ecstatic, dizzying, yet anything and everything can and will happen in between. Between is where the moment waits.

We struck up a conversation with an older couple in the next booth. They live in eastern Iowa, West Point, it's called. They were in town to watch their son compete in the Iowa

Championship Rodeo Roping that was taking place in Afton, 20-some miles west, but there's nowhere to eat there. "Don't get me wrong, it's a good rodeo arena," the father said. They have six kids—four boys, two girls. Two are away at Kansas State. One is on a full rodeo scholarship to a two-year community college in Kansas. The younger boy, who is competing this weekend, and the two girls all rope and barrel race and compete in other rodeo events. "It's not like football or baseball, which is just part of the year. Rodeo is year-round," they both said. "It helps keep them from getting in trouble. It keeps them occupied. There's so much drugs out there," the mom continued, but trailed off nodding her head.

After more talking, we discovered that they both had been to Roanoke three years ago for an auctioneering contest. They lit up when they heard this was our honeymoon. When they started to leave, the man grabbed our bill and paid it. I was humbled by this kind gesture.

On down the road, we stopped for a bathroom and quart of milk. The cashier observed our bikes and biking clothes and deduced we were touring. He asked where from. We told him. Where are you going? Likewise, we told him. He asked how long we had been on the road, we told him. We're on day 82. Then the inevitable comes. He tells us about a guy that came through, heading east. He'd left Washington thirty days earlier. This obviously impressed the cashier, yet I don't know what to say. "I'm sorry," might be appropriate.

This time/speed issue raises its wiry little head quite often, either from bikers that go tearing off down the road or from those that stand by and tell the stories of speed and endurance. This bores me and is completely irrelevant to what we are doing. I don't want to race through this country, and I don't want to hear how long it took somebody to bike from A to B. I want to know what they experienced, what they felt, what they saw, who they talked to, the human and the physical geography, any feelings of place, all this and more. I'm as interested in racing across this big diverse country as I would be in sprinting through a room full of scantily clad beauties. Or more to my liking, rushing through a room of people having coffee, talking about things that interest them, playing music, etc. You get the point. Cathy, my new wife, says I'd *better* run through that room of scantily clad beauties.

5:42 at Red Haw State Park. These trees we are in are Eastern Woodlands species. We are under oaks and eastern cottonwoods looking up through the canopy to the evening lighted sky. It seems the canopy is thinner, not as lush as the woods at home. We see more sky here than in Virginia woods. The cicadas are very loud. Their rasping pulsates and blankets the campground, a remnant of summer.

In the last ten miles of our ride today the landscape became more wooded with very little farmland visible from the road. We passed an Amish man with his two-horse wagon selling produce by the side of the road. The last two towns we rode through were laid out around a square with the courthouse, circa 1890s, in the middle and businesses lining the perimeter. In both cases, the scene was of struggling shops, second-hand stores with names like Kay's Korner. There were no obvious community meeting areas, such as cafes. These have moved to the supermarkets, the Casey Stores, and fast-food joints out on the highway.

Sunday, September 8, 1996

Noon. It rained hard during the night. We were expecting it and had our gear in the tent with us. When it stopped, we washed the mud off the tent, dried some things, and were on our way. We stopped at the Lucas County Welcome Center, talked with the proprietor, and got some brochures. One informed us that John Wayne, alias Marion Morrison, was born just southwest of here in Winterset, IA, May 26, 1907. The brochure had a picture of Ronald Reagan visiting the Duke's childhood home in 1984. Another brochure informed us that the city of Chariton hosted the World Unicycle Championships this year, July 26-28. The winner and holder of the World Unicycle speed-record lives in Chariton. She is 18-year-old Amy Edwards.

2:45 Albia, IA. We are in the Dairy Bar having a snack and resting a bit. The day is improving from rain early this morning to little patches of blue trying to seep through the grey clouds. We have a bit of a tailwind, and this helps a lot. We're averaging 14 mph. We have 21 more miles to Ottumwa where we'll camp at the City Park.

The owner of the Dairy Bar brought some brochures to the table. He sold his motorcycle, but not before he and his wife traveled on the Blue Ridge Parkway and through the South. He had a Kawasaki 1300; he liked twisting the handle but couldn't pedal like us.

About 17 miles back, west of Albia, the odometer turned, telling us we had ridden 3,000 miles since Seattle. To commemorate, we stopped by the road and took a picture looking back from where we'd come. It happened to be in front of an old farmhouse and barn. The man in the backyard working on his farm equipment waved and probably wondered what we were doing taking a picture there as we marked this milestone.

When we got to Chariton, we rode around the square then out through an old neighborhood. A couple, our age, was sitting out on the big front porch of their sweet old house. We waved to each other. He asked, "Where are you going?" "Virginia," I said. "Wow," the woman intoned, enthralled and appreciative of the journey. I felt like she knew enough of what we were doing, understood well enough to say, "Wow." That is enough.

Last evening at Red Haw, we walked down to where Glen and Rick and their families were camping. We had passed Glen in Chariton. He was tooling along in sandals and shorts on a bike with an empty baby seat on the back. He was on the sidewalk as we passed on the road. He said, "You guys must be trippin'." When we got to Red Haw State Park, we caught up with Glen. He invited us down to their campsite.

We were close to not going, after setting up camp, showering, cooking, eating, cleaning up, writing in the journal, and playing the guitar. We were about ready to hit the sack, Cathy more so than I. But I decided we would go be neighborly. I took the guitar along.

It was a typical car camping scene, folding chairs, an electric light washing across the campfire, a table piled high with baskets and bugs. We introduced ourselves and were greeted nicely by all—four kids, grandma, and two couples. Glen and Karen had been to Australia two years ago for a church conference on the Gold Coast. They liked the Australians they met, finding them friendly and that they said, "exactly what they mean." They said they thought Australia was, "just like America was in the 60s."

One of the couples had lived in Roanoke, in 1970-71. He worked at a supermarket on 9th St., and they lived around Highland Park (which is near our house), though they couldn't remember the street name. They spent a good while entertaining everyone with their stories of the country folk of Roanoke and their southern accents. The woman mimicked southern women saying "crowns" when referring to the "crayons" their kids were using. They did imitate southern slang pretty well. They told of meeting another Iowan upon first arriving at their apartment building and the other Iowan shouting, "Thank God, another person speaking the King's English!" I could tell things weren't going too far with this group.

Glen's gang turned off the radio and asked me to play, and Cathy said, "Go ahead, you should play them something." Well, that was all I needed. Cathy sang and I harmonized on the chorus of "The Night They Drove Old Dixie Down" by the Band. "Ginseng Sullivan" by Norman Blake (I think he and his wife are from Iowa) and "Sunny Side of the Street" were my other songs. They enjoyed the music, and I enjoyed giving it.

I learned that Chariton was named because it is near the headwaters of the Chariton River. I mentioned we had entered a different landscape about 10 miles back, more woodlands, less corn fields. Rick said that the soil conditions change in this area and are good for woodlands but not for farming. They said the Amish were starting to move into Southern Iowa from Pennsylvania because, "they didn't have enough folks in their family tree. They were having too many special children. I've seen them," he testified. "They came here in the last few years to increase their gene pool," Glen said matter-of-factly.

I thought about this, about southern Iowa already being a repository of the Midwest's "post-institutional era" residents. Several people had alluded to Iowa's brain drain and many times, "Nothing," is the reply to my question, "What goes on in this area?"

9:30 p.m. We're in our tent in Ottumwa City Park Campground. We've been snacking on grapes, apples, peanut butter, crackers, and water. We got here to Ottumwa around 5:30, found the campground, and stopped at the host's trailer to pay our fee ($7). The tent sites are in a grove of trees a couple hundred yards from the RV part of the campground. The host said, "There's one other tent over there. Just don't set up in a valley; it could rain." We rode over and discovered there were no picnic tables, just a grove of oak trees encircled by a dirt road. Water and bathrooms were a short bike ride away. Otherwise, the place was nice.

The guy from the other tent walked over to where we were setting up by a fire pit surrounded by three upended logs that we hoped to use as chairs and tables. He said the guy who was camping there previously had to leave in a rush to tend to his sick dad, and he'd asked him to not let anyone burn his logs. (Not a problem.) He and his girlfriend have been camping here for about a month. They have a car and he's got a job now. "I'm trying to get out of here and get a place; can't quite make it yet," he said. They pay $7/night to camp here. We asked wouldn't it be cheaper to rent a place. His answer was that places rent for $300 a month. I said the campground ought to at least provide them a table. "Yeah, I been thinking about trying to get one," he said, scratching his back.

We went to the closest laundromat and washed our clothes and sleeping bag. The area seems rough, depressed, blue collar, a different feel from what we have been riding through.

When we were stopped at the light on Highway 34 getting ready to turn into the campground, a truck honked as it pulled beside us. It was the couple who'd paid our tab yesterday in Osceola. Through the window I asked how their son did at the rodeo. He got a second place and a third place. They seemed pleased. He said, "That's not bad for a state championship rodeo." The light turned, we said bye, best wishes, and parted ways. I glanced back at their truck pulling a trailer, their horse's chestnut-colored rump showing out the back. The wife must be cold-natured; she had a quilt piled in her lap. She had a nice smile; even her eyes smiled. There they go, accelerating back home to West Point, Iowa.

Now Cathy is asleep. The Burlington Northern train is blowing at some crossing across the Des Moines River from here, and a nice breeze hums through the leaves above. Over this is the locust's call like the roar from an ocean shell, there but ephemeral. The front passed through last night, and today we've had clearer air. Cooler temperatures should be in store tomorrow.

Retrace 2022

We had driven most of this part of our route (in reverse, east to west) in 2018, on our way to see my nephew in Denver and to visit Colorado's National Parks. On that trip, we found very little that stood out as recognizable from our bike trip. We stopped in Stanton. The Swedish Coffee Pot was no longer a functioning water tower, and it had been moved next to the Historical Society building which was closed. We were unable to find Don, Wayne, and Mary, or any of the other folks we fondly remembered.

On this 2022 retrace trip, we didn't make an effort to stop anywhere along Highway 34 until we got to Red Haw State Park. The park had been devasted by a tornado in the spring of 2022. The clean-up had begun, and the park was partially reopened. Behind the closed gate to the campground, we could see the tall piles of felled trees and debris from the storm's massive damage.

After a picnic lunch, we veered off our bike route to stay a couple of nights with my old college friend Jack and his wife Lois at their amazing farmstead just outside Knoxville, Iowa. They have several gardens along with goats in the barn and hogs in their pens. They make the effort to help their neighbors and have nurtured a wonderful community of friends. We left their farm with big smiles.

Monday, September 9, 1996

Up at 6:45 a.m. We picked up the Adventure Cycling maps at the Post Office and sent a package of exposed film home. We rode downtown to the Plaza Hotel and Restaurant and ate a great breakfast for $7.50.

Ottumwa was first settled in 1844. It is an Indigenous term meaning "rippling waters." Native Americans camped by the river before whites came. The first steam train came to Ottumwa in 1859. By 1889 Ottumwa was one of the first US cities with electric street cars.

Looking at our new maps, the bike route through Kentucky is awesome. We have quite a bit of riding in front of us. One day at a time. This morning the Canadian Geese out by the campground were honking and circling the area. There are several small lakes they are congregating on, preparing for winter migration.

The sky is clear this morning. The front has cleared the air of its mugginess. It should be a good riding day as we start angling southeast toward Hannibal, Missouri.

2:30 p.m. Corner Cafe, Keosauqua. As we ride, Cathy wears a visor to shade the top of her glasses. She fashions this out of maps we no longer need, or AAA information of a state we just passed. She sticks the stiff paper in her bike helmet, then puts it on and adjusts the paper so that it just covers the top of her glasses. It is a cool, retro-utilitarian look, though she says, "Nerdy." Sitting in the Corner Cafe, she tells me that today, while riding, she needed to adjust her visor, but the phrase that went through her mind, then stuck for many pedal revolutions, was, "Devise, da visor, device." Over and over. Riding can do this to anyone.

We took Rt. 16 south, a less busy road off Rt. 34. After an hour or two of biking we came to Eldon, Iowa, home of Grant

Wood's *American Gothic* house. Wood was in Eldon in the late 1920s with a fellow artist and native of Eldon, John Sharp. Wood was inspired by the modest one-and-a-half story house and its Gothic style window. He sketched the house on the back of an envelope and used it as the backdrop to a painting he called *American Gothic*, which conveyed the irony of the stern no nonsense father and plain dour daughter set in front of the pretentious house. (People assume the couple in the painting are husband and wife.) The models Wood used were his sister Nan, and his dentist, Dr. B. H. McKeeby.

We rode up to the Gothic House on Finney Street. It's set across the street from a big field and two big metal farming equipment storage buildings. We could see the famous gothic window across this field, and we rode over to it. Beside the Gothic house, across a side street is a less pretentious asbestos-shingled house of the same vintage being disassembled by man and nature simultaneously. I talked to the guy building a small deck on a double-wide trailer beside this crumbling house. He waved, and I asked how it was living by the *American Gothic* house. He paused from his figuring, and looking over to the little white house said, "Busy, but it's all right." I said (tongue-in-cheek) I thought he had a good marketing angle as "the house beside the *American Gothic* house." He considered that and said that behind the old house he is tearing down is the barn that is also in the painting, "But it's too old to do much with."

He was in a wreck in Roanoke in the '50s. He was hospitalized, "but no one was killed." He was stationed at Fort Bragg, NC and was up "just driving around in Roanoke, on 220 I believe it was." He has two tattoos, which were in the wreck too, judging from the faded blue lines of the full-bodied blue blobs on his left arm. He's a nice guy. He goes to the races in Bristol, TN some years.

Before we left, we rode over to the gravel turnaround in

front of the *Gothic* house. From this vantage point, we posed our bikes for a picture, BOB's flag filling in for the pitchfork, grasshoppers in the foreground, and the famous background in the background.

Eldon's other claim to fame was that Tom Arnold and Rosanne Barr bought 2,000 acres and a restaurant in Eldon. Somehow it doesn't surprise me that they liked Iowa. As far as I can see, they must have fit right in, so to speak. We didn't go by their place on purpose, not after the way she sang the National Anthem!

What a fine ride we've had through the Des Moines River Valley farmland and up into a wooded hill terrain. We're in the Corner Cafe having the Special—beef and noodles, mashed potatoes and gravy, mixed vegetables (cooked to within a breath of existence, the southern way), and a roll. Carbo City!

A couple of men came into the restaurant and spoke to us, "These must be your bikes." One of the men, middle-aged and fit, loved hearing of our trip and destination. A big knowing smile came over his face and he said, "Ahh." Looking sideways and slightly down at us, his face lifted, and he gave a short click with his mouth and a thumbs-up. He didn't linger; he got a lemonade and left. When we tried to pay our bill, he had already paid for the beef and noodles specials for us. The lady said he was a nice guy and liked to bicycle himself.

A farmer came in, a big man in a feed cap and overalls. He had a coke and sat at the table beside us, and we talked about Keosauqua and the Des Moines River. Keosauqua is in Van Buren County, one of Iowa's first counties, and its courthouse is the oldest in the state. The town was formed in 1837. Many old brick and log homes are still in use. The Des Moines River passes through the county, and the Mississippi is to the east. Established before railroads, the rivers were the parents to the town, transporting and supplying all the things one needed.

During the Civil War period, the rivers transported escaped slaves on the Underground Railroad; Keosauqua was a stop. The farmer said, "You see, Missouri was a slave state, but Iowa was free. They brought a lot of Blacks up this river on the way to Canada."

He said his grandparents homesteaded up west of Fort Benton in Montana. "Why?" I asked, remembering the dry desolate land we passed on our canoe trip. "It was free land. They were poor. After the '30s, during the war, wheat went up, everybody was trying it," he said.

He left the restaurant when we did and stopped to look over our rigs. I think he figured we were crazy but having fun. He said my gloves were "awful fancy," but when he heard the distance we've ridden, it seemed to make the gloves all right. He told us of a scenic route to take out of town to go through two more old river towns. We took his advice and thanked him for it.

We rode up to the Pearson House, which was a safehouse where escaping slaves could stay, undoubtedly stealing up from the river under cover of darkness, to rest and eat, and await further transport further into Iowa and on to Canada.

10 p.m. in Farmington at the Indian River Park. Riding across southern Iowa, before coming into the Des Moines River valley, we've noticed the terrain was hilly, but each hill was level with all other hills, so that when we were on a hilltop the land appeared flat out to the horizon. When the railroad came into Iowa in the mid-1800s, they built the RR lines along the tops of the ridges, preferring this divide between two drainage systems. This means the railroad tracks were located up and away from the rivers and creeks. This is different from southwest Virginia's mountain valley terrain, where the railroad tracks were laid in the level bottomland along the rivers.

In Iowa, towns that sprung up around the railroad lines were not on the best or most easily watered land. These towns have a boom/bust look and feel, mostly after the boom.

Sunday, we dropped down into the Des Moines River valley, the landscape changed to a richer farming area and the city of Ottumwa started showing signs of life with its riverside parks, the old town still facing the river.

As we progressed southeast along the river, the feel of the land, the people, and the towns changed. In this bottomland there was more human history, lush fields, nice yards, people fixing up old homes. Cathy noticed that the nicest flower boxes we'd seen yet, across all America, were there in Keosauqua. In Bentonsport, riding across the bridge over the river into town, kids were playing on a small dock, swimming in the late summer day, home from school, playing by the river.

In Bonaparte, the old town stretched along the river like an old friend. I parked my bike and walked between two old buildings to look at the town from the riverbank, like a traveler of old would have seen it. There aren't as many paths to the riverbank and fewer landings on the river, and the road traffic has turned the old town's attention away from the muddy Des Moines River up toward the main street, but you could see the connection still. A sign at the bridge says Brigham Young and a band of Mormons crossed the river there on their way to Utah, March 5, 1846.

We rode to the Indian Lake Campground; no one was around to pay. We only had one quarter for the showers, so we showered together, soaping and rinsing quickly so as not to be left soapy when the water ran out. We both snacked. I ate a quarter of a watermelon we bought in Farmington. Cathy had chocolate milk and peanut butter crackers. Ah yes, it is a beautiful evening.

Tuesday, September 10, 1996

We crossed into Missouri after a fifteen-minute ride from Indian Lake Campground, and we are in Kahoka, in Clark County. This is the first county established in Missouri in 1836 and was named for William Clark. It's had its set of skirmishes. In 1839, Iowa Territory and the state of Missouri mobilized troops in a boundary dispute called the Honey War (named for the nearby bee trees) before boundaries were settled by the Supreme Court. Then, in 1861, during the Battle of Athens, five hundred Union troops under Col. David Moore routed eight hundred Confederate guards under Col. M. E. Green and saved Iowa from serious Civil War action.

1:15 p.m. We stopped by the Canton Historical Society office in a remodeled storefront. The nice folks there were happily keeping the past of Canton alive as best they could, and they shared brochures on the Battle of Athens and The Honey War.

The Parmalee Brothers Boatyard built three steam paddle wheelers in Canton. As that phased out, one of the descendants invented a pickle sorter, still manufactured today. They are made of wood, and the design has remained the same for three generations. They are painstakingly crated and shipped all over the world.

In 1993, for five weeks, the Mississippi River threatened to submerge the towns along its banks in its muddy water. Older citizens in Canton moved to a college on higher ground. Able citizens worked sandbagging the levee, raising it by four feet. Canton was one of only three communities north of St. Louis whose levees held. All others were breached, and the towns were flooded. As we rode through Canton today, the high levees hid the Mississippi from our view.

In LaGrange, we finally beheld the Mississippi River for the first time on this trip. We both whooped at the big river. We felt the river to be a milepost, a marker, as it has for countless travelers who have crossed this sprawling land. We could see Illinois lining the far bank.

Cathy just counted our traveler's checks. We have $820 left; we might have to use the credit card some. Like everything in our life now, one day at a time.

Wednesday, September 11, 1996

Mark Twain's Cave Campground, Hannibal Missouri, 9:30 a.m. The campground is a nice spot, not many campers here. There are two tent campers beside us and about 20 RVs. We've finished breakfast, and I am having a second cup of coffee. I'm strumming the guitar, relaxing. We are going to take the day off from riding.

We're sitting in the gift shop of the Mark Twain Cave waiting for the free tourist trolley into Hannibal. We're giving the cave a pass; admission is $9 each. In the 1800s, people came to these grounds for outings, picnicking, and exploring the cave for free—much more my style. An interesting collection of old photos is on exhibit here. There are photos of Indian Joe, who denied he was Injun Joe of Mark Twain's writings. Indian Joe died September 30, 1923. His old house still stands in the Douglasville area of Hannibal, known here as the area in which Negro people built houses. Becky Thatcher was modeled on Laura Hawkins, who also denied it, yet she admitted that the incidents associated with the fictional Tom and Becky had indeed been part of her relationship with young Sam Clemens. An autographed photograph of Jimmy Carter visiting the cave with Rosalynn and

226

Amy, when he was President, was added more recently.

Noon at the Bird Street Cafe, a small hole-in-the-wall restaurant filled with locals, mostly older folks. The men wear work clothes—overalls or jeans. The silver handles of a pair of pliers stick out of one man's back pocket. I overhear him tell another man that work is slow; he seems to be comfortable with the idea. The food is good, and servings are ample. The waitress comes around several times filling our coffee cups. It has the feel of a community meeting place. On the wall are several Twain-isms: "Make sure you get the facts straight and then you can distort them," and "Always tell the truth and then you don't have to remember anything."

Getting off the trolley earlier, we found that Hannibal is full of Mark Twain. We started to get confused as to what was fictional and what wasn't. A five foot, white-washed fence holds a historical marker that officially states, "Here stood the board fence that Tom Sawyer persuaded his gang to pay him for the privilege of whitewashing ..." This blending of fact and fiction would please the humor bone of Sam Clemens, were he alive today to see all the hubbub over Mark Twain, from the shops displaying first edition publications of his writings to the corny Tom Sawyer Creek minigolf course along the river, two miles south of town.

We sat for a while on the bank of the Mississippi watching the river flow, not saying much, just sitting. The *Mark Twain* riverboat docked near us after its hour-long cruise. It was a fake paddle wheeler, a gaudy tourist event, but if we squinted our eyes and imagined the river of the 1860s, it's good enough. Maybe.

Now, the river smells foul, and swimming is not advised. This is the grandest river in the Northern Hemisphere. Its basin covers one and a quarter million square miles, second only to the Amazon River in area drained. This jewel of our continent is a slow-moving cesspool as it passes the levees of Hannibal. Yet who is to blame?—There is no one single answer. This is the sad resolution of those who stand on her banks and are old enough to remember a time when the river was clean enough to swim in. This is a national—no, world-scale—disgrace. She still is mighty, still transports goods to and from America's heartland. Yet, from this same heartland, she is poisoned. The nation is hemorrhaging into the Gulf.

The ride back to the campground on the Hannibal trolley was guided by an impish seventeen-year-old who talked into the microphone with a high-pitched voice, each word ending with a rising tone. She rattled off story after story with practiced precision while studying her fingernails. The tidbits of information are interesting: Young Frank Sinatra sang at the dedication of the baseball park; Three boys lost in a cave were never found despite efforts of rescuers from around the world; Samuel Clemens was born when Haley's comet arrived and died when it returned seventy-five years later; Only five and a half ounces of fish per week are recommended eaten from the polluted Mississippi River.

Today, we stood on a bluff 800 feet over the river, looking south down the Mississippi. On the right, the west, the state of Missouri stretched down to St. Louis and beyond; Illinois lay on the left, the east side of the river. What immediately struck us was the Missouri side was edged with bluff after wooded bluff, overhanging the river, while on the Illinois side, the land was flat to the horizon. Until that moment our plans had been to follow Rt. 79 down the Missouri side, along the river, even though we had asked people about it, and the report was, "hilly." After seeing the terrain, we concurred and altered our plans.

Before going to dinner near the cave at Olivia's Restaurant (Samuel Clemens' real wife's name), we mapped out the next leg of our trip—crossing the Mississippi here at Hannibal to the flatter Illinois side, skirting East St. Louis, then biking down to Carbondale where we will pick up the TransAmerican Bike Trail. We transferred the bike trail route onto our Illinois, Kentucky and Virginia Highway maps using an orange highlighter. Then we lined them up on the picnic table and stood back so we could see the whole squiggly orange line from Hannibal to Roanoke. We laughed at the markings that seemed to be approaching randomness.

Still, it is beautiful, and we say the names of places along our projected path: Cave-In-Rock, IL; Berea, KE; Haysi, VA; Damascus, VA and on and on. How wonderful this journey is, each moment, each day, one instant after another, one breath at a time, one heartbeat after another, one dream evolving, growing, knowing.

Thursday, September 12, 1996

9 a.m., at Becky Thatcher's Restaurant. This morning we'll cross the Mississippi River on the Mark Twain Bridge, commemorated at its opening by President F. D. Roosevelt. It cost two million dollars at that time.

We will leave the West, the land of opportunity, in our wake. Our thin trace over the land is imprinted there forever. Ahead, in our uplifted faces, lies the land of promise, the rising sun, the new day dawning.

Riding out of the campground this morning, up over the bluff of Lover's Leap, coasting down in the fall chill into lazy Hannibal, I wore a mischievous grin as I felt a camaraderie with ole Huckleberry Finn—a love of moving on down the river, embracing whatever comes, and making it ours. There is no failure here. The curious open mind is the key, the strong heart.

Our river is this long black tide that stretches before us.

Ours is not the paddle wheel, but the pedaled wheel. But the call is the same, "Roll on, Big River, Roll on." It matters not the vehicle; the journey is the transporter through the mystic beyond.

11:22 a.m. Kinderhook, IL seems a nice old farming town, though empty amongst the cornfields at the edge of the Mississippi River's flood plain. The ride across the Mark Twain Bridge was scary; traffic was too fast and too close. Holes in the pavement gave us clear views to the river below. But we made it, white-knuckled, but safe.

Pleasant Hill, Pike County, in Pam's Cafe. We've ridden along some beautiful Illinois countryside, passing through the small old towns of Rockport, Atlas, and New Canton. We decided to have lunch. A nice man sat with us at our table. The place is warm and buzzing with locals having lunch. We all had the roast pork lunch special which was very tasty. He is retired from working with the county as a grader and equipment operator. "I'm physical," he said grinning, equating operating a bulldozer with biking across the country. He looks like many of the bulldozer men I've known. He's a big beefy guy, easy going—too easy, as if one screw is loose, the one that makes a saner person be timid or tentative lest they dig too deep and sever the power line to the whole east coast. Because of this loose screw, the bulldozer driver appears to have nerves of steel as he digs like there's no tomorrow.

This man's wife has Alzheimer's and is in a nursing home. "It's bad," he says into his roast pork, shaking his head. He's just returned from Colorado, visiting his son and only grandson. He tells us with pride how his grandson won second place in the State Pedal-Power Tractor Pull for 9-year-olds. He was there to see it and spoke with admiration about how "he just got on there, went where he wanted to, got off, and walked away like it

230

was nothing." Sounds like that screw might be coming loose on another one. We headed on south, the bulldozer man giving us a laughing wave.

We saw our first presidential election poster of the trip. It was along Rt. 96, tacked to an old corner fence post under a tree. DOLE DOLE was its message. We saw one more, a Dole/Kemp one, and that has been it. But there's a lot of local election yard signs—Knight STATE ATT, Simpson 4 Coroner, etc.

9 p.m. Pere Marquette State Park. We got in around 5:30. What a beautiful fall day, cool crisp sun, a breeze off the river pushing us southward. The breeze rattled the dry leaves of the thousands of cornstalks all along our way. A timeless feeling of fall permeated my being and I reveled in the day. We biked along the eastern edge of the Mississippi River flood plain which is about 8-12 miles wide on the Illinois side. Then we crossed the Illinois River at Hardin and continued in its flood plain. Both flood plains are planted mostly in feed corn, thousands of acres of river bottomland chattering in the fall breeze.

Retrace 2022

As we headed south from Jack and Lois's, we circled through the city campground in Ottumwa. We had stopped here in 2018, and then, like now, we found little had changed, except now there were picnic tables present in the tent camping area.

In Eldon, a visitor center now sits opposite the American Gothic house, although it was closed the day we passed through on our retrace.

The drive that day felt bland and wearisome. And we weren't encouraged when we couldn't find Indian Lake Park. Our sense of adventure was muted, and we realized that we longed to be home.

We drove through Hannibal and out to Mark Twain's Cave Campground. In the gift shop we looked for the photo of the Carters. It wasn't there, and the young employees didn't know anything about it or any of the other historic photos. After perusing the trinkets, we headed up to Lovers Leap for a windy lunch on top of the bluff overlooking the Mississippi. The old Mark Twain Bridge had been demolished, replaced by a new bridge carrying I-72. I don't think we could cross here on bicycles today.

Friday, September 13, 1996

We are in Pere Marquette State Park, having breakfast at the lodge. Last night, I played some evening guitar music in the tent, the acoustics great. Cathy hummed along. As we were readying for much needed sleep, suddenly outside near the tent a struggle for life commenced with the growling grunts of a fox and the whimpering sad calls of something already caught in death's jaws and knew it. There was not much to do or say, just quietly witness nature.

The Lodge's restaurant is a wonderful place to sit and write. In the spacious lodge common room, we admired the four beautiful hanging tapestries representing the flora and fauna of the area. They are shaped like the wings of the mythical Piasa beast.

Yesterday, we crossed the Mississippi River at Hannibal, Missouri into Illinois. About ten miles before Hull, we stopped to read a historical marker about Illinois and George Rogers Clark's bloodless taking of this territory into the State of Virginia in the 1780s. Just before getting to the marker, I noticed a car following us on the two-lane road for a couple miles, staying back 100 yards or more. I told Cathy, "There's a car back there, but it's not gaining on us. Maybe they're having car trouble."

Little did I know that we were being tailed by the remarkable Rienebach Brothers, Lewis and Lester, "The Admiral." (Lewis was quick to confide to us that, "Lester just gave himself that name, same as he put that feather in his cap.") When they eased into the pullout for the historical marker, both their heads poked out the windows. The Admiral, who was driving at the time, was saying, "We're so intrigued by what you're doing." They were out in a jiffy. The Admiral, proud of his cunning, crowed, "I was just following. I knew you'd have to stop for a rest sometime."

He grinned at himself.

The Admiral wore a ball cap with a long turkey feather stuck up in the back. They are both in their 80s and don't see or hear too well, which causes them to get right on you to see and hear. Lewis, wearing thick glasses tied around his head with a nylon cord, grayed with use, his beard stubbly with a half inch square spot of hair an inch long projecting under his chin, confided to Cathy, "I can't see so well, so when I drive, I turn the lights on so they can see me coming." Well, they swarmed all over us, touching and shaking our panniers, studying BOB the trailer. By their reactions they approved. They'd be bent down looking, then with their hands on their knees, lift their heads back and say, "Oh yes, wonderful, wonderful!"

I knew we were being visited by angels themselves. Their faded gray Nova had a two-foot-long air horn mounted on the front hood back toward the windshield. On the front grill, on each side, were tied horizontally two husked ears of field corn. The back windows on each side had newspaper clippings taped on the inside so you could read them from outside. There was a picture of their mom and dad on their wedding day, a beautiful handsome couple (though the Admiral just said, "This is my dad, in 1910, on his wedding.") Another clipping showed his dad in his two-horse buggy. "That's the way it was, there weren't no cars out here then," the Admiral happily said, gesturing with his hands, another masterpiece of an encounter.

He equated and liked to think of his car as some kind of carriage, though it frosted him to have to put gas in it. In fact, that's why the Rienebach Brothers were out on this beautiful morning. They'd driven down to get gas. "Ten dollars," the Admiral says with disgust. He got immense joy from the fact we didn't have to stop at a gas station. His hands went up in a hallelujah fashion when he realized this. Somehow, we were getting one over on the gas stations.

The Admiral had on timeless white pants and a white shirt with a button, "Old Thresher's Reunion, 1996 Mt. Pleasant, Iowa." I commented on the button. "Yes, yes, the Thresher's Reunion, fantastic," they exclaimed.

They are retired, farmed all their lives. They grew corn, beans, pigs, and cows in that order. They spoke in that wonderful way where each sentence would be a personal revelation to the joy of the world, their hands always moving in flowing gestures. These men are in touch, I thought. They made me grin.

I got their address. Lester, "the Admiral," wrote it into the back of my journal, leaving his brother Lewis out the same way he left out his mother earlier. I took a picture of the Admiral by his car, he in an exuberant pose. "Let's get your brother in," I said. "Naw, just me," he said, waving off his brother Lewis who was over leaning close to Cathy, talking in his red nylon windbreaker.

As we got ready to go, I said that this land used to be part of Virginia, where we are going. The Admiral said "Wonderful," and walked over to read the marker. He began reading aloud to himself, his hands tracing the embossed words. We stood into our first stroke of forward movement, always a delicate moment on loose gravel. The Admiral got to the part about Virginia, "The Great Commonwealth of Virginia!" he yelled out, praising the sign and life itself. We rode off saying good-byes sincerely.

About a mile down the road, here came the Reinebach Brothers, this time gaining on us, the air horn honking. They pulled alongside us, nearly running us off the road. Another car, impatient at this reverie, blew its horn and passed in angry acceleration. The Admiral, driving (fortunately, I think) was reaching over across Lewis' lap, trying to hand me something. I slowed to a stop with them. "Here Jim, this is for you," and I took the "Old Thresher's Reunion" button he offered. They drove on, the back window sporting a "Plant Trees" and an "Old Beekeepers Don't Die, They Just Buzz Off" sticker. We last saw them turning off to the left down a gravel road, disappearing into fields of feed corn hailing their passing with raspy fall waves.

Noon, at the Chantilly Cake Company, Alton, IL. We're at the confluence of the Missouri and Mississippi Rivers. Out the window spans the Clark Bridge, hanging like a trapeze act under strobe lights. Riding our bikes from Pere Marquette State Park to here, we were on wonderful bike paths along the Mississippi. I had a flat on BOB caused by glass from some jerk tossing bottles at the river from his car or pickup truck. I've seen this occur with my own eyes. It is unbelievable though.

We rode right by the site of the last Lincoln/Douglas debate on the riverside below the town. Now the site is commanded by a riverboat gambling operation, its electronic sign proclaiming " 5 years of success, 5 times the fun, 5 times the winnings, 5 times..." This modern-day predator of the wayward sojourner, its blazing sign enticing the traveler into its lair, is apparently in good company.

On the bluffs overlooking this legal chicanery used to rest the petroglyph of the legendary monster, the Piasa Bird. Reportedly, the petroglyph was seen by Father Marquette in the 1600s when he and Joliet and company passed through this area. Illini Indian legend claimed that many thousands of years ago, there was a bird creature with deer antlers, the face of a bearded man, and four clawed feet that craved human flesh. The petroglyph has since faded off the bluffs. A replica was painted, but modern paints didn't hold to the sandstone, and it sloughed off. Presently, the town is trying to install another Piasa replica. Maybe they should just redecorate the gambling boat and rename it the *SS Piasa*. The river has always been the transporter of people and ideas and those that prey on them.

Today it is pure joy to ride through this new territory draped in the mantel of human history and a living crossroads of four of America's great rivers—the Mississippi, Missouri, Illinois, and Ohio. Here the paths and journeys of human endeavor, explorations, and commerce have proceeded for 14 thousand years, just a wink in the ancient rivers' lives.

9 p.m. Eldon Hazlet State Park, Carlyle Lake. We are camping on the shores of Illinois' largest man-made lake. We rode 90 miles today. It is hard to believe that we were at Pere Marquette State Park just this morning. Alton was quite a historic area, yet the museum was in the process of moving to a building on the Dental School grounds. That building was the oldest building in Illinois continuously used for education, according to Paul, our guide through the museum.

Alton was the birthplace for two of America's giants; one literally, one figuratively. Robert Pershing Wadlow was born February 22, 1918, and died from a blood infection July 15, 1940. He is listed in the *Guinness Book of World Records* as being the tallest human in recorded history. He was just over eight feet, eleven inches tall. The people at the Alton Museum are quick to impress how kind and normal a person Robert was. He was seven feet tall in his fifth-grade class photo. Robert posed with classmates, friends, police officers, and dignitaries. Everyone seemed to want a picture taken with Robert, the gentle giant.

The other giant from Alton is the jazz great, Miles Davis, born May 26, 1926. Miles' trumpet ushered in the cool jazz era of the late 1950s. One of the all-time classic jazz albums, recorded in 1959, and my favorite, is Miles' *Kind of Blue*.

We rode due east out of Alton on Highway 140, trying to get away from the traffic of St. Louis. This was the most urban, congested riding we'd done since riding from the SeaTac airport to North Seattle. Most of the road away from Alton didn't have a paved shoulder. The road gradually became less trafficked and more rural.

Finally, we were back in cornfields and soybean fields. At Hamel (pop. 440), we turned onto old Route 66 for a half a block, stopping at an ice cream and video store. The woman owner was a sweet Illinois farm woman. When she heard how far we'd come, alone, she asked, "Youse guys don't have nobody tailing ya to help with emergencies?" We both answered, "No, we're on our honeymoon. You don't want to be tailed on your honeymoon." She agreed and gave us a little price break to celebrate. We paid for a small and a large shake, though we'd had two larges. We left her smiling as we climbed back in the saddle with 45 more miles to pedal.

We passed through Alhambra (pop. 550) where the Elementary School, the Alhambra Tigers were urged on the school sign to "Read a Comic." Lenny Bruce came to mind, but I kept pedaling.

Somewhere near Greenville, in a sea of corn and soybeans, a carload of college dudes passed us within inches—too close—even though there was plenty of room and nothing coming from the other direction. The pickup behind this car had politely pulled over into the other lane. I worked through my anger at such ignorance, but it took several miles and remembering the Admiral and his winsome curiosity. Then I was back.

Retrace 2022

September 26, 2022, (continued)
Kinderhook, IL to Pere Marquette State Park, IL

Sometime in the early 2000s, I put my journal entry of meeting the Rienebach Brothers on my webpage. I received this email March 7, 2008.

> *Hey Jim,*
>
> *Great story about my Uncles Lester and Lewis. I found that on your website. Very perceptive. They were great fun when I was a kid...I moved back to the area where you saw them in 1999. I helped them some, and my mom especially took care of Lewis later. I live on the farm now, where they grew up, helping my mom enjoy her remaining years despite Alzheimer's.*
>
> *My Uncle Lewis passed away in 2001, and I have his house rented by someone who enjoys the rustic nature of his house, which reflected his nature. Lester passed away in July 2006 and hardly slowed down the whole time. He ran all over the grounds of the Vets Home with his motorized scooter that he named and labeled "Prince" after one of the old farm horses. He died on his own terms, refusing medication and dialysis, saying, "I've lived long enough." He was 91. He did cause his share of trouble, but the side of him you saw was what was enjoyed by those that didn't invoke his wrath.*

His tombstone is high on a bluff in Kinderhook, with a picture of him juggling. The tombstone has etched in "Two balls out of frame", he wanted to be sure it would be forever known that he could juggle four balls. And I can attest that he did that at halftimes, weddings, and even in a courtroom, before being removed by the bailiff.

Hope your other ventures are going well. It is nice to read what you wrote. It is a fine tribute.

On our retrace, we stopped briefly at the historical marker where we met the Admiral and Lewis. Then we continued on our way.

Earlier, in 2018, on the way out to Colorado, we stopped by the Cemetery "high on a bluff in Kinderhook." We easily found Lester's tombstone with the enameled photograph of him juggling. We placed some wildflowers Cathy had picked on his gravesite. Our empathetic dog, Jetta, seemed to understand the nature of this side trip. She lay beside us as we toasted Lester with shots of Irish Whiskey and paused in silent remembrance of this remarkable man.

At Pere Marquette State Park, we reminisced in the expansive log lodge over dinner. The now faded tapestries hanging from the tall ceiling seemed to emphasize the elapsed time between our visits. We walked out to the Illinois River at twilight, the peaceful old river rolled smoothly on. We spent the night in the tent camping area. In the morning, surprisingly, there was no dew on our tent even though the river was only a hundred yards away.

Saturday, September 14, 1996

7:30 a.m., Eldon Hazlet State Park, IL. Breakfasting by the lake with the sun rising over it; a foggy mist dances above the surface. We're in the great eastern hardwood forest—hickory, walnut, white oak, red oak, dogwood. The campground stirs awake; souls wander up to the pit toilets.

Noon in Nashville, Illinois, 26 miles down the road. We've been riding straight south on Rt. 127 with a crosswind. As we've ridden along, I've been thinking about traveling. Cathy and I are travelers that choose to travel on bicycles, not bicyclists per se. I think bicyclists tend to focus on the mode of travel more than the why of travel. To me, this mode of travel is more on a human scale. It is faster than walking, and I can carry more gear to make the experience more varied and comfortable.

One drawback from biking is that we almost exclusively use paved surfaces as our path of possibilities. The why of our travel is curiosity, to experience new places, new people. It is not based on the physical, in fact physical holds only a minor part in this play. This travel is the geography of hearts, the vital center and source of our being, emotions, and sensibilities.

We got into Murphysboro around 4:30 and decided to go east into Carbondale and get a motel room. We have ridden 250 miles in 3 days, which is long riding. We've decided to treat ourselves.

In Pinckneyville, we stopped in the T-Bear Pizza and Ice Cream Parlor, on the square. It was a beautiful sunny fall Saturday. Football was in the air in southern Illinois, and their high school team, The Panthers, was ready to play. We walked in and the place was filled with excited, vibrating Jr. High kids, almost all girls. Glasses full of water were spilled, giggles bouncing off the walls, braces shining. We hadn't been around that much raw energy from so many congregated kids in many months. Cathy laughed at one point. "Look at the name on their shirts." There we were, eating with the Pinckneyville Marching Kittens!

Sunday, September 15, 1996

We're up early in the motel room, watching the Weather Channel forecasting rain, leftovers from Hurricane Fausto that hit Baja and Mexico. So, we're wrapping everything in plastic for rain.

We are a few miles down the road enjoying the Shoney's breakfast bar—good watermelon! There's not much else open on this grey Sunday morning. We've decided to stay on Rt. 13, a divided highway that runs due east. That way, we can be close to a motel when it starts raining. We will probably connect with the TransAmerica Bike Route Tuesday at Cave-In-Rock on the Ohio River.

We are at Giant City State Park in our little cabin by the edge of the woods. We hadn't planned to be here, but this morning as we sat in Shoney's, spread out in a corner booth studying maps, a nice couple across the aisle started talking to us. They said that Giant City State Park was nice, had a lodge, and was close. We really liked the lodge at Pere Marquette, so this idea hit home. As I have mentioned, flexibility is an important quality to the traveler. We changed plans and rode 15 miles south to Giant City.

A cabin was available, and with our bikes it was better than a lodge room. We unpacked, and since the rain held off, we took an unloaded ride to a trailhead and hiked an hour through

242

hardwood forest into the sandstone bluffs and narrow canyons that define this park. There were names carved in the rocks dating back to 1829. Others, more hastily scratched, dated back a few weeks. (This is called graffiti because it is very recent. If it lasts a hundred years, it too will be history.) The bluffs have caves and overhangs that were used by Native peoples back to 400 BC. Confederate and Union soldiers used the bluffs as a haven during the Civil War.

Monday, September 16, 1996

We're at breakfast in the lodge. It is a grey and foggy morning, the trees dripping. We're going to stay another day in our cabin. Last night we had a fine meal here, then retreated to our cabin and watched the Ken Burns' film, *The West*, which was excellent. Dayton Duncan, author of *Out West*, was interviewed in the film.

This area of Southern Illinois is a unique cultural-geographic region. The Ohio and Mississippi Rivers to the east, south and west, and the Ozark Mountains to the north form the natural boundaries of the region. Culturally, the region is Southern. The architecture, language and agrarian roots are linked to the Old South via the Cumberland Trail. Thousands of Southerners migrating westward through the Cumberland Gap, following the Cumberland Trail, settled this region of Illinois. This area is called Little Egypt, due to its being a grass-rich area in times of famine. The city of Cairo lies at the southern-most tip of Illinois at the confluence of the Ohio and the Mississippi Rivers.

Tuesday, September 17, 1996

We've packed up in the room and walked up to the cold restaurant for breakfast. The sun is poking through fuzzy white clouds, and the day looks promising.

Last night, we watched the second segment of *The West*. It is amazing, the early history of this country. Our own slow passage across America has increased my understanding and curiosity of its multifarious history.

Our two days here have been very restful. Our bodies needed the break. I'm looking forward to this eastern portion of our trip. I know there is an even more wonderfully mysterious journey ahead.

Eddyville, 3:30 p.m., Hick's Shawnee Mart. Two of the three round tables are filled with folks. When we walked in, a gregarious man said loudly, so everyone could hear, "All right, where'd you come from and where're you going?" I could see everyone looking and smiling. I gave them the short and sweet of it, and they were mighty impressed. When I told them that it was our honeymoon, this seemed to relieve them of any lasting doubts as to our sanity.

I asked, "How's the coffee?" trying to get off the hot seat and a cup of coffee with one stone. "You got to be pretty strong to handle that stuff, but I reckon you can," the gregarious one said.

The thought of coffee suddenly appealed to a woman named Sarah, and she beat me to the pot. We started talking. She's from south central Illinois, visiting her cousin, Marie, who also joined us at the table. Marie has land here and in Arizona. This is a historical and wilderness area and land prices are still pretty good.

Our conversation touched several topics. They'd been trail riding on horses for 4 hours today, travelling about 20 miles.

A horse walks at 4 mph and trots at 8 mph. They later looked at our loads and said a horse couldn't carry the weight we had on our bikes.

Sarah told us about the Crenshaw Mansion. John Crenshaw owned and operated a salt mine near here. Salt was like gold, a valuable commodity to preserve meat. Though a "Free State," the Illinois legislature, in the 1830s and 1840s, gave Crenshaw special permission to own and use slaves in his mines. He and his men would go to an often-used part of the river near Cave-In-Rock and wait for escaping slaves to cross the Ohio from Kentucky. In those days before locks, the river often was shallow enough to walk across. Crenshaw and his men would pick up the newly escaped slaves, putting them in the back of their covered wagon. The people were led to believe that they were part of the Underground Railroad and happily got in; after all, they were in the free state of Illinois. Crenshaw drove them to his mansion which had a huge basement with large doors they could drive the wagon through. Once in the basement, he would slam the doors shut." He'd break the women in the house and sold slaves along with using them in the mine. And he didn't even have to," Marie said incredulously, "He made over a million dollars a year in those days."

This led to a discussion of problems we still have, bigotry, racism, sexism. Sarah said women in her mother's generation (Sarah looked to be 48-50), had experienced more social change than any previous generation. Sarah thinks that the biggest problem society faces is drugs.

The story of the Crenshaw Mansion above is how Marie related it. Another source has it that the upper attic was where Crenshaw kept the slaves. The current owner of the mansion has been offering tours to see inside, including the small wooden cells in the attic. The owner is financially strapped and is appealing to the legislature for funds to keep the Crenshaw Mansion open as a

245

reminder of the horrors of slavery.

Crenshaw had one slave, Uncle Bob, who was his "breeder." Uncle Bob actually drove the wagon to the river to pick up the fleeing slaves. He fought for the South in the Civil War. He lived until 1949, to the ripe old age of 114, and sired 300 offspring.

Crenshaw's story is one of greed, racism, and the power of money. Interestingly, in 1840, Abe Lincoln (later to be President Lincoln, reluctant emancipator of the slaves), stayed with John Crenshaw while campaigning for Whig candidate William H. Harrison.

In Golconda, the campground we planned to stay in had been taken over by the state from the National Forest Service and was closed to camping until they improve the water system. We discovered this after riding down a gravel road and encountering the "No Camping" sign.

As we were consulting our maps back at the highway for our next option, a woman pulled up on the gravel road. In another of the many coincidences of this journey, her in-laws own the Deer Run Campground, the only campground in this area. We had to ride through Golconda, where we saw the Ohio River for the first time, then beyond for two miles of steep hills. We got to the campground about 5:30 p.m. Nobody was there, and the bathrooms were locked. A sign said they'd be back soon. We set up and cooked spaghetti with Five Brothers sauce and dried vegetable protein. I'm battling a sore throat, so I ate a clove of garlic in bed, after cleaning up. We were asleep when the owners arrived. They'd driven 50 miles one way to get tires for their truck, and it took longer than they'd thought. We are obviously in the boonies. We got up and showered and felt much better.

Wednesday, September 18, 1996

The dew is extremely heavy this morning. It took us an hour to dry out the tent enough to pack. Dew has drenched our shoes and socks. Still, it is a sunny fall morning by the Ohio.

We rode back into Golconda and are at the Dari Bar for breakfast. The waitress, a mom in her 40s, smells of a splash of perfume. Five tables are filled with locals eating and chewing the fat.

I asked the waitress about Golconda. She said, "It's quiet." She didn't know much of the history except it was, "founded back in the 1800s." But she gave me a menu with a corner portion containing Golconda facts. We learned: Golconda is in Pope County, established in 1816; The first Courthouse had a log dirt floor and the present courthouse, the third, was erected in 1871; The *Herald-Enterprise* is the oldest newspaper in southern Illinois, established in 1858; The first steamboat, *The New Orleans*, landed at Golconda in 1811, 903 river miles below Pittsburg; The first train arrived in Golconda in 1902; Golconda is on the Trail of Tears. (The winter of 1838-39, twelve thousand Cherokee Indians, in ten groups, crossed the Ohio River here. Thousands died from the harsh conditions during their forced march toward their new "home" in Talaqua, Oklahoma. They spent the remainder of that winter in Jonesboro IL, waiting to cross the Mississippi River.)

Our waitress told us to look up Mildred McCormick at the Not So New Shop down the street, beside the insurance company and in front of the grocery store.

We found Mildred in the Not So New Shop run by the Golconda Historical Society to fund its projects. Mildred is retired from teaching but "works even harder now." She's a stately woman, careful to greet all that enter the store. While we talked, the place was busy, mainly women browsing and finding things to buy. The waitress at the Dari Bar said, "After Mildred goes, the town will lose so much. The kids don't care, and the old people are just too old."

I tell Mildred she was highly recommended to us by the waitress at the Dari Bar. She chuckled and said, "Oh, that must be Wanda. She's president of my fan club," and chuckled again. Mildred is used to being asked questions and loves the role. She doesn't mind my turning my tape recorder on, which is good because she talks in bursts of information. She gave us some booklets, one that she had written.

Out on Main Street, with its historic slow river town vibe, we took our still soaked shoes off and changed into dry socks. This Ohio River dew is serious!

We rode out the levee to old dam 51, a quiet ride in the fall splendor. Across the way, Kentucky waits peacefully. It is hard to imagine the crossing of the Cherokee, uprooted, cast out of their homeland due to the discovery of gold. Gold has been the catalyst of tremendous suffering in this country.

We stopped to talk to a man selling Golden Delicious and Jonathan apples, cucumbers, tomatoes, and green peppers from the bed of his pickup parked under a sprawling oak tree. We rolled out of town in the crisp sun, past the wall with the mural depicting the Trail of Tears, up the hill, out of the river bottom, and away.

We came upon Elizabethtown, another river town, and had lunch in the Town and Country Restaurant. The folks there were familiar with seeing touring bikers and immediately got us huge red plastic cups of ice water. They had us sign their biker register. This was a fine little town, and the restaurant was the meeting spot for lunch. Farming is the main occupation of these folks. Outside, we mailed some letters from the storefront post office and paused to watch a tugboat push a barge of coal up the Ohio.

In Marion, Kentucky at the Coffee Shop. We crossed the Ohio River at Cave-In-Rock on the state ferry, our third ferry ride on this trip. It was a fitting way to enter Kentucky.

Coming into Marion, the road was predictably hilly, as it climbed out of the river valley and onto a rolling landscape with woods and cleared farmland. The feel of the place seems poorer than across the river.

Retrace 2022

Downtown Alton was sleepy even at 9 a.m. On our drive in, we noticed a new gruesome looking Piasa painted on the cliffs. At the Brew House on Main Street, we stopped for coffee and pastries. Signs in the storefronts spoke of reviving Alton, the old river town. One storefront had posters in the windows so you could view architectural drawings depicting what they hoped to do with the old city. Riverboat gambling was still successfully operating on the waterfront.

We headed on through southern Illinois. We stopped at Eldon Hazlet State Park and picnicked by the lake. Jetta enjoyed a nice walk through the tent camping area with us as we reminisced. Lake Carlyle was beautiful and peaceful.

At Giant City State Park, the road we were following through the park was unexpectedly closed. Our GPS was not working, and our maps were too large scale to be helpful, but we eventually found the lodge. Cathy was surprised when she didn't recognize it. We had spent two nights in a cabin nearby and neither the outside of this CCC-built lodge nor the inside seemed familiar. One lobby wall was filled with portraits of elected officials. The top row of presidents made us realize how much time had passed. GHW Bush was president when we were here last. Now, photos of Clinton, GW Bush, Obama, and Trump hung in the top row. Biden had not been added.

Next to the lobby, we peeked into the dining room. Finally, a little light of memory flickered. We remembered our mornings with coffees, as I sat there and wrote in my journal.

Our stop in Golconda began at the Dari Bar. I asked the waitress about Mildred. The waitress said that Mildred had passed away, but the "Not So New Shop" was open. We had just enough time to locate it before it closed for the day. The volunteer inside was not keen to begin a conversation on anything. It was just minutes before she had planned to lock the doors. Slightly disheartened, we started our car and continued through town, out past the levee, and headed east toward Cave-In-Rock.

The host at Cave-In-Rock State Park., in his conspicuous MAGA/Trump ballcap, assured us that there were no level sites for our tent in his loop. We drove around the tent camping loop as he suggested. The pit toilets there were located well away from the unappealing eroded sites. We found a suitable grassy, level campsite in the RV section and opted to pay an extra $10 to stay within walking distance of real restrooms and showers. I'm sure he was disappointed when we set up our tent a couple of sites away from his RV.

We had time that evening to drive over to the historic cave. A short path along the Ohio River led to its entrance. We were alone to explore the nooks and crannies of the short multi-tiered chamber, and we imagined the many uses of the cave throughout time. Native Americans used the cave as a haven and safe connection to the river. From the late 1700s, when rivers were important means of transport throughout America, the cave became a tavern, gambling den, and brothel. Outlaws hid out in the cave, luring river travelers in, then robbing and often killing them. Back out along the river, we watched the little Cave-In-Rock ferry on its run over to Kentucky.

The next morning, we packed up our gear and were ferried across the Ohio on the Becky-D. We were tickled by the warning sign mounted on the railing of the ferry; "To prevent loss of stability, keep bilges dry." Good advice all around.

Thursday, September 19, 1996

11:20 a.m. We're in Clay, Kentucky having lemonade. We stayed last night at Myers' Bed and Breakfast, "Your home away from home" run by Merle and Jim Myers. We had a fine blueberry pancake breakfast with melon, OJ, coffee, and bacon cooked by Merle. Bubba and Randy ate with us. Randy works around Marion at a power plant, but his home is near St. Louis. He drives home on the weekends and lives at the B&B during the week.

Bubba and Jim are starting to work on the brick walk behind the house. Bubba, Jim's son-in-law, lives with his wife and kids in Texas. He comes up each year to help Jim around the house. He has a diamond stud earring in his left ear, smokes, and loves fast driving in his Corvette.

The house was built in 1880, a beautiful wood frame Victorian home. When Merle and Jim bought it a few years ago, they gutted the interior walls and redid the woodwork, doors, and windows. The interior doors have operable transoms to compliment the 12-foot ceilings. We slept in a separate duplex out back. We had a TV and enjoyed a program on Frederick Douglas called *When the Lion Roared* on PBS, which corresponded to much of the history we have been reading about and bicycling through.

The ride this morning has been magnificent, through rolling hills, past Kentucky woods and farmland. We stopped in Dixon, at the hardware store, and got a drill bit to clean the clogged cotter pin holes on the trailer. This worked perfectly and the rig is back in good order.

I asked a man at the hardware store if there was a restaurant in town. From what we could see, which seemed to be all of town in two blocks, there wasn't any. He said, "Yea, just over that knuckle, it's on the left." The knuckle was a little rise, just enough you couldn't see over it, yet not really a hill. Indeed, there was Gardener's Cafe, Dixon's only restaurant. A 1950s vintage building, it was a combination restaurant and convenience store, but thankfully, a wall divided the two.

There were two older women having the lunch plate specials of sloppy joes and corn chips. One of them lives down by Clay on Rt. 132, which we'd just come through 12 miles ago. She looks like anyone's grandma, white hair, rounded face, short but nattily dressed for a luncheon outing with her friend.

The conversation touched on the fact that we are taking the Bicentennial Bike Route through Kentucky. Earlier in the morning, I had wondered to myself why we weren't seeing the reassuring little green signs with the white bicycle and white lettering: 76 BIKE ROUTE. They were all along the route when we picked it up near Carbondale, but there haven't been any in Kentucky.

She said, "I live on Route 132. It used to be the Bike Route." I said, "It still is. That's what we're taking." But this didn't seem to register. Instead, she continued, "I wish I would have gotten one of those bicentennial bike signs, you know, before they took them. They stole every one of them." This last bit of information she delivered with full indignation. I said, "I wondered why we haven't seen any in Kentucky." "They took every one of them," she said with disgust.

I asked them what goes on around Dixon and they said farming is the main occupation of folks in these parts. There is some coal mining, "but coal mining is depressed. There're no new jobs for young men." When I tried to follow up on this, the women's demeanor changed and they left shortly, as if the condition of coal mining, and talking about it made them uncomfortable.

The best thing about this lunch experience was the introduction to the geographic term, *knuckle*. We used this term with abandon for the rest of our trip.

After lunch, riding through Kentucky woodlands, we passed the Dorea Coal Mine, operated by Sextet Coal Company. Coal trucks rumbled out of there, grumbling from their load. The side of the road near the mine was strewn with gravel-sized coal and the roadside weeds were blackened with dust. The trucks rumbled past us steadily, crashing and banging on the lumpy road. They seemed to be taking the coal to a railroad line a mile or so off to the south. Later, when we crossed over the Green River, coal trucks were unloading where a conveyor belt filled barges moored in the river. Downstream in the distance was a coal-fired electric generation plant. All of this brought John Prine's "Paradise" to the forefront of our minds, and we sang several verses as we rode along.

We saw several tobacco drying barns filled with hanging tobacco plants. A newspaper article we saw yesterday talked about Kentucky tobacco farmers getting higher prices for tobacco due to the hurricane damage to crops in the Carolinas.

We are camping in the picnic pavilion of a schoolyard park in Utica. We cooked macaroni and cheese for dinner, washed dishes, and bathed sponge-bath style in the clean women's bathroom nearby. We waited to pitch our tent until six high-school boys finished shooting hoops. It was well after dark.

It was a beautiful sunset of oranges and lavenders as Cathy played her violin. My cold is doing great. I'm hoping tomorrow it will surrender and be gone.

Friday, September 20, 1996

7:30 a.m., Marvin's Cafe, convenience store and gas station. The scene in this cafe is of truckers and farmers, cigarettes, and snuff. We got cups of coffee and a sweet roll.

Last night, around 2:30, a police car pulled up beside our

tent, stopped, spotlighted our tent, got out, got back in, and drove off. Phew, that's too early to start riding!

After a good night's rest, we packed our gear on the bikes and rode off. The sky looks good, promising another great fall day. We are just ahead of a cold front towing thunderstorms in its wake across the Midwest.

We have our maps out. It's about 640 miles to home, through hilly terrain. Maybe fifteen days of riding left. Still too far away, I argue, for Cathy to start adopting stray animals. She's petting a cute, white-eyed mutt out by the bikes now! We have about $400.00 cash left in the till. My cold is slowly fading away; it hasn't bothered me much. I've enjoyed riding every day since Giant City where the bug jumped aboard.

The terrain and weather are beautiful. I love fall, the feeling of change, the crisp nights, the first hints of color. What a fine time to come through Kentucky. Our odometer reads 3,647 miles, an almost unfathomable figure. The past three months are like one of those "snakes" where you light the pellet, and it burns a long stream of expanding carbon. Our memories are getting longer with each new day.

Noontime in Fordsville, KY. We're at The Diner, a very busy spot here on this sparkling fall Friday. Outside, the townspeople are busy preparing for Fordsville Days this weekend. Across the street, three or four carnival rides are in different stages of erection and on the corner, a dunking pool is being installed. Signs advertise the Baby Beauty Contest. A mile back out of town, down along Adams Fork Branch Bottom, they are preparing for a Mud Bog event and a Demolition Derby set for tomorrow. These are the youngest people we've seen since the Pinckneyville Marching Kittens.

Back about 18 miles, south of Whitesville, along the bottomland of the South Fork of Panther Creek, we came upon three men putting up tobacco. Curious, we pulled to the left shoulder of the road and stopped to watch them. They were on a tractor pulling an empty drying rack trailer to a section of tobacco that had been cut and stacked upside down in little pyramid stacks, the stalk bottoms sticking up. They'd run a 5-foot-long stick of oak through about 5 of these bunches and hang the ends of the sticks over the trailer's metal rack. Once it was filled, the plants were taken to a well-ventilated wood barn and hung to dry. This is air-dried tobacco, different than the heat-dried tobacco of the Carolinas, so the farmer told me.

As I pulled to a stop, lo and behold, the farmer stopped his tractor and cut the engine off. His two helpers were riding on the trailer, a barrel-chested young lad with a NY Yankees t-shirt and worn jeans and an older skinny man in teal work pants. Both helpers avoided eye contact. This was obviously a stop on the whim of the owner. When the motor coughed silent, he yelled up to us, "Is this unethical what we're doing here?" He asked this with a devilish grin. Caught a little off guard by his question and his waiting for a reply to this smoky issue, I said, "I guess that depends on whether you smoke or not," realizing immediately the slippery logic of this line of reasoning. "Well, Bill Clinton thinks it is," he laughed, getting to his point. I countered with, "I guess the problem is that society ends up paying the medical costs of smoking." I really didn't want to debate smoking and neither did he. He wanted to bash the government and Clinton, and I wanted to talk about his work, his life.

He talked about how the government sets tobacco prices and how he's not making much money (this latter is more for the benefit of his underpaid help, I figure). He has ten acres in tobacco, burley tobacco, a yellowish green plant used in smoking blends. The darker green tobacco we've seen is a chewing tobacco, which is only grown in nine or ten counties around here. He will plant more acreage in tobacco next year, he said. "Believe it or not, there's a worldwide shortage of this burley tobacco." This news was probably the source of some of his grinning. In the eight-acre field he's working here, he has soybeans, feed corn, and tobacco. I told him good luck. He exclaimed that we are going through Kentucky the "longest way" and warned us of upcoming hills. Then they went back to work. I took a picture. They laughed at life. We rode away.

We have seen more churches since entering Kentucky. At one intersection, on Rt. 54 and a gravel road named Sunnyvale, there were three church signs pointing up the gravel road: The Pleasant Grove Bible Baptist Church; The Sunnyvale General Baptist Church; and the Sunnyvale Church of Christ. That's some mighty intricate carving of a niche in the ol' theological landscape.

Today's ride was superb but hilly towards the end of the day. The hills here are short and steep. We are in granny gear a lot. Oh, Granny Gear, we entrust the rest of Kentucky to your care. We are deacons in the Church of Up and Down.

This is happy riding. I love looking ahead watching my new wife riding through this flushed-cheeked fall countryside. This is the intersection of fantasy and life, right here in rural Kentucky. Back in Whitesville, while drinking her malted chocolate shake, Cathy said, "I'm looking forward to getting to the mountains." I didn't say anything, but I'm storing that comment for later retrieval. Before coming to rest at our home on Thirteenth Street, we will have crossed every ridge of the Cumberland, Allegheny, Appalachian, and Blue Ridge Mountains.

6:30 p.m., Axtel Campground. We've set up, showered, and made chili for dinner. I've been playing guitar. Cathy's lying down, resting. We're camped by Rough River Lake. As we were heating some coffee earlier, Cathy told me, "I smelled my grandmother today. It was a faint odor of Ivory soap and Clorox.

257

My eyes teared up before I even realized why."

This is a rural portion of Kentucky. You hear "ain't" a lot spoken with a southern drawl. Folks are friendly overall. But occasionally people try to be invisible, like the old man we passed getting his mail at his roadside mailbox. We were right there beside him, in the middle of beautiful countryside, no one around for miles, yet he refused to make eye contact; he just kept his head down. Still, several folks have waved from their porch swings or chairs today, and I enjoyed waving back, sometimes saying "Howdy," loudly. I know we must be a sight but we're a friendly sight.

At one point today we rode over new pavement for five miles. The surface was fresh, and our tires stuck as they rolled, producing swishing sounds and moans from us as we climbed a doubly nasty hill. Thankfully, our route turned off this new construction and we continued more smoothly, up and down, up and down.

At a convenience store, about eight miles from here, we stopped for a drink and to call some campgrounds: How much? Do you have showers? A van full of Mexicans folks were buying sodas. I asked the clerk what they were doing. She said either harvesting tobacco or peppers or working on a new golf course going in down the way.

Saturday, September 21, 1996

We're in the tent. We're pretty socked in, but thus far it is a light, steady rain. Plans are formulating for breakfast, but as I write this, it is raining harder. We'll stay put and eat granola bars.

Noon at Boots and Vada's Chicken Coop Restaurant. We walked up here on top of the knuckle during a pause in the rain.

258

We've been reading the *Louisville Courier-Journal,* a good read, and eating a big breakfast. It's still raining, but the forecast is for partly sunny tomorrow.

Two old boys are busy rubbing lotto game cards and talking about once, when they won $100, or somebody they knew won something. This rain came at a good time, we can use the rest. Cathy's butt was sore, so this will help in that arena also.

In the tent, late. The rain cleared out around 4 p.m. today, from dark grey drizzle to blue skies and sun in about 30 minutes. We were in the tent reading and emerged with other campers into the sweet fall evening. We were like prairie dogs after the "all's clear" signal bark. The kids started their bike escapades through the puddles, smoky campfires started, and an easy feeling of calm settled over the hills. We played music, Cathy playing "Shenandoah" on the violin, sounding good and mellow.

Since entering Kentucky and the knuckles of the Western Alleghenies, the land and people seem settled in old patterns. People seem stuck. There is a palpable feeling of stagnancy. Coal mining is still king in this region. These old mountains absorb the assaults from outside economic concerns that extract their carbon riches, transporting it by truck, train, and barge into the Midwest's industrial pall. This land and its people are mortgaged heavily against the American Dream. With the motion of three-year-olds with crayons, people scratch lotto tickets at convenience stores, like the lady buying 27 dollars' worth of a-snowy-day-in-hell on her way home from the laundry mat, her old Nova listing as she pulls out. Is it any wonder rubbery lotto shavings dust these back-lane nooks and crannies?

Retrace 2022

Once in Kentucky, we keenly felt the pull of home. We passed the old B&B in Marion, now called the Iris Inn Bed and Breakfast. We did not stop. Instead, we drove on through Utica; the park shelter where we had camped was no longer there.

Axtel Campground was open, people were camping, but the gate across the road was down, and the office was closed for lunch. We walked into the campground and had a light lunch.

Fortified, we prepared to branch off our bike route and plotted our course to Mammoth Cave National Park. We had reserved a site there for two nights. This would give us time to take a guided tour of the cave while Jetta stayed in a provided kennel run.

At the park, we shared the tent loop with dozens of young students participating in a creationist science field trip. The leaders taught their alternative to the park ranger's scientific explanation of the geology of the cave, fitting it to their religious perception of the age of the earth.

The pull toward home intensified when we checked the weather forecast. Hurricane Ian was in Florida and would be storming north in a couple of days, sure to sock in the rest of our trip. We decided to cut our stay at Mammoth Cave short and make a direct run for home instead of following our bike route through Kentucky and Virginia. We still had time to take the superb two-hour tour of the cave before we headed down the road. The weather was still good, and we would have one more night on the road, in Berea, before finishing our trip.

<<<<< >>>>>

Journey: End

Appalachia

Sunday, September 22, 1996, Autumnal Equinox

4 p.m. We crossed into Eastern Time this morning. Just south of Hodgenville we stopped at Lincoln's Birthplace near Knob Creek. We viewed a film and walked to the old cabin, which is inside a granite monument that looks and feels like a giant mausoleum. It isn't the actual cabin, but the sinking spring, the Lincoln family's source of water, still flows nearby.

I thought it was telling that when Abe was two years old, his family moved to the Knob Creek farm and lived there until he was seven. His first memories were from Knob Creek. Abe's father took care of the road that passed through their property. The road stretched from Louisville on the Ohio River to Nashville and certainly connected with the Natchez Trace. Abe was exposed to many travelers during that time, people stopping and staying over, talking of other places and peoples. Those must have been important early influences on him, preparing him for his later role in history.

We are camped out under a huge box elder tree behind the Cruise Inn just down the road a half a mile from the birthplace monument. We've showered and checked our maps. I had to true my rear wheel from a mishap caused by avoiding a car about four miles back. I got it straight enough to make it home, I think, but the rim is stressed from the weight.

Today was a splendid, exciting day of riding, not too hilly and a bit of a tailwind to boot. The sun was radiant, the sky awesomely blue. We rode through farmland, tobacco, corn, and beans. We passed an Amish farm. Two men were out in their white, straight brimmed straw hats with black bands which glowed in the fall Sunday sun. Around the side of the barn four boys peered into a shed. They wore the same glowing hats and overalls as the men. A road sign nearby cautioned motorists that horse-drawn carriages traveled these roads.

We stopped in a convenience store in Hudson just before the timeline. Six men sat in the corner jawin' and talking car prices. One of them was trying to sell a van. They were working over the youngest cub amongst them, a carrot-topped young man who they goaded as being "too cheap." "I'll buy anything if the price is right," Carrot-top drawled. "Yeah, free!" they retaliated, laughing. I asked them if the Natchez Trace passed anywhere near here. This initiated a vigorous discussion about roads and such, for they needed something to talk about. But they didn't include me in the conversation. The owner had us sign his biker logbook, a medium-sized composition book. The most recent entry was nine days ago by a couple heading to Virginia Beach. They must be traveling light, or just joshing because their comment was, "One week to go." Hmmm, we've got about two weeks and we're just going to Roanoke. Oh well. Bet they didn't stop at Lincoln's birthplace.

Monday, September 23, 1996

9:30 p.m., Chimney Rock Campground, Harrodsburg, KY, in the tent after a good day of riding. It started out cool and sunny in Hodgensville. We had a hard time finding a restaurant in town and settled for the Duck Inn, a small joint with homemade fried pies and home cooking. An older couple ran the place, more as something to do than for income. She talked about taxes, city stickers, school taxes, all with this Limbaugh-ish fatalism, a lot of "They say this," or "They say that." She used to work "down to the sewing plant." Now her daughter does. She had a sad edge

263

to her as if she only felt good if she were hearing about how bad things were. She said, "One guy was in here talking about how, you know, teachers have assistants and now the assistants have assistants. I don't know..." She let this lie, not knowing how we came down on the issue of public education, or perhaps she sensed we didn't go for all that right-wing caterwauling.

We left there happy to be out in the beautiful fall morning. It's a blessing, a privilege for us to be able to do this, pack all we need onto our bikes and head off silently down the byways of America, seeing what lies before us, working as we go, feeling the landscape.

We stopped to photograph little piglets doing their cute pink tiptoe rooting in the grass with mom. The slightly older piglets were outside the fence; one of them was working on something in the road, probably smashed chewing tobacco, knowing the habits of this region. From around the bend came two Budweiser beer trucks, rolling down the country road. The lead driver saw the adventurous piglet about the time the piglet saw him. The piglet turned and ran dead in the middle of the road in front of the trucks, heading for mom and family. Such earnest running; he really gave it all he had, little ears flapping, curly tail pulled back. All this gutsy effort was just feet ahead of the Mack truck's grill and wide piglet-creaming tires. But, by God, he made it. At full piggy-gallop he careened off toward his kin, continued right past them through a wire fence and into the woods. The others quickly followed, seeming to want to hear all about it. As the first truck passed us, we were still laughing joyfully at that scene. The driver, a young mustachioed fellow, wasn't as amused, having to slow his rig to a piglet gallop then down-shift and carry on up the road.

We stopped at the Fifth Wheel in Raywick, the only place open. The park across the street was locked up with a 12-foot-high chain-link fence. We got the feeling the boys get rowdy around here. The bar owners, Jimmy and his wife, are sweetly gregarious. We have a couple of Pepsis, a bag of chips and some popcorn she popped in the microwave. They get a lot of bikers coming through.

Mackville, at a local grocery store. It is a vintage wood-sided building with a porch roof covering the front sidewalk. A couple of seats from a school bus provide a makeshift bench. I was ready to head in when the door opened and out shot some chewing tobacco spit. Then the door closed, a Dole/Kemp sticker pasted to its window. There was a respectable amount of spit on the wood sidewalk in front of the door. Inside, six or eight men sat around, saying nothing to my "Howdy. How're you doing?" No problem, a cold Gatorade will suffice.

Tuesday, September 24, 1996

8 a.m., having breakfast at Chimney Rock Campground. We'd moved under a patio roof to keep dry last night. It drizzled a little, but this morning the sun is out with clearing skies.

The terrain is interesting here. Yesterday we came through the Knobs—an apt description. There haven't been mountains, just rolling hills and "knobs." Only occasionally do we get a view off in the distance, and when we do, it is a level hilltop view, no peaks or ridges.

1:15 p.m., Berea, at Papa Leno's on Main Street having lunch. We've come 41 miles today. We climbed out of a few hollows, not real long hills, but steep; they took about all we had.

4:45 p.m., in Berea Coffee and Tea. We just toured several of the craft shops in Berea including Charles May's gallery of fine woodworking, where Appalachia's eastern hardwoods are displayed in all their polished, planed, turned, and carved beauty. This connection with the traditional mountain culture and crafts gives Berea a museum vibe.

Berea College's charter is to educate the children of Appalachia tuition-free. In exchange, the students work as apprentices, making Appalachian crafts, ranging from brooms, pottery, and wood toys, to quilts and furniture. This arrangement galvanizes this little city in the western edge of the Appalachians into a beacon of hope as it mines its cultural past, passing it along to a new generation.

When we run our hands over a finished and oiled piece of cherry, walnut, hickory, or oak furniture, we sense the timeless Appalachian region and the character of those who crafted a life from the hard scrabble of wooded hills, hollows, and meadows. This touching, this laying on of hands, of heart, reveals the essence of the crafted wood. It is much the same with the breadth of this country. To feel its rich contours, its folk history, its possibilities, you must touch its timeless grain, its magnificent form. Our bicycle journey is but a glimpse into the country, but a glimpse none-the-less. For this we give thanks.

We have taken a room at the historic Boone Tavern Inn, in the heart of Berea. The hotel clerk asked if we wanted a dinner reservation, and we said we couldn't meet the dress code. (We'd read it was coat and tie.) He said that had been relaxed to casual attire, but we assured him we would not be able to meet that either!

Berea is near the northern point of Boone's Trace which Boone surveyed in 1775 and is part of the Wilderness Road—the "poor man's way west." The expansion of southern America into the west followed the trail onto the central Kentucky plateau and the Cumberland Gap at the border of northeast Tennessee, southwest Virginia, and southeastern Kentucky. Long hunter

Daniel Boone had crossed into Kentucky from North Carolina many times by 1773. This region was still the wilderness home of the Shawnee Indians at that time, but with Boone's Trace came settlers and conflict and more settlers.

Entering the Appalachians, we begin a new phase of our journey. The tug of home becomes a constant hum in our breast. But herein lies the delicate balance we hope to achieve. We foresee two weeks of riding left. This will be our hardest, most strenuous bicycling. The increasing pull of home will be matched by increasingly mountainous terrain. Knowing this, we are mailing back all nonessential gear including books, maps, brochures, tape recorder, tapes, guitar capo, the Outdoor Kitchen, frying pan, swimsuits, some toiletries, exposed film, songbook, and a bag of sage from Nebraska—fourteen pounds!

Through this difficult terrain, with each bend and smell reminding us of home, we still are only here. To experience eastern Kentucky, to learn from it, to be changed by it, is perhaps our greatest challenge. When does a journey end? How do I keep the consciousness of the traveler as I increasingly look forward to being home and to our new life together?

I love the journey. I will always have this in my soul. I am a traveler. We all are, spinning through space, galactic miracles of infinite dreams. I am happy in this dream. I revel in the passage. I cherish the here, the now, the zaniness of present life. Yet, with each hill and valley, I also dream of the future. I view its images over and over, touching and savoring them like smooth planks of cherry.

A day or so ago, I crested a hill. There, in the hill's shadow, was a dead rabbit, its dismembered body parts scattered. "Rabbit parts," my mind intoned, then in a chain of consciousness, I thought of a VW Rabbit and how to some people, "Rabbit parts" would mean car parts. The instant "Rabbit parts" flashed through my mind, a faded grey VW Rabbit materialized on this lonely

Kentucky road. Just as quickly it was past and gone. This chain of events lasted a couple heartbeats. A confluence of thought and matter that has no meaning, except that we see it—our "little thoughts" along with the "little events." Coincidences are the back side of possibilities. We are forever one with them, we just need to see.

Retrace 2022

We took time in the morning to hike around the woodlands of Mammoth Cave, waiting for our reserved time for the Historic Tour. When the time came, we joined our tour group of a hundred or so folks and entered Mammoth Cave. Our guide, a National Park Ranger, did a fine job keeping us informed and curious. It is a massive cavern, the longest cave system in the world with over 400 miles of charted tunnels. Our two-hour climb through the cave gave us a mere glimpse. We both felt invigorated as we climbed back up to the mouth of the cave into brilliant daylight.

After our tour, we picked up Jetta in the kennel and headed straight to Berea. Boone Tavern Inn allowed dogs and it was tempting to stay there again, but there was a $75 pet fee. We opted for the Motel 6 a few miles out of town. We drove downtown and got our bearings, as we walked around the College area, past Boone Tavern. The shops were closed by the time we got there, so we did a bit of window shopping. We ordered a takeout pizza at Papa Leno's and headed to our motel room for the rest of the night, our last night on this retrace journey.

Wednesday, September 25, 1996

This was our 100th day on the road and what a fine day it was, good bicycling through the Cumberland Mountains for 90 miles. I am in our tent. It is 8:30 p.m. We're at Buckhorn Lake Dam Campground—very nice. We rolled in around 6:30 with still enough light down in these hollows to set up, shower, and cook a fine meal of stewed tomatoes, pinto beans, a bagel with peanut butter, raisins, and Gatorade. A screech owl called from the trees during dinner, and the night became a cacophony of rhythmic sounds. I think of Mom and her book *Night Comes to the Cumberlands* by Harry Caudill. She liked that book and being here, I think I know why. This region is isolated, so cultural patterns can mature. These mountains insist that you adapt, make do, improvise and persevere—all traits of Mom.

This morning before we left Berea, we breakfasted at the local deli—a regular spot for some of the faculty and town folk. We left town on a perfect fall morning, 57 degrees and sunny. Today for the first time I noticed leaves falling on the road, brittle yellow/brown curled and expired leaves. I enjoyed running over them, the crisp crunch under my front tire. Also, under walnut trees I noticed the road was stained by their crushed shells. It looked like chewing tobacco stain in copious amounts. We saw kudzu and we both thought of our home by the railroad tracks, our little back field covered with the menacing green vine.

In Bighill, we passed the Wilderness Road Outdoor Theater, and I thought of Daniel Boone in these woods. We paralleled several streams and rivers as we wound through the mountains. Near Irvine, we rode five miles up Red Lick Creek, then we crossed the creek and rode five miles back down before curving east—10 miles of biking to get a quarter of a mile east.

We had four long climbs over passes on ridges and four great descents as we dropped into stream basins. I enjoyed watching Cathy barreling down at 38 mph around these twisting country roads. I laughed at the fun of it, though we had to be careful about too much open mouth laughing, or we'd surely be eating bugs! There were lots of turtles on the road today. Maybe yesterday's rain created perfect turtle conditions.

Farmers were putting up their tobacco today, the larger operations had workers cutting and stacking. The other day coming into Berea, we saw three Mexican workers in a tobacco field. As we waved, one yelled out to us "Hola. Como estás?" I yelled back, "Bien!" with a thumbs-up sign, and we were past them.

The camp attendant here told us there are three mountains to climb in the first ten miles tomorrow. She is comfortable around bikers; some people aren't. It's like we were from Mars the way some people react, almost repulsed by our presence. I guess we seem strange in the spandex clothing and bike shoes that we wear.

Cathy is asleep and I'm fading fast. What a great day. It's a blessing to be in the Cumberland Mountains.

Thursday, September 26, 1996

7:45 a.m., waking up. A brief thunderstorm rolled through during the night. We scrambled out and brought a few things into the tent. Thunder bounced around the mountains and rolled through these hollows.

8:35 a.m. We wrapped BOB and the guitar in plastic, though I don't think it will rain. Earlier, I stopped and talked to the old fellow camping in his Shasta trailer, a funky old trailer that he has used and kept in good shape. His old German shepherd dog sleeps under his trailer on a chain. He asked about our trip.

When I told him it was our honeymoon and we we're having fun, he patted me on my shoulder and said, "That's good. I'm glad to hear that."

9:00 a.m., at the Dairy Queen in Buckhorn. When we arrived the manager was sitting out at a table getting ready to open. He is now fixing us four sausage, egg, lettuce, and tomato sandwiches. The coffee is good. He informed us that the first mountain we will cross "is a doozie."

We're having fun looking at the maps. We just got the Virginia map out, which means we're getting close. We have a cold front coming east. At last report, it will be here by Saturday. We're thinking it would be good to be in the Breaks Interstate Park for the rain. We have some mountains to climb.

11:30 a.m., in Chavies, having beans, cornbread, and milkshakes! The mountains weren't too bad; just get in low gear and pedal. Each mountain took around 20-25 minutes to ascend to the top, then two minutes to go down, then start back up again. We are seeing more fall colors. The brilliant reds are outrageous. From one ridge crest we could look out to the east and see the flattened treeless ridges of strip mines. This was the first strip mining we'd seen. We dropped down into Chavies at a coal transfer point. The road and everything are blackened from the coal dust.

We stopped at a small convenience store along the road. A middle-aged woman walked up the aisle with a loaf of bread. "Stay in your sleeping bags of a night?" the lady asks us. She is from around here, Perry County, and says this coal is from strip mining. Cathy asks if the strip mining is just in Perry County. "No, all these counties around here, but they're good companies. I like the railroad company." She says the pollution isn't bad here, and "That Delaware takes the cake." She'd just returned from Delaware today. Leaving she says, "It's been nice talking to y'all. I got to get back up to home."

The rest of the day we will have to be extra careful with these coal trucks on the road. Some have short semi-truck beds; others are huge dump trucks.

The ride from Chavies was a tough haul. We had a steady climb and lots of traffic with 60-ton coal trucks passing, hissing, and pounding just inches away. The last 15 miles was somewhat less steep, but the traffic was still heavy.

We rode by a film shoot of the movie *Fire Down Below* starring Steven Seagal. They were getting ready to wreck a coal truck. We rode through the scene, seemingly invisible, passing a Kentucky State Trooper paid to sit at the side of the road in his patrol car. He seemed to be a moment away from a nap. I said, "Howdy," as we passed him. He managed a dull, "Yep."

The clerk at the convenience store five miles down the way filled us in on the movie's storyline, how many wrecks they'd filmed (three), and that she'd seen Seagal. "Of course, they're going to make us look like hicks," she said laughing with a pat of her hands as she leaned toward us. "There's a brand-new house right there, but they are shooting scenes in the 100-year-old house next door," she said in a can-you-believe-it tone.

9:05 p.m., Pippa Passes KY. The odometer clicked past 4,000 miles back in Dwarf, Kentucky. We're at 4,019 now. At about 5 p.m., up a very steep single-lane road, we met Ed and Charlotte Madden and arranged to stay overnight in their Hostel. It's a popular stop for cyclists on the 76 Bike Route.

We are in Knott County, the second leading county producer of coal. They are strip mining on two high coal seams. One reaches a thickness of 30 feet in areas. At one time, Charlotte's father, like everybody else around here, dug coal out of the hillside just 30 yards in front of where we sat on the porch talking. He used it for heat. "He'd dig in 30-40 feet, then move over and dig in some more," said Ed.

Ed has been in education administration for 43 years, a principal for 20 years and now is working in County Education—Head Start, etc. He told us that Kentucky has adopted a Performance-based system that is very experimental and does not stress the fundamentals of spelling or math. A student multiplied 4 x 4 and got 17, but since he had three different "logical" explanations as to his thinking process to achieve this answer, the answer "17" was not considered incorrect. Ed couldn't remember any of the logical explanations, unfortunately.

We walked down the steep road to the Alice Lloyd College campus and ate in the dining hall. The college has about 500 students. Alice Lloyd came from Boston in the 1920s and started the college as a community center on the model of those established in New York city "to help people learn to live."

We just came in from viewing the beautiful lunar eclipse. Ed asked if we'd heard the Sonic Boom from the Space Shuttle this morning around 8:05. We had. I thought it was dynamite. What a world we live in—orbiting spheres shadowing each other, space shuttles flying from the earth, life in a tiny hollow in the Cumberlands called Pippa Passes.

Friday, September 27, 1996

At breakfast at the ALC dining hall. This morning, we counted the number of bikers that signed the Madden's register—around 100 this year. We slept well, down in the dank basement room with its 6-foot ceiling. It is a grey day with rain in the forecast. We will just see what happens. The Breaks are 60 miles east.

Kentucky has been an experience. Eastern Kentucky is very poor. People live in shacks along the road, the steep mountainous terrain leaving few choices. Many times, we would see people sitting on their porches (often a mobile home) and could tell that they saw us, but they would divert their eyes and not make contact. I waved and said hello every chance. Sometimes they'd say hi back, mostly silence was their offering. This behavior is very curious to me. Young males shoot us the finger—the last one was yesterday. I just grinned at the absurdity as the old pick-up truck passed us, growling under stomped acceleration, the driver with his left hand sticking up beside the top of the cab, giving us a tight-fisted gig.

We've also encountered lots of dogs—hound dogs, shepherds, and mutts of all shapes. Most of them are chained by the house or in the yard, the length of chain determining the size of the barren dirt in which the dog lives. When we'd get within 100 yards, the howling would commence, growing more frantic as we neared apogee to their orbits, until they and their chains would raise a most righteous commotion. All this raises the alarm for the canine population throughout the steep hollows. Often we uttered thanks aloud that a chain held back the especially fearsome ones. Of course, they know they can't get to us and maybe a lot of their exhibition is for the benefit of the other dogs, sort of like the guy that says, "Why I oughta..."

For the dogs not on a chain or leash, I have the best defense—my wife. The flashing, blood-tipped, steely, "No!" that she can fire off, startles even me. I've witnessed big dogs, all a-bluster and fearsome in their across-the-yard charge screech to a stop on a dime when that "No!" hits them. Why, I sometimes feel sorry for them, and I never smile so they'd see it because it could embarrass them so bad it could alter their personalities.

Another curious southern icon peculiar to Kentucky and

some parts of southern Illinois is the yard trampoline. I know we've seen over two dozen in the last two weeks. I have never seen anyone bouncing on one, or anywhere near one, unless they were mowing the grass.

Yet another observation from Kentucky, the more rural, the better—tanning salons. These are almost always in someone's home, be it a wood frame or brick house or a trailer. The sign might read, "Gail's Tanning Salon," then below it might be "turbo face tanning" as an extra feature. I can't say as I've noticed many tan people though.

11 p.m., in Breaks Interstate Park. What a day! At least five monster hills. Coming down the first mountain, the road snaked and dropped precipitously. The road was wet which made it necessary to go slow. In braking, both my rims heated up, warping my rear rim, and cracking the place that had already been stressed. I tried to true the wheel and succeeded in straightening it some. The rest of the day, I limited my use of the rear brakes. The climbs were indeed steep. The road was narrow and potholed. We played cat and mouse with 60-ton coal trucks. A black and white dog came after Cathy on one downhill, miscalculated its speed, and came sliding, toenails scratching the pavement, right in front of me. I cut my wheel to the right but hit the dog with a glancing blow. He ran off. Luckily, I stayed up and it didn't buckle my front wheel. It was one of our hardest days of riding.

We got to the Breaks around 5 p.m., got a room in the Lodge, and showered. We ate here in the room and enjoyed lounging and watching the tube. The wind is howling up the gorge outside and rain is forecast for tomorrow.

Virginia

Saturday, September 28, 1996

8:30 a.m., up early. Cathy tried to photograph the view from our deck overlooking the gorge. Clouds created a white river of mist that flowed through the horseshoe canyon below us. Rhododendron covers the ground at the precipice's edge. Cathy is washing some clothes in the bathroom sink, probably the last road washing before home.

I'm excited about being close to home and the route we will take to the Blue Ridge Parkway. I like the idea of this quieter rural route into Roanoke, rather than the route published on our TransAmerica map that parallels Interstate 81 in places.

We've finished breakfast at the Lodge with its beautiful view. Its huge window wall pulls us into the vista. Maple, sourwood, oak, and hickory trees are changing color on the ridges. This is a fine time to tour into our home mountains.

Because someone else has reservations, we need to move out of this room and into another room soon. We have packed our things, except for our wet clothes. It is a sauna in here as Cathy is drying socks on the radiator.

We are in our new room in the Lodge, which is even neater than the first one. We have an upstairs end room with a private covered porch overlooking the gorge straight down off the back. It has rained hard all day, but it is lifting. Clouds fill the gorge. Just the ridge tops show horizontally across the canyon. What a special place to be rained in.

Out on the deck we met brothers, Wesley, and Toby. They are riding recumbent bikes from Yorktown, VA to Indiana. They are with their father, Jack, who is riding support in a van. They are staying in motels. They are having a great ride. They looked our rigs over and were in disbelief at the loads we carry.

We spent a few hours in their room. Jack has toured with his wife on their Harley, and he understands traveling on country roads. He enjoys being their support but commented on the general lack of meeting people. He said, "I squirrel hunt and have hunted in this area. I thought I'd be able to sit and talk to some other old boys, sitting around in a store, you know, relate while the boys were riding." Instead, he's forced to sit by the road waiting on them.

It has been fun talking with them. They have been on the road for seven days. We all told stories and laughed the laugh of comrades. Wesley, 42, is twenty years older than his brother Toby. They ride with some tools and snacks. Jack carries the rest, including a laptop which they use to e-mail daily reports back home. They both are riding recumbents and like them a lot. This morning, they disassembled each bike and cleaned them so they glowed.

Wesley and Toby are just starting to mellow to their trip, the rituals of travel just starting to crystallize from the brew of their activity, both mental and physical. Any trip has three basic stages—beginning, middle, and end. The beginning is an awkward time, a testing of self, equipment, and mission statement that only can be answered upon beginning and accruing experience. Even the most experienced traveler still must pass through the beginning. I sense this edge in Wesley and Toby. They've begun and are thrilled by it. Some things will be let go and others added even in a 14-day trip. This is one of the blessings of traveling.

Cathy and I are in the final stage of our cross-country quest. We are on our 103rd day, three or four days away from our 1904 Queen Anne home. We have quietly begun looking back, signaling the beginning of the end. We are only doing this for brief periods of time. Soon we will be looking back on our trip in total, and whether we recognize it or not, a new quest will have begun.

Sunday, September 29, 1996

When we got up, we were socked in—fog thick as pea soup. We planned to ride with Wesley and Toby, and they didn't want to ride in the fog either. So, we waited.

It was 11:00 by the time the four of us rolled away. The recumbents looked wild! It was a fun eight miles riding with them. We had a couple good climbs, which is a weak point for recumbents. I was able to easily keep up with them and I was carrying over 100 pounds of gear. When we reached their turnoff, we stopped and said so longs all around.

Soon, at one mountain top, Cathy and I came upon our first long view into Virginia's beautiful valley and mountain terrain. Cathy got weepy, overwhelmed by the beauty and the feeling of being home, the trip almost over. It all welled up in her.

We rode hard, because of the late start and we had a long way to go. The section through Hayter's Gap was beautiful. We crossed the Clinch River and the north, middle, and south forks of the Holston River. Wonderful riding.

8:30 p.m., Quincey's Pizza, Damascus Virginia. We pulled into The Place right at dusk, the temperature dropping to 55 degrees. The Place is a hostel run by the local Methodist Church for Appalachian Trail hikers and TransAmerica Route bikers— $2/ night. The Place needs a thorough cleaning. A flea jumped on my leg in one room, so we relocated upstairs to one of three rooms furnished with bunk beds made from two-by-fours and dingy foam pads. It does provide a needed service for the traveler, though.

We talked with a guy hiking part of the Appalachian Trail. He's an Interlochen kid, a violist. He played Cathy's violin a bit. I was so tired, I arranged the bed on the floor and was soon asleep.

So Close

Monday, September 30, 1996, Cathy's 37th Birthday

This morning, it is in the low 40s, chilly but a sparkling day. We're at TJ's Deli and have ordered breakfast. The folks here are friendly and talkative. The guy across the room rides a motorcycle and is relating to our trip. Some cyclists have walked in. I've yet to talk to them. I need to do some stretching. I felt like I was pulling something in my left thigh yesterday. Just three days of riding left!

9:30 p.m., Super 8 in Galax, Virginia. We got into Galax around 5:30 p.m.

The day had many faces and moods. The ride through Mt. Rogers Recreation Area was awesome in the morning chill. We rode by mountain streams, waterfalls, and pools of clear water. Sunlight backlit the falling leaves drifting, spinning, and flipping down to the road like thousands of golden memories.

We stopped for a snack on the roadside by the New River, our first sighting of this ancient sojourner. Scientists estimate the New River is approximately 250 million years old. It flows northward from North Carolina and Virginia into West Virginia, where it connects with the Kanawha River which then joins the Ohio River on its the way to the Mississippi River and finally into the Gulf of Mexico.

As we ate, along walked a bearded fellow with long grey hair and a burlap bag on his shoulder. He was curious about our travels, and we engaged him in conversation. His name is Dean. He is 64 years old and has two small farms, one in Virginia and one across the river in North Carolina. He walks the four miles between his farms and was on his way to his North Carolina farm when we met. Dean grows tobacco and raises sheep; he gets a good price for his sheep, about the same price as a cow. Dogs are killing his sheep, 17 thus far this year. He thinks the dogs belong to "newcomers."

Dean was born around the bend, one of thirteen kids. His mom died when he was three. His sister died of fever when he was five and he remembers riding in the hearse. Dean remembers old men begging for food in the '40s and '50s on this road. He pointed out the old Mouth of Wilson Post Office now decaying in the woods and weeds. He had a story about some friends who had walked here from Texas for a funeral. People gave them shoes along the way.

I took a picture of Dean standing by our bikes. I realized we are riding through this man's life; along this road, we ride by thousands of his memories, a gift of time.

Tuesday, October 1, 1996

8 a.m., in the lobby of the Super 8. We're eating English muffins, drinking coffee, and looking out the window at the cold grey rain. We've changed plans; tonight, we will stay with our friends, Frank and Ann, 40 miles away in Floyd. When I phoned and asked if we could stop by their house late this afternoon, Ann asked if we'd be spending the night. We laughed and said, "Yes, please." I guess it is hard for her to imagine we wouldn't want to continue on when we seem so close to home. After all, to her it is only an hour drive—but that's a day's bike ride for us.

The Super 8 coffee and muffins are hitting the spot. Outside, it seems to be getting lighter, lifting somewhat, and the rain has slowed to a drizzle. We've wrapped the BOB bag, guitar, and violin in plastic and my two journals have their own Ziploc bag too. The camera goes in a dry bag—the most secure bag we have. We're off into the mists of Southwest Virginia.

11:05 a.m., in Hillsville, 25 miles to Floyd. We looked hopefully for a nice coffee shop, the kind where people worked because they loved it, with homemade breads and good coffee. A coffee shop with these qualities is like a homecoming, a warm promise of well-being and solace. I asked two women we met if a place existed in Hillsville that had good coffee, wooden chairs, and a warm interior. They looked at me like I was from Mars. After all, there was a Hardees, McDonalds, and a Burger King within 100 feet of where we stood. "Naw," she finally said. I asked if there was anything further down the road, "Yeah, there's a Dairy Queen and a convenience store down there," she said, pointing toward Roanoke.

So, we stopped at Express Stop or something like that. They had local apples in boxes. We bought a Winesap and a Red Delicious and had a warming cup of coffee. I picked up *The Roanoke Times*, the first one I've read in 106 days. Ray Reed's column had a letter by a jogger suggesting closing Wiley Drive to traffic. Ray said some folks had suggested a one-way drive but closing it would be harder than riding cross-country on a bicycle! Funny that this was the first thing I read.

The rain has stopped. The air is misty-wet but fine. I find myself humming "Ashokan Farewell" and smiling a lot. How great it is to be alive.

4 p.m., at Frank and Ann's. We rode down their gravel driveway in the grey mist around 2:30. Our last 10 miles really let go with rain. It was the wettest we've been on this whole trip outside of a shower stall. (The last time that we rode in the rain was back in May, on one of our two training trips to the Peaks of Otter.) The temperature has been in the low 50s, which means the downhills were frigid events, given that we're nearly naked,

soaking wet, with 30 mph wind created by our decent. The road, Floyd Pike, is consistently hilly, and on the uphills we got a chance to warm up some.

It is great to be among friends. We are nearly home, 4,262 miles thus far, about 60 miles to go. The trip is nearing its end, but isn't over yet, even though we are in very familiar surroundings—I made the knotty pine cabinets and pantry in this kitchen. In part, home for us is being back here in southwest VA. But our old house on 13th Street shelters our home heart. There, too, is the home of our familiar life, our memories together. Cathy is such a part of the house. She makes it a home for me now. For both of us, Roanoke harbors family and friends. What wealth we have that nurtures our minds, bodies, and souls.

For the last 106 days, home has been our small tent, housing all our possessions. We have been snug in storms and on starlit nights with the rainfly off and the door open so we could stare up at the stars. How many times have we packed all we have into our panniers and BOB the trailer and rolled away? We never went back. The places we've left in our wake have receded into the past.

Retrace 2022

September 30, 2022
Berea, Kentucky to Roanoke, VA

We should have been excited for the last day of our retrace trip (plus, it was Cathy's birthday), but we were exhausted from two months on the road and wanted to be home. Google Maps told us we were around six hours away.

By traveling the fastest route home by car, we missed most of the route we had taken on our bike trip, but we have visited much of it over the years. We've camped at Breaks and driven the winding, hilly, pot-holed road up to Pippa Passes. We learned the Maddens had passed away, but they were still remembered there. We often camp at Grayson Highlands, passing through Floyd, Galax, and Mouth of Wilson where we met Dean by the New River. We adopted Jetta nearby in Hillsville. Floyd, VA is a vibrant destination and remains a draw for us although Frank and Ann have moved to a neighborhood near us in Roanoke.

Leaving Berea on our last morning, heavy fog obscured all but the road in front of us, concealing the views as we wound through the mountains. After an hour driving in heavy mist, the fog began to lift, revealing the dark blue mountains surrounding us.

We continued through Hazard, past small communities that had been catastrophically impacted by flooding in July, 2022. It was heartbreaking to see. Forty-three people had died, and many homes were destroyed. The clean-up had begun, but there was much more to do.

This whole trip, we had favored small rural roads. At Abingdon, VA we left that mentality behind and chose the faster paced Interstate 81N. The rain from Hurricane Ian began closing in on us.

We were exhausted when we arrived home and headed straight to bed. We didn't begin unpacking Evee for several days. A week later, we were still unloading.

Home

Wednesday, October 2, 1996

8:00 a.m. On this, our last traveling day, we are excited. Cathy said she slept, "somewhere between like a rock and like a kid on Christmas Eve." I slept erratically too, going over the trip in my mind, arriving, imagining our house, friends, pets, all in a warm symphony of thoughts.

Last night, we had a fine time visiting, eating homecooked food, and drinking single malt scotch. So good to be among friends.

Thursday, October 3, 1996

Home in Roanoke, VA. I will try to recount our homecoming, for a triumph of body and soul it clearly, unashamedly was. At Frank and Ann's, we waited for the rain to diminish. The grey morning only heightened the anticipation we both felt swelling in our hearts. We had breakfast, sipped coffee, and danced around the promise of home. Finally, the rain let up, and we rode off up their gravel drive, our last morning of this bicycle odyssey.

We rode on country lanes to Route 8 and then turned onto the Blue Ridge Parkway. This is a jewel of a road that traverses the mountain ridges with overlooks designed to give timeless views of the land. How we loved seeing the misty streams and hollows. Pileated woodpeckers streaked through massive rhododendron thickets in their sweet, dank niche. Turkey vultures circled craggy ridges.

The day had much in store for us. We rode on the asphalt

band into miles of pea-soup fog, shrouding us in its moist arms. White-tailed deer, startled at the road's edge, sprung toward the woods only to stop within view, curious of our silent forms gliding by. A soft rain fell, soaking us. Our tired legs pushed us over hills then we'd blindly careen down through the crazy greyed universe. Sometimes we'd shout or sing. "Ashokan Farewell" again visited my mental band, now a full orchestra with cannon and fireworks. In the fog, we were lost, up and down sensed only by the body— up, pedal harder, down, glide. No matter, we were almost home, a thought at once unbelievable and passionate in its world of inflection. Home.

We dropped off the highlands toward the valley, descending out of the thick mass of grey clouds. Across the valley we could see patches of blue sky and the sides of mountains. Just below, the valley was awash in a fantastical sea of white clouds that splashed up into this clear band of light.

And now, Cathy, in front of me, is crying at the beauty. I feel a moment of clarity. Behind, in the amorphous clouds, lay the expedition we are ending. Below lies the home toward which we voyage, harboring our future, our past, and our desires. I am grinning such that the light enters each pore of my being. Indeed, we are getting close.

Down the mountain, we fall back into the mist. We come to our friends David and Carroll's home that borders the Parkway. Just a year ago, I was building this house for them, along with my brother Dan, and Cathy's brother Ken. Now, a lifetime later, we stop and yell from the road. David is first out, running through the woods to us with hugs and re-hugs. Then Carroll comes out of the woods with a rainbow-colored umbrella and a small cooler. The closer she gets, the faster she comes. "Oh!" she cries, the umbrella thrown up and away. Cathy and she embrace, both crying with joy. We walk back to their house to quickly see the beautiful landscaping they planted this summer. Then we ride on.

The next 18 miles of the Parkway is very familiar. Down the road, David and Carroll pass us on their way to the welcome home party we know is awaiting our arrival. We pedal on as if levitated; the world is a fantastic sparkle now; nothing is normal. We're laughing at the joy. Two more hills to climb. We drop down along the Roanoke River. Two miles to go. We are unconsciously pedaling, the weight we carried these 107 days dissipated. We reach the last incline atop the river bluff and pause a second before drifting down to Memorial Avenue and Memorial Bridge.

We start across the bridge, gliding, wide-eyed, joy welling up like an aching volcano. I see a figure come down from our house just around the bend at the bridge's end, 200 yards off. It is my sister. "There's Helena!" I tell Cathy through the huge lump forming in my throat. Across the bridge we drift. As we enter the last bend, we come into view of our house with cars parked along the road and a throng of people responding to our appearance.

A lifetime has progressed in each of our lives since our journey began. Here is a goal being attained, a journey's end, a homecoming, a celebration, a welcoming home party of universal design. On the sidewalk, three teenagers who are walking by this unfolding scene get caught up in the moment and yell, "All right!"

And there is Mary across the street photographing us, trying to get the whole event in her lens. Oh, we're home! There's Ron, clapping his hands above his head, coming out in the road to greet us. Everyone moves forward, clapping and cheering. There is my dad, smiling, smiling. There is brother Dan, another camera in hand, smiling. Betty comes toward me as I pull onto the sidewalk from the road, her eyes moist and happy. We hug and I relinquish my bicycle to her for the first time in four months and move to Cathy, surrounded by family and friends. We kiss as we mark our incredible love and jubilant journey together.

Friends are everywhere. Ken gives me a high five amid a swirl of exuberant joy. Hugs and more hugs. Everyone is wet on their fronts from hugging our rain-soaked bodies. The house is radiant with flowers exploding in the yard.

On the porch, Ron has taped a 4'x 6' photograph of Cathy and me at the moment of our marriage, turned to face our family, friends, the world, with our hands raised above our heads. Ron has inserted in our upraised hands a banner as if we were holding it aloft. The banner reads: "TransAmerican Honeymoon We Did It!! 6/18 through 10/2, 1996." Below this picture, by the front door, is a U.S. map on which Ron has artistically traced our route across the continent, pieced together from our phone calls from the road.

I look at this map with its familiar erratic squiggly line to this very moment, I turn back to look out at this group, at our lives of joy here. Cathy is by my side. I put my arm around her. "Let's take a shower," she says. This journey is over.

Epilogue

Almost 27 years have passed since Cathy and I began our marriage and embarked on our honeymoon journey. It's been eight months since we retraced that epic trip in our car. Despite my grandmother's advice, "Never go back," I am overwhelmingly glad we did go back. Our retrace trip replayed and reinforced amazing memories and provided new experiences for Cathy and me to share. I am so thankful that on our long-ago honeymoon I had the luxury of time and the discipline to record our crossing in my journal.

My memories have become a significant focus for me now. Two months ago, I was diagnosed with Alzheimer's Disease. The thought of losing these precious moments is horrifying. But Cathy and I are strong. We are still having fun. We feel very lucky to have each other. Our life is full of love. Our journey is not over. We continue to explore the Geography of Hearts.

Scrapbook

Above: Fish that Dick gave us, July 8, 1996 (p. 55)

Right: BOB with flat tire July 11, 1996 (p. 61)

Going-to-the-Sun Road, July 15, 1996 (p. 70)

*Trail to Vimy Peak,
July 22, 1996 (p. 86)*

*Gravel road "short
cut," July 28, 1996
(p. 102)*

*Mt. Rushmore, August
22, 1996 (pp. 159-160)*

American Gothic House,
September 9, 1996
(pp. 220-222)

"The Admiral," September 13, 1996 (pp. 233-236)

Cave-In-Rock Ferry, September 18, 1996 (p. 249)

Family and friends at the finish, October 3, 1996 (pp. 289-290)

About the Author

Jim Crawford has lived a varied and unconventional life. A musician and songwriter, Jim has also worked as a carpenter and cabinetmaker, taking time off to sail in the South Pacific and bicycle through Australia and New Zealand. In the early 1990s, Jim spent time in Central America notably studying the demise of the traditional fishing culture in a Belizean village. He received his MS in Geography from Virginia Tech in 1995. Jim loves talking with people about their lives and has shared their stories as a writer and through several documentary films he has produced, including *Down in the Old Belt: Voices from the Tobacco South*.

He and his wife, Cathy, live in Roanoke, VA.

Cathy, Jetta, and Jim at Diablo Lake
Retrace Trip, Aug. 26-28, 2022 (p. 25)